The Veneration and Administration of the Eucharist

The Proceedings of the Second International Colloquium on the Roman Catholic Liturgy organised by the Centre International d'Etudes Liturgiques

Translated and edited by members of CIEL UK

The Saint Austin Press
Southampton
1997

THE SAINT AUSTIN PRESS
P.O. BOX 610
SOUTHAMPTON
SO14 0YY
Tel. (01703) 235966
Fax (01703) 346953

© Le Centre International d'Etudes Liturgiques

ISBN 1 901157 15 6

A catalogue record for this book is available from the British Library

Printed in Great Britain by BPC Wheatons, Exeter.

For UK and Eire Enquiries relating to CIEL:
CIEL UK
P.O.Box 180
Hemel Hempstead
HP3 0UJ

Dedicated to Our Lord Jesus Christ,
Sovereign Priest.

Contents

Introduction

M. Loïc Mérian (France)

Mr Loïc Mérian, aged 30, is a former student of the Ecole Nationale Supérieure des Télécommunications. After a career as a telecommunications engineer, he undertook university studies in history. Having directed the Jeune Chrétienté *movement for several years, he is today president of the International Centre for Liturgical Studies (CIEL) which is responsible for the organisation and promotion of the colloquium at Notre-Dame-du-Laus.*

In the introduction to the first Colloquium on 4th October 1995, we recalled to what extent the success of this first scholarly meeting devoted to the traditional liturgy could be considered a real miracle; a fruit of Divine Providence.

At the risk of repeating myself, I am convinced that today's opening of this second Colloquium is once again a real miracle, perhaps still more extraordinary than that of last year. In fact, perhaps on that occasion we benefited from the natural goodwill which many of our friends freely bestowed on an enterprise whose existence and future might, to say the least, have seemed uncertain. Nevertheless - and we were very touched by it at the time - the support of eminent people gave us the courage to pursue our project.

Today, as last year, we must thank first of all Bishop Georges Lagrange who by his interest and friendship, has agreed to this meeting being organised once again in a diocese of France under the patronage of the local Bishop. In addition, he has done us the honour of agreeing this year to introduce our meeting with a message. How can we bear a more definite witness to our desire to place ourselves as clearly as possible in communion with the Church? Is it not by responding to the wishes which the Holy Father expressed recently when he hoped that the Catholics of France would be finally reconciled to the essential truths of the faith?

Before opening this second Colloquium, I would like to outline briefly our activities during the year. Our first task, already announced last year, was to commit ourselves to the publication of the Proceedings of the first Colloquium: we did not fully appreciate all the problems of such an enterprise. That is why some people, who showed their confidence in us by subscribing to this publication, were rather surprised at not receiving a document that we had promised them - no doubt a little rashly - for November 1995!

The international character of the Colloquium, the fact that the contributions were in various languages; all this involved setting up translation, correction and proofing arrangements which caused numerous delays. It was in April 1996 that the volume containing the work of the first Colloquium was eventually published. As an anecdote, if we were ourselves very upset about this delay – sentiments shared by some of our friends, the subscribers – we were still happy to receive a letter from Rev Fr Blet congratulating us on the prompt arrival of our publication, since he himself waited some six years for the publication of the proceedings of a Colloquium, in which he had taken part, in the setting of the Ecole Française in Rome!

We printed more than 1500 copies which have been distributed widely, and the sale of them has enabled us to establish an operation which must have seemed risky to some people.

Since then, in order to enter into contact with, or strengthen our links with ecclesiastical authorities, we have sent a free copy of the Proceedings of our Colloquium to all the French-speaking Bishops of Europe, as well as to superiors of the great religious communities and to university libraries. About 400 copies have been distributed in this way. We have no misgivings about this since the mail-out has allowed us to establish friendly contacts with more than 50 people - largely ecclesiastics (Cardinals, Bishops, Superiors of communities, professors...) who, for the most part are not known for their attachment to the traditional liturgy. Thus we can say that already our first Colloquium has allowed us to establish contacts with the laity and with religious which we hope will deepen and be enriched in the future.

This unexpected result following the publication of the Proceedings has persuaded us to undertake to produce the Proceedings of this year's second Colloquium not only in French, but also in German and English and perhaps in Italian and Spanish, in order that the largest possible number of Bishops and ecclesiastical and university authorities can be informed of our activities.

This ambitious project, which we are determined to carry out, can only be achieved thanks to the productive and exceptional links established over the year with numerous groups who share with us a love for the traditional liturgy and the mind of the Church. These groups in Germany, Italy, Great Britain, Spain and North America allow us today to establish something which up until very recently has been almost unthinkable. We are thus in a position to affirm that the Centre International d'Etudes Liturgiques, initiated by a group of mainly French and French-speaking people as "god-parents", is set to become in the future a truly international association, soon perhaps universal! That is to say fully catholic.

This international character which CIEL has already achieved, is demonstrated by the audience whom I have the honour of addressing today. However this miracle, renewed this year, would not have been possible without the generous help of hundreds of benefactors, who by their donations have allowed us always to have at our disposal the means necessary for the realisation of our projects, and the dynamism of the activists of *Jeune Chrétienté* who have not spared themselves, so that today, in the best conditions possible, a Colloquium can be held devoted to studying a liturgy to which they are devoted, not by nostalgia, nor by aesthetic consideration, but because it sheds light magnificently on their faith and their Catholic convictions, and each day enlivens their missionary zeal amongst other young people today, all too many of whom still do not know of Christ and His Church.

Now I must bring this quickly to a close to allow the contributors to speak. Monsignor Schmitz who is present with us here, will be responsible over the three days for introducing each of the contributors and their affiliations. However, I can already tell you that we are happy this year to welcome amongst us people whose credentials are so beyond question that this second Colloquium – no doubt even more than the first, which was above all a Colloquium of friends – will be able to carry out fully its function as a platform for those who are faithful to the Church and wish to remain firmly attached to the traditional liturgy.

To achieve this ever more securely we have chosen this year to devote the whole Colloquium to one theme which we hope will allow us to achieve deeper and richer results. If God wills, we will steer future Colloquiums in this direction, since given the success already achieved by this second meeting, we wish to improve the meetings more and more each year. Thus we hope that from year to year, it will attract large numbers of especially high calibre people, clerics as well as laity seeking to enrich their knowledge of their heritage of traditional liturgy. We hope also that these people will thus become ever more ardent defenders of a celebration which we firmly believe – thanks to the spiritual and theological treasures that it expresses in a magnificent manner – can make the Church loved by many of those who have left it or who know nothing about it.

Eucharistic devotion
in the teaching of John Paul II

Mgr. Georges Lagrange, Bishop of Gap.

Mgr. Lagrange was born 23rd November 1929 at Châtillon-sur-Chalaronne (Ain, France). Ordained priest the 29th June 1955 in the Belley-Ars diocese, he was, at first, curate in the parish of Notre-Dame in Bourg-en-Bresse (1955-1958), then diocesan chaplain of the JAC-JACF (1958-1964), national chaplain of Algerian rural Catholic Action (as Fidei donum) *(1964-1966), joint-national chaplain of the Christian Movement in the Rural World for the liberal and technical professions branch (1966-1972), parish priest of Saint Didier of Aussiat, Saint Sulpice and Curtafond (rural parishes in the Belley diocese) and chaplain of the upper school at the Sacré-Cœur School in Bourg (1972-1983) ; he was then named diocesan director of the cathedral of Dakar (Senegal), as* Fidei donum *(1983-1986) and finally parish priest of Montluel (Belley diocese) (1986-1988). He was called to the episcopacy then named Bishop of Gap by Pope John Paul II in 1988.*

Neither the time that I could find to prepare this talk, nor the time in which I have to give it, allow me to scrutinise all the teaching of John Paul II and to discuss everything in it that concerns the Eucharist. I have therefore kept myself to a few texts which seemed to me the most important, and have tried to delineate in these the characteristic emphasis of our Holy Father the Pope. I hope therefore that you will excuse the limited scope of this lecture. If I may, I should like, before tackling the subject itself, to thank the organisers of this colloquium for having asked me for this contribution, and also to underline the significance that I myself attach to that request, and to the response which I give it. It is quite clear that it is not because of my particular competence in the proposed subject that you ask me to address your colloquium: it is obviously in my role as the local bishop that you have sent me this invitation.

And in another way, when you ask me to speak to you about the spirituality (and therefore also about the doctrine) of our Holy Father Pope John Paul II, you make plain your desire - lest anyone should doubt it - to place your reflection on "the veneration and the administration of the Eucharist" at the heart of the Catholic Church of today, in union with the successor of Peter, by whose will I am bishop of Gap. More important than what I am actually going inadequately to tell you - at least as much as it will really be me, as I will do scarcely more than quote some writings of John Paul II - is the very fact that at your request I am addressing you today on this subject. For there I see your desire to affirm that it is as sons and daughters of the one holy, catholic and apostolic Church, in union with her hierarchy and with the teaching of her Magisterium, that you embark upon this reflection.

Eucharist and Priesthood

Clearly, the thought of John Paul II on the Eucharist is in the first place that of the Church in all of her tradition, but it is not surprising that it should be strongly marked by the teachings of the Second Vatican Council, to which he often refers. And it is certainly there that one must look for the source of the key point which seems to me to constitute the originality of the Pope's teaching on the Eucharist: appreciating the close link between Eucharist and priesthood, and a priesthood conceived of in conformity with the teaching of the Second Vatican Council, which underlined simultaneously the close link and the clear distinction between common priesthood and hierarchical priesthood. We are aware of the passage in the dogmatic Constitution on the Church *Lumen Gentium*, section 10:

Though they differ from one another in essence and not only in degree, the common priesthood of the faithful and the ministerial or hierarchical priesthood are nonetheless interrelated. Each of them in its own special way is a participation in the one priesthood of Christ. The ministerial priest, by the sacred power he enjoys, moulds and rules the priestly people. Acting in the person of Christ (*in persona Christi*), he brings about the Eucharistic Sacrifice, and offers it to God in the name of all the people. For their part, the faithful join in the offering of the Eucharist, by virtue of their royal priesthood. They likewise exercise that priesthood by receiving the sacraments, by prayer and thanksgiving, by the witness of a holy life and by self-denial and active charity.

Eucharist, Redemption and Penance

To begin with, however, I should like to emphasise the important position, in all the teaching of John Paul II, which is held by the mystery of the Redemption. Without entering into an analysis of everything the Holy Father has said and written on the subject, I mention to you simply those pontifical documents which, in their title, include the words *Redemption* or *Redeemer*, beginning with his first encyclical which, for every pope, is indicative of his important emphases, and is generally considered as a 'manifesto' encyclical. For Paul VI there was *Ecclesiam suam*, and for John Paul II *Redemptor hominis*, in March 1979. In 1984, during the Jubilee Holy Year of the Redemption there was the apostolic Exhortation *Redemptionis donum*, on religious consecration in the light of the Redemption, then the apostolic Letter *Redemptionis anno* about Jerusalem, the sacred patrimony of all believers. Then *Redemptoris Mater* in 1987, *Redemptoris custos* in 1989 and *Redemptoris missio* in 1990. This insistence is evidently also to be found in the the the teaching of John Paul II on the Eucharist, which he loves to bring together with the sacrament of Penance, as for example in paragraph 20 of *Redemptor hominis* :

> 'Let everyone put himself to the test and let him eat of this bread and drink of this chalice.' This exhortation of the Apostle indicates, at least indirectly, the close link which exists between the Eucharist and Penance ... Thus the Eucharist and Penance become, in a certain sense, two closely linked dimensions of an authentic life according to the spirit of the Gospel, of the truly Christian life. Christ, who invites us to the Eucharistic banquet, is always the Christ who exhorts us to repentance, who tells us again and again "Be converted." Without this constant and always repeated effort for conversion, participation in the Eucharist is deprived of its full redemptive efficacy; in this there would be absent, or at least weakened, that particular disposition which enables us to offer to God the spiritual sacrifice in which the essential and universal manner of our participation in the priesthood of Christ is expressed.

This text is important because it gathers together the essential emphases of John Paul II with regard to the Eucharist in its link with the Redemption, with Penance, and with the priesthood of Christ from which spring the baptismal priesthood and the ministerial priesthood, both commissioned to unite the spiritual sacrifice of the baptised to the perfect sacrifice of Christ.

The following year, in his second encyclical *Dives in misericordia*, the pope takes up this perspective again:

> Of great significance... is constant meditation on the word of God, and above all conscious and mature participation in the Eucharist and in the sacrament of penance or reconciliation. ... "For as often as we eat this bread and drink this cup," we not only proclaim the death of the Redeemer but also his resurrection.

We also find important explanations of the links between Eucharist, Penance and Redemption in the apostolic Exhortation *Reconciliatio et Paenitentia*, following the synod of bishops on penance:

> In section 7: It is ... legitimate ... to concentrate the reflection about the entire mystery of Christ on his mission as reconciler. And one must proclaim once again the faith of the Church in the redemptive act of Christ ... I invite you specifically to look at the mystery of the cross as the highest drama in which Christ perceives the depth - and experiences the suffering - even of the tragedy of man separated from God. ... Our sights fixed on Golgotha should constantly remind us of the "vertical" dimension of the division and of the reconciliation of the man-God who, in the eyes of the faith, always prevails over the "horizontal" dimension, that is to say, the reality of the division

among men and the necessity of the reconciliation between them.

In section 27, the Holy Father recalls the definition of the Eucharist that St. Augustine gives us in his commentary on St. John: *sacramentum pietatis, signum unitatis, vinculum caritatis*, which "casts light on the effects of personal sanctification (*pietas*) and of communal reconciliation (*unitas et caritas*), which flow from the very essence of the Eucharistic mystery as the unbloody renewal of the sacrifice of the cross, source of salvation and reconciliation for all men." But he does not forget to recall "that every Christian conscious of having committed a grave sin may not receive the Eucharist before having obtained God's forgiveness." Then citing the Instruction *Eucharisticum Mysterium* (May 1967) : "every man aware of having committed a mortal sin, however contrite he may feel, may not approach the Eucharist without a prior sacramental confession; if he finds himself in a case of necessity, and it is not possible for him to make his confession, let him first make an act of perfect contrition."

Let us also note that with regard to the family founded on the sacrament of marriage, a theme so dear to his heart, John Paul II, in his admirable apostolic exhortation *Familiaris consortio*, emphasises the close link between Eucharist and marriage:

Number 57: The duty of sanctification which is incumbent on the Christian family has its primary root in baptism and its greatest expression in the Eucharist, to which Christian marriage is intimately linked... The Eucharist is itself the wellspring of Christian marriage. For the Eucharistic sacrifice represents the covenant of love between Christ and the Church, in as much as she has been sealed by the blood of his cross. It is in this sacrifice of the new and everlasting covenant that Christian spouses find that gushing spring which inwardly models and constantly enlivens their marital covenant. As a representation of Christ's sacrifice of love for the Church, the Eucharist is a source of charity. And in the Eucharistic gift of charity the Christian family finds the foundation and soul of its 'communion' and 'mission'.

The Letter *Dominicae Cenae*

It is, however, the Letter of the Sovereign Pontiff to all the bishops of the Church on the Mystery of the Cult of the Holy Eucharist, for Holy Thursday 1980, which is to this day the most complete document by John Paul II on the Eucharist, under the title of *Dominicae Cenae*.

From the beginning of his Letter, the pope is keen to establish the close link with his Letter of the preceding year where he had dealt with the priesthood : "Again this year, for Holy Thursday, I address to you all a letter that is directly linked to that which you received last year."

He returns to it in section 2 :

> The present letter that I am addressing to you, my venerable and dear brothers in the episcopate - and which is, as I have said, in a certain way a continuation of the previous one - is also closely linked with the mystery of Holy Thursday, and is related to the priesthood. In fact I intend to devote it to the Eucharist, and in particular to certain aspects of the Eucharistic mystery and its impact on the lives of those who are ministers of it...
>
> In reality, the ministerial and hierarchical priesthood, the priesthood of the bishops and priests, and, at their side, the ministry of the deacons - ministries which normally begin with the proclamation of the Gospel - are in the closest relationship with the Eucharist. The Eucharist is the principal and central *raison d'être* of the sacrament of the priesthood... In this way our Eucharistic worship, both in the celebration of Mass and in our devotion to the Blessed Sacrament, is like a life-giving current that links our ministerial or hierarchical priesthood to the common priesthood of the faithful, and presents it in its vertical dimension and with its central value. The priest fulfils his principal mission and is manifested in all his fullness when he celebrates the Eucharist.

In section 4, where he recalls that just as "the Church makes the Eucharist, so the Eucharist builds up the Church", he makes a fresh insistence on the "vertical" dimension:

> This drawing together and this union, the prototype of which is the union of the apostles about Christ at the Last Supper, express the Church and bring her into being. But the Church is not brought into being only through the union of people, through the experience of brotherhood to which the Eucharistic banquet gives rise. The Church is brought into being when, in that fraternal union and communion, we celebrate the sacrifice of the cross of Christ, when we proclaim "the Lord's death until he comes,"... Only in this way, through that faith and that disposition of mind, is there brought about that building up of the Church, which in the Eucharist truly finds its "source and summit," according to the well-known expression of the Second Vatican Council.

Source and summit of the life of the Church, centre and summit of the whole Christian life : in fact it clearly seems that John Paul II, following on again from Vatican II, is telling us that the Eucharist only appears in all its grandeur when seen in relation to the entirety of the Christian mystery. To a certain extent it is also true of every aspect of faith, of every event in the history of salvation, of every sacrament. And it is indeed this that makes it difficult to set forth a particular point if it only acquires its full meaning when placed in the greater context. At every turn it would be necessary to reduce everything down into a synthesis. As this is in fact impossible, one supposes *a priori* that this synthesis is known and that everyone has the same synthesis. Now in reality, this is not always the case. And the

14

incomprehensions or divergences on a particular question are due, most of the time, to the fact that basically we place ourselves within different syntheses. To set forth and explain an entire synthesis, however, would take an enormous amount of time. How does one escape from this impasse?

This central position of the Eucharist is indeed brought to light in this Letter to the bishops. For example in section 5, we read :

Eucharistic worship constitutes the soul of all Christian life. In fact Christian life is expressed in the fulfilling of the greatest commandment, that is to say, in the love of God and neighbour, and this love finds its source in the blessed sacrament, which is commonly called the sacrament of love... As we thus become adorers of the Father "in spirit and in truth," we mature in an ever fuller union with Christ.

And in section 6:

The authentic sense of the Eucharist becomes of itself the school of active love for neighbour... Let us learn to discover with respect the truth about the inner self of people for it is precisely this inner self that becomes the dwelling place of God present in the Eucharist.

And in section 7 :

From this concept of Eucharistic worship there then stems the whole sacramental style of the Christian's life ... Now, of all the sacraments, it is the holy Eucharist that brings to fullness their initiation as Christians ... in this way Eucharistic worship is the centre and goal of all sacramental life. In the depths of Eucharistic worship we find a continual echo of the sacraments of Christian initiation: baptism and confirmation.

The pope then goes on to mention the link which the Eucharist has "with the sacrament of family life and the sacrament of the sick", and then "the close link between the Sacrament of Penance and the sacrament of the Eucharist. It is not only that penance leads to the Eucharist, but that the Eucharist also leads to penance. For when we realise who it is that we receive in Eucharistic communion, there springs up in us almost spontaneously a sense of unworthiness, together with sorrow for our sins and a desire for purification. But we must always take care that this great meeting with Christ in the Eucharist does not become a mere habit, and that we do not receive him unworthily, that is to say, in a state of mortal sin."

Today when many Christians receive Communion so readily, and yet approach so infrequently the sacrament of penance, such a remark cannot fail to prick our conscience with regard to the grandeur of Him whom we receive in the Eucharist. And that introduces us to the second part of the Letter, which bears on the sacredness of the

Eucharist and the sacrifice.

In section 8, the Sovereign Pontiff draws attention to the notion of *Sacrum*, recalling that throughout history "secondary elements have undergone certain changes, but the essence of the *Mysterium*, instituted by the Redeemer of the world during the Last Supper has remained unchanged." He continues :

The Second Vatican Council also brought to it some modifications, as a result of which the present liturgy of the Mass is different in some ways from the one known before the Council. We do not intend to speak of these differences: It is better that we should now concentrate on what is essential and immutable in the Eucharistic liturgy.

There is a close link between this element of the Eucharist and its sacredness, that is to say, its being a holy and sacred action. Holy and sacred, because in it are the continual presence and action of Christ, "the Holy One" of God... For it is He who, represented by the celebrant, makes His entrance into the sanctuary and proclaims His Gospel. It is He who is "the offerer and the offered, the consecrator and the consecrated." The Eucharist is a holy and sacred action, because it constitutes the sacred species, the *Sancta sanctis*, that is to say, "the holy things (Christ, the Holy One) given to the holy," ... The sacredness of the Mass, therefore, is not a "sacralisation," that is to say, something that man adds to Christ's action in the Upper Room, ... The sacred character of the Mass is a sacredness instited by Christ. The words and action of every priest, answered by the conscious and active participation of the whole Eucharistic assembly, echo the words and action of Holy Thursday.

In section 9 it is the idea of *sacrificium* which is stressed:

The priest offers the holy sacrifice *in persona Christi*; this means more than offering "in the name of" or "in the place of" Christ. *In persona* means in specific sacramental identification with "the eternal high priest" who is the author and the principal subject of this sacrifice of his... If separated from its distinctive sacrificial and sacramental nature [it] simply ceases to be. It admits of no "profane" imitation, an imitation that would very easily (indeed regularly) become a profanation. This must always be remembered, perhaps above all in our time, when we see a tendency to do away with the distinction between the "sacred" and the "profane," given the widespread tendency, at least in some places, to desacralize everything.

In section 10 a paragraph on the "table of the word of God" touches especially on the concerns of your colloquium :

The fact that these texts are read and sung in the vernacular enables everyone to participate with fuller understanding.

Nevertheless, there are those people, who, having been educated on the basis of the old liturgy in Latin, experience the lack of this "one language," which in all the world was an expression of the unity of the Church and through its dignified character elicited a profound sense of the Eucharistic mystery. It is therefore necessary to show not only understanding but also full respect toward these sentiments and desires. As

16

far as possible these sentiments and desires are to be accommodated, as is moreover provided for in the new dispositions. The Roman Church has special obligations towards Latin, the splendid language of ancient Rome, and she must manifest them whenever the occasion presents itself.

In section 11, after having expressed regret that one sometimes encounters "a lack of Eucharistic 'hunger' and 'thirst'", the Holy Father denounces once again the laxity of some people who approach the Eucharist without having had the requisite concern to purify their consciences, and he goes on :

But there can also be, at least at times, another idea behind this; the idea of the Mass as only a banquet in which one shares by receiving the Body of Christ in order to manifest, above all else, fratenal communion.

Regarding communion in the hand, John Paul II says that he "hears mention of deplorable cases of a lack of respect towards the Eucharistic species." "It also sometimes happens," he continues, "that one does not take into account the free choice and the free will of those who, in those places where communion in the hand has been permitted, prefer to keep to the usage of receiving in the mouth... Touching the sacred species, distributing them from their own hands, is a privilege of the ordained, which signifies an active participation in the ministry of the Eucharist. There is no doubt that the Church may concede this faculty to persons who are neither priests nor deacons or [to] other lay people who are chosen for this to meet a just need, but always after an adequate preparation."

In the subsequent section he recalls that "every priest who offers the holy sacrifice must remember that it is not only he, with his community, who prays, but the whole Church that prays, expressing thereby - notably in using the approved liturgical text - her spiritual unity in this sacrament."

And he continues: "I should like to beg forgiveness - in my own name and in the name of all of you, venerable and dear brothers in the episcopate - for everything which, for whatever reason, through whatever human weakness, impatience or negligence, and also through the at times partial, one-sided and erroneous application of the directives of the Second Vatican Council, may have caused scandal and disturbance concerning the interpretation of the doctrine and the veneration due to this great Sacrament."

And finally one may read in the conclusion:

We shall continue in the future to take special care to promote and follow the renewal of the Church according to the teaching of the Second Vatican Council, in the spirit of an ever living tradition... Above all I wish to emphasise that the problems of the liturgy, and in particular of the Eucharistic liturgy, must not be an occasion for dividing Catholics and for threatening the unity of the Church.

One could find again in many other texts the insistence on these same important themes of John Paul II concerning the Eucharist, amongst others in the Wednesday catechisms. Here are just a couple of examples:

> The full expression of this communion of life with Christ is the Eucharist... This sacrament is the enduring sign of the presence of His Body given up to death and His Blood shed 'for the remission of sins;' every time that it is celebrated it makes present the saving sacrifice of the Redeemer of the world.
>
> > 13th July, 1988. Catechesis on "Jesus, founder of the sacramental structure in the life of the Church."

> According to Vatican II, it is in the Eucharist that the Church as a priestly community is truly realised; a community that is realised by means of the Sacraments... The participation is common to all the 'priestly people', admitted to unite themselves in the sacrifice and in the communion. But it is different according to the condition of the members of the Church in the sacramental order. The priestly minister has a specific role which does not suppress, but rather promotes the role of the common priesthood.
>
> > 18th March, 1992. Catechesis on "The Eucharist in the Church : a priestly and sacramental community."

Conclusion

To sum up the central message of these texts of our Holy Father the Pope, let us say that the Eucharist accomplishes sacramentally that which is itself the heart of the eternal design of God as it unfolds in the history of salvation. The glory which, according to the priestly prayer of Jesus in St. John chapter 17, the Son in the bosom of the Trinity, receives from the Father and in turn gives to the Father : "Glorify Thy Son that Thy Son may glorify Thee;" and according to Gregory of Nicea : "That the Holy Spirit is called glory, no-one who examines the subject can deny." (*Homily on the Song of Songs*.) The Son having assumed human nature, gives to His Father this same glory at the heart of the world so that the vocation of creation, which is to render glory to God (according to the definition of Vatican I), might be fully accomplished. Thus the sin of the one who did not give to God the glory and thanksgiving which are His due (Romans 1, 21) is atoned for. Thus is wrought creation's "return to God." That was clearly accomplished on the Cross when Christ "gave up the Spirit." And it is this supreme sacrifice which is made present *hic et nunc* in every Eucharistic celebration, and to which every baptised person unites himself when he receives communion with the correct disposition. This perfect sacrifice consummated on the Cross

18

in the earthly Body of Christ goes on for ever in the risen Body of Christ, the Lamb that is slain, and communicates itself to men in the Eucharistic Body of Christ in order thereby to build His ecclesial body, the earthly seed of the Kingdom of Heaven where Christ will be, in all truth, "all in all." (1 Cor. 12, 28.)

The Church's theological responses to the most important heresies concerning the Eucharist

Father François Clément (Switzerland)

Father Clément was ordained in 1981. He is a priest in the Fribourg diocese in Switzerland. He has been a curate and parish priest in this diocese and, at the local bishop's request, is now chaplain of the Tridentine Rite for the whole diocese. He also has a degree in liturgical sciences.

Outline

Introduction

On June 9th 1996, His Eminence Cardinal Etchegaray, Papal Legate to His Holiness John Paul II, celebrated Solemn High Mass in the Basilica of St Martin of Liège on the occasion of the 750th Anniversary of the Feast of *Corpus Christi*. The feast was first celebrated by the Bishop of that city, Robert de Thourotte, in 1246 - at the inspiration of two nuns, St Julian of Cornillon and Blessed Eve of St Martin. After the death of the Bishop, the decree permitting the feast was no longer applied, and it was Pope Urban IV who re-established the festival in 1264, giving it universal application.[1] This anniversary seems to be a most suitable moment to hold this Conference, as an important witness to the development of Eucharistic Dogma through the ages. My talk must be limited in accordance with the time allowed me. I intend to keep to the essentials without oversimplifying or exaggerating.

The great heresies of the ancient Church were at first Christological and Trinitarian, concerned with the mystery of God and of Christ, the Son of God, *image incarnate of the Invisible God* - a radical novelty *vis-a-vis* the religions of antiquity. Eucharistic dogma thus remained outside the field of discussion for many centuries and was chiefly expressed in the liturgy and preaching which prepared the faithful for the Sacrament (cf. the various mystagogical homilies). After the Peace of Constantine and the great invasions, the Church settled down to a public and visible existence in the East and West. It was appropriate, therefore, that a theology of the Church and her sacraments (of the visible means of salvation which translate and transmit invisible grace) should have developed. Theological difficulties would be centred on the two above-mentioned truths: on what constitutes the visible continuation of the Incarnation, which is, and always will be, the fundamental core of Christianity.

It seems to me that one may fix the moments when these problems first became apparent within two critical periods: periods which reveal certain common characteristics and a kind of agreement, for there is nothing so old-fashioned and so constantly recurring as heresy. These critical periods are chiefly to be indentified in the eucharistic controversies which reached their apotheosis with Berengarius of Tours and the elaborate theories of the Reformers. Far from threatening the Church's faith, objections and controversies served to inspire the development of theological ideas. We could say that the Church's response is threefold and interdependent, in accordance with the adage *Lex orandi, lex credendi*: vocabulary is refined, evolves and becomes more precise, and, in consequence, theology is enriched (this is particularly evident in the context of the Carolingian and Berangardian controversies, and in the debates which resulted from the Reformation) and the liturgy translates all this into the prayer of the Christian people. We can, therefore, deduce from this, that language and philosophy will be of great importance in our understanding of this subject.

"The Eucharistic mystery poses problems for reasoned belief, which it is the role of theology to solve. Faith does not depend on this initiative, nor on its consequences, but supports it and judges the result. These questions can be divided into four categories: In what way is the Eucharist a sacrifice? How can we grasp the Presence of Christ within it? How do we understand the action by which the gifts "become" (fiunt) the Body and the Blood of Christ? And finally, how does the Eucharist guarantee the mystery of the sustained and vital Presence of Christ in his Church?"[2]

1   Vocabulary: Evolutionary and Patristic origins

Using classical language, the Fathers who followed St Augustine spoke of three "bodies": the body of the Church, the body of Christ in HIs historical reality, and His sacramental body made visible in the Eucharist.[3] Amalar of Metz, in his *De*

Ecclesiasticus Officiis speaks of the *primum corpus* (i.e. the Church), *alterum corpus* (i.e. Christ incarnate), *tertium corpus* (i.e. the eucharistic Christ).[4] Therefore, in speaking of the unity of the body, one thinks first of the Church, and only secondarily of the Eucharist - particularly since Berengarius. Until this time, the expression *sacramentum Dominici corporis* was the equivalent of *corpus mysticum* and applied principally to the Church. Following the patristic period, a sort of ambiguity surrounded the word "corpus" with its chosen epithet; for example *unum corpus*[5] for "the Church": *corpus Christi* for the Eucharist[6] The Eucharist was therefore seen as the mystical basis revealing the unity of the body of the Church.[7] The term "mystical" has gradually come to be associated with the Sacrament and other terms used to denote the body of the Church. It appears that the stages overlap: there were prophetic forshadowings and also old concepts which remained in use. A typical example is that of Peter of Troyes who wrote his *Sentences sur les Sacrements* between 1165 and 1170. Following St Jerome, he distinguishes two understandings of the term "the body of Christ". To the first, he attaches three soubriquets: *vera* denoting reality, *propria* establishing its identity with the flesh born of the Virgin, *sacramentalis*, that is, the eucharistic species. The second Incarnation, fruit of the first, is the *caro mystica*, that is to say the Church united by the power of the Sacrament. We notice how *sacramentalis* and *mystica*, previously synonymous, have now become separated and conflicting. In the second half of the 12th century, the Church became known as the *"corpus mysticum"* and it seems that the use of this term spread rapidly.[8]

2　From the Carolingian period to the controversy of Berengarius of Tours

In 831, the Abbot of Corbie, Paschasius Radbertus, wrote his *De Corpore et Sanguine Domini* which may be accepted as the first theological treatise on the Eucharist.[9] Its fundamental argument concerns the identity of the historical figure of Christ with His sacramental presence, notwithstanding the different modes of being of the two bodies. In the Blessed Sacrament we acknowledge His spiritual presence. However, the Eucharist is both a truth and a symbol: a symbol of all that is outwardly visible (*exterius sentitur*), a truth acceptable to everything that intelligence may grasp or faith affirm (*interius recte intelligitur aut creditur*). The professions of faith of the primitive Church simply affirmed eucharistic realism, without much explanation of the spiritual nature of the presence.

This treatise, although devoid of polemic, was to attract the opposition of Ratramnus, a monk of the same abbey, who wrote a book bearing the same title. In it, he denied the identification of the eucharistic body of Christ with His historical one, and seemed to oppose the idea that the Eucharist can be simultaneously symbol and truth. If it is difficult to identify any formal heresy in his arguments (given the lack of precision of the period), it is certain that a century later, Berengarius of Tours was inspired by him, as were the Reformers of the 16th century. All of these tend to ignore the Real Presence, without actually denying it, and prefer to consider the Sacrament in metaphorical terms, and in its role in the spiritual life. So we find that from the first there were two streams of opinion that could be defined as *realist* and *spiritualist*, both of which have their adherents and their descendants.

Berengarius of Tours, already swamped by the crisis, took a further step. He denied the "Real Presence" and reduced the Eucharistic presence of Christ to mere symbolism. For him, theology (like any other science) can only admit purely rational knowledge (or *dialectic*). It is, therefore, a contradiction to state that the bread disappears whilst its accidents remain. Lacking the knowledge of the distinction between substance and accidents, he did not understand that the essence of a thing is not the same as its external appearances.[10] Here, beyond mere semantics, we encounter a problem that is more philosophical than theological.[11] The two ideas which are difficult to state with precision concern transformation (the Real Presence) and identity (the sacrifice of Christ). Against Berengarius, Lanfranc proposed his eucharistic doctrine as a *realistic* reinterpretation of his adversary's pure symbolism. *For both of them, the* res sacramenti *belongs to the order of absent reality and therefore exists only in thought and concept, whilst the* sacramentum *is of the order of present reality, concrete and material. But this* sacramentum *which,in the opinion of Berengarius,is only consecrated bread and wine,is in Lanfranc's view, the actual flesh and blood of Christ. The difference is fundamental*[12] Lanfranc soon became the *official theologian* of this subject. He took tradition as the basis of his argument for substantial change (i.e., a fundamental change touching the very reality of the bread and wine), which he judged to be an article of faith, anterior to all explanation. He insisted upon both the reality of this change, and the mystery which veiled it. This represented a tangible advance on the theology of the Fathers and Paschasius: if the bread becomes the Body of Christ, this change can only be understood if the bread ceases to be bread. His work was approved by the Council of Rome in 1050, so he may therefore be accepted as the exponent of the opinion of the Roman Church at this time. It is more than likely that he was behind the formulation imposed on Berengarius in 1078[13]. Pope Gregory VII thought the term *substantialiter* expressed the fundamental meaning of this text.

It was then found necessary *to add* a doctrinal precision to clarify the meaning of Christ's words at the Last Supper, so that their essential truth might be expressed without ambiguity.   Here we encounter the problem of the relationship between Scripture and Magisterium. The phrase "This is my Body", taken literally, may be understood as   Berengarius undertood it, or given a realistic interpretation.   The rôle of the Magisterium in this case was to guarantee the authentic meaning of the phrase, as it has been transmitted by Tradition, in conformity with the *whole* of the scriptural evidence.[14] Berengarius raised objections which others would take into account and which were later to be satisfactorily explained. For example, the problem of the simultaneous presence of Christ on different altars, of Christ truly present in a large number of Hosts (Guitmond used the simile of a word which reaches a great many hearers), of the separate consecration of the bread and wine implying two Christs, of the permanence of the appearances (*qualitas et forma* according to Lanfranc and Alger, *accidens* according to Guitmond). It is, by this time, already apparent that the heretical rejections which had multiplied in response to problems which reasoned argument had discovered, did not destroy the mystery of faith, but rather assimilated it, and demonstrated that in this mystery there was nothing self-contradictory.

From this period it is safe to assume that the understanding of the first two bodies was complete, but a new danger loomed: doctrinal scrutiny moved away from the Church and onto the Eucharist in order to distinguish between the two more than ever before.[15]

3   The major dogmatic definitions

3.1   The Golden Age of Scholasticism

The term "Transubstantiation" was first used in theology in 1140, in a work sometimes attributed to the theologian Roland Bandinelli, who became Pope Alexander III in 1159 (reigned1159-1181). The idea had already occured in the writings of Guitmond: he talked of *substantialiter transmutari*.[16] It should be noted that this term was not imposed by authority, but rather coined because it was considered most suitable to defend the true faith, in the same way as the term *homousios* was introduced at the Council of Nicea. The word "transubstantiation"   takes up and defines *conversio*, used by St Ambrose, who himself was translating the Greek *metabole*. The 4th Lateran Council employed it in its definition of faith, as part of its creed;[17] canon lawyers then borrowed the term from theologians. Later   Councils did likewise,   thereby hallowing by usage both the terms themselves, and the ideas which were the basis for them.[18] We have come a long way since Ratramnus and Berengarius!

St Thomas Aquinas is clearly the theologian *par excellence* of the Eucharist. We all know about the famous occasion when he, along with St Bonaventure, his rival in holiness and humility, was called before Urban IV to discuss the celebration of *Corpus Christi* with; how the latter tore up his own notes as the "Angelic Doctor" was reading his. Whilst it is true that his treatise is not an act of the Magisterium, the Church has, however, been so inspired by it that it is impossible not to consider it, albeit briefly.

The treatise is contained in questions 72 to 83 of the "Tertia Pars". It leans heavily on patristic ideas rather than on Holy Scripture and makes use of Aristotle more discretely than in some of his other works.[19] However, the eucharistic change posed an ontological problem - he was obliged to employ an analagous division of being into substance and accidents. He pushed this ontological analysis as far as it would go. It was at once seductive and deceptive, in that he himself realised that the rational argument used here is too compressed. He came to the conclusion that these distinctions did not exclude the mystery revealing the true power of God. The originality of his treatise lay in an application of the general doctrine of the sacraments, to the particular case of the Eucharist (Q73). He clearly explained the nature of the Eucharistic sign (Q74 on matter and Q78 form) and also his theology of realism (Q75-76). We rediscover ideas dear to the Fathers, now arranged systematically. He located the sacrament in the past (the passion of Christ), in the present (the unity of the mystical body), and in the future (its effects, and future glory). He defined three levels of sacramental understanding of the mystery: *sacramentum* (the sign: the species of bread and wine), *res et sacramentum* (the Body and Blood of Christ really present; efficacious signs of grace), *res tantum*, (that which is fully realised; grace). His theology stemmed from the sacramental life of the Church, rather than from philosophy. It was more a realisation of the philosophy of being (Q83). The Nominalists and Reformers never understood this.

3.2   The Reformers and the Council of Trent

It is not possible to present a succinct synthesis of the opinions of the Reformers. The general impression they give is one of confusion, with everyone expressing differing opinions as their thoughts led them. By way of illustration, we could cite the important episode of the Conference of Marburg in 1529 where Luther and Zwingli met. They could not agree about the Real Presence. Calvin wrote sadly to Melanchthon: *"It is of great importance that no suspicion of our differences should pass on into the next century, for it is above all ridiculous that having broken with everyone else, that we should get on so badly together right from the start of our Reformation."* [20] All were agreed on the rejection of the Catholic doctrine of sacrifice: according to them, the Eucharist is not a propitiatory work which man can offer to God. But the fundamental quarrel concerned their understanding of the repitition of the Sacrifice of Christ. They raised philosophical problems of time and space. Another important question conerned the identification of the offerings with the Body and Blood of Christ. Calvin, for example, delved into an unresolved paradox: on the one hand, he insisted on the *sign* at its most precise and most spiritual, (a symbol of the Body of Christ), which lead to an insistant denial of transubstantiation and even of the ancient idea of change.[21] On the other hand, he professed his esteem for the Eucharist, by which we communicate with Christ our Saviour, not by an act of faith only, but also by eating[22].

The essential difference sprang from general sacramental theology: Catholics say that the sacraments *contain* grace, while Protestants maintain that they *confer* it.[23] The difficulty arose from a faulty interpretation of "transubstantiation" according to which Christ undergoes a change. He was unable to conceive of transubstantiation except in a spatial or localised form - hence his objects against multilocation.[24] (Cf. Berengarius's difficulties).

Luther was, in general less extreme. He prided himself on being (like the Papists) a defender of the literal meaning of the Real Presence. However, he rejected transubstantiation, as such, in the name of biblical fundamentalism; St Paul talks about the "Bread which we break". Hence he spoke of the simultaneous presence of two substances: the Body of Christ *with, inside, and beneath* the bread (the three prepositions are used indiscriminately). That is the reason why this doctrine is termed "impanation" (*Christus impanatus*).

The Decrees of the Council of Trent provided a response to all these errors. There are principally two series of pronouncements separated by ten years:

On the Eucharist: Session 12 on the Real Presence
        (11 October 1551)

On the Sacrifice of Mass: Session 22 (15 September 1562)

The twenty-first Session on 16 July 1562 contained definitions on Communion under both species, and childrens' Communion.

The impression is given that the Fathers of the Council were working in a scholastic context, whilst avoiding wading into the mire of theological controversy. Perhaps they were aware that they were making their pronouncements at the end of a period marked by a certain decadence in Eucharistic theology, which had begun in the 14th Century with Ockham: the Reformers made great play of denouncing what they believed to be Catholic theology, but which was all too often nothing but a caricature.[25]

26

3.2.1 The Real Presence

The dogma of the *Real Presence* was concisely expressed in Canon 1.[26] It defined the reality and integrity of the Presence of Christ in the Eucharist (*totum Christum, vere, realiter et substantialiter*:Christ is entirely present where there is a part of HIs glorified Being). It also explained the form of this Presence, with its basis in Scripture and Tradition. We find here only a wish for a general reaffirmation (of the doctrine), not a detailed response to each error. The Presence of Christ is something apart, imperceptible to the senses: a living Body, but one without any material accidents.[27]

3.2.2 Transubstantiation

Transubstantiation, a consequence of the Real Presence, was dealt with in Canon 2.[28] Two truths were affirmed here: after the Consecration there is nothing left but the outward semblance of bread and wine. The literal meaning of Christ's words is thus adhered to. But there is a new reality, known only to faith. By the divine power of Christ's words, His Body and His Blood take the place of the bread and wine. Then there is the change of substance properly termed transubstantiation. The Council, however, left room for further explanation by theological investigation. The definitive statement was almost, word for word, that of St Thomas (IIIa q.75, a.4). Three terms are to especially highlighted; terms which surpass in importance any theological system:

- a "change" (conversio),

- of one substance into another substance, and

- a "change" which nevertheless retains the substance's original appearance.

The Franciscans and Dominicans argued over many points, distinguishing in the main two separate theories, but the Council did not take sides.[29]

3.2.3 The manner of the Presence

The whole Christ is present in each species and in every particle: Canon 3.[30] This is simply a consequence of Canon I: after the teaching on the Eucharist in general, Christ's presence in each species is affirmed. His humanity is inseparable from His divinity as a result of the hypostatic union; it is therefore the whole Christ which

27

is present, in His glory, under each species. A distinction made by St Bonaventure shed light on one difficulty: the soul is completely contained in the body it animates, and complete in each part of it; the soul is co-extensive with the body, although limited by it.[31] So it is with the Eucharistic body of Christ - which, like the soul has no dimension in space, and thus, is not subject, as bread is, to the laws of bodies which occupy space. The Canon went no further than the Council of Florence.[32] It was a practical necessity that was envisaged here: in the presence of a particle of the Host or a drop of the consecrated Blood, the faithful could be sure of receiving the whole Christ.

3.2.4   Permanence and consequences of the Real Presence

The permanence of the Real Presence, and the consequences of this permanence were dealt with in Canon 4.[33] The Reformers tried to restrict the Real Presence - when they believed in it at all - to the actual celebration of the Sacrament: Christ is only present during Communion, because His promise was given only to the man who receives HIm (tantum in usu).   Here follows for time what was said about space in the preceding Canon: the change remains so long as the species are not substantially altered. Canon 6[34] talked of the cult of "latria" addressed to Christ as to God Himself: Christ is adored whenever He is present, not only during Communion, but also by other means, of which the most solemn are the Feast of Corpus Christi, processions and public adoration; and the most personal involve adoration of the Reserved Sacrament, especially for the Communion of the faithful in case of need (which takes up on this point Canon 13 of the Council of Nicea: thus the argument from Tradition is important here).

In conclusion, from this overview we can see that, as in matters liturgical, the Council of Trent did not create anything new, but rather ordered and perfected what was already there. The texts attempted to remove anything equivocal, and to identify what was necessary for the safeguarding of the Faith, whilst at the same time carefully avoiding sterile polemics. If people had been content to remain with the clear explanations of classical scholasticism (for example, presence per modum substantiae), the complicated and dangerous theories of later commentators would have been avoided.   An excessive concern with realism, by way of reply to the Reformers, lead to immolationist theories or, at the other extreme, to theories which excluded any idea of immolation, even of an unbloody kind.[35] Other attempts at explanation in a Cartesian manner rejected scholastic philosophy: doomed to failure because of this, they are totally abandoned nowadays.

It is not until the twentieth century, that, following the

Liturgical Movement, we encounter fresh interventions of the Magisterium.[36] In his encyclical *Mediator Dei*, His Holiness Pope Pius XII noted the positive achievments of the liturgical movement, but very firmly recalled traditional doctrine: Transigrification and Transfinalisation were declared insufficient to explain the Eucharistic mystery,[37] and transubstantiation, in the sense of a change concerning the ontological reality of the bread and wine, was reaffirmed.[38] Following the discoveries of atomic physics which analysed matter in its minutest elements, the encyclical *Humani generis* questioned if this posed a problem for transubstantiation. Descartes and his successors had already looked for an explanation in terms of physics (the corporeal inclusion of Christ into the dimension of the host, or the application of a dualist anthropology to the sacraments, by which the soul of Christ would inform the matter of the bread and wine). The Pope opted to maintain the scholastic categories. In its constitution on the liturgy, the Second Vatican Council took up and developed the teaching of *Mediator Dei* (Consitution on the Liturgy, no. 7).[39]

4   Cult and Rite

As far as most of the faithful are concerned, the Faith of the Church, which has been refined and perfected to the highest degree, is only encountered in public prayer and preaching. The Liturgy is therefore of capital importance to the people of God - Pius XI used to say that it could be considered as the first act of the ordinary Magisterium - and the sacramental presence of Christ organises and informs this prayer of the Church. The final Canons of the Council of Trent clearly indicate that theological concepts call for a liturgical *mise en oeuvre*.[40]

The *Ordines Romani* have for many years codified the rituals of the Mass and the celebration of the Sacraments. At the time of the Carolingian Controversies, the Emperor - helped by Alcuin - made them normative throughout the Empire, in particular, through the use of the Sacramentary of Adrian. A little later, the *fusion of the two rites* was solemnised, energetically promoted by Cluny and the Monastic Reform, by which the old Roman hieratism was joined to the luxuriance of the Gallican rites. All this took place in symbiosis with the prevailing medieval theocracy. Since the Peace of Constantine, many years before, the cult of saints allowed bishops and the Church generally *to offer their own definition of the urban community, and to provide the rituals which would help to make this definition clear.*[41] From then on, the Church came to identify herself with organised society. This is why the tradition of the patristic era of the *three bodies* became increasingly important: the relics beneath the altar are a sign of a society united by a common bond, both tangible and emotional. In the East as in the West, an allegorical interpretation of

29

the Eucharistic mystery (and its ancilliary rites)[42] became widespread. It was at the time of the Carolingian Renaissance, when the West established its feudal structures, that Paschasius and Ratramnus worked out their theology of the Eucharist. During the same period, from the IXth to the Xth Centuries, an important innovation took place: the change from leavened to unleavened bread,[43] a change in the nature of the offerings, from bread made by the faithful to bread made by a *specialist*, which was considered more suitable as an expression of the purity and the sanctity of the Eucharist, which in future would be approached only in fear and trembling. Thus was obliterated a whole network of social customs, which had survived for more than 800 years, maintaining a bond between earthly nourishment and the Bread of Angels, as well the work of the laity and the ministry of the Clergy. The result was that Communion was received less often, a process that had already begun at the start of the Constantinian era, when the ardour of piety chilled with the ending of persecution. Religious were the only exception to a rule that was so general that the Fourth Lateran Council imposed, by way of a canonical obligation, the duty of yearly Easter Communion. In the long run, popular piety which sought marvels of every kind, would experience nothing but frustration. It was at this time that the Elevation started, as a rite which exhibited Christ, from now on more contemplated than received. Theological opinion reflected this dichotomy: either an excessive realism, or a disincarnated spirituality. Now and again miracles refuelled the fires of devotion. This central action of the Mass, breaking the silence of the Canon, enhanced by incense and bells, was in harmony with the soaring grandeur of the sanctuary and with that cathedral of the mind which was scholastic theology. It is significant that it was Paris, at the time one of the chief centres of theological reflection, which was first to introduce the practice of elevating the Host, during the last years of the XIIth Century. This place of urban culture, with its high intellectual level and highly developed liturgy, prepared for the dawning light of the Feast of *Corpus Christi*. *Liturgically, the Feast sprang up at first like an amplification, from the choir, of the gesture of the Elevation; and, from the nave, like an orchestration of a rising paean of adoration, which grew from the individual exercise of piety. Both are expressive and enduring memorials to the names of Urban and Thomas.*[44] In fact, the ceremony endowed the culmination of Roman and Gothic culture with a perfection which would sustain it through the rupture of the Reformation.

The surroundings in which Julienne de Cornillon grew up are those of the "Beguinage", the feminine framework of wives and widows abandoned by their husbands for the Crusades; it owed much to the piety of the German mystics, amongst whom prayer often swelled into ecstasy and all kinds of exultation, and in which the

30

centre of attraction was often focused on the reserved Sacrament. So, by contact, what started as a very private devotion, became a public one, transformed into a general devotion which was at once demonstrative and organised, flourishing in the body of a previously feudal society now breached by the growth of disparate communities and economic upheaval. It was now necessary to endow this development with a religious and symbolic presence, a Christian model to strengthen the whole fabric. An obvious parallel is here suggested by the reasoning of the Prince-Bishop of Liege, who stated his meaning plainly, and which may be summarised thus:

Once a year, publicly, and in all places,
the Feast of the Body of Christ *will be* to the feast of His saints
what
the Real Presence *is* to the cult of the saints,
every day, in places uncommon or private.[45]

What Saint Ambrose and Saint Augustine had achieved in their time by integrating the cult of the Saints with Christianity in order to give stability in a disintegrating society, Robert de Thourotte and Urban IV, faced with a similar problem, were to repeat nine centuries later, developing the meaning of the Eucharist and giving it a popular image. Both therby baptised deep popular movements, which henceforth became agents of supernatural cohesion, assisting the change from a rural, feudal and monastic society to one which, albeit already Christian, was developing an urban life both commercial and intellectual, of which the mendicant orders would soon become the masters. It was not unusual to display statues and relics of the saints during *Corpus Christi* processions. These processions would make a round tour of the city visiting four temporary altars situated at strategic points, symbolising the unity of the hallowed enclosure. The heart of the procession would be arranged in a concentric formation around the Blessed Sacrament, rigorously graded according to the prestige and standing of the participants.[46] And so on the altars, the dead presence of the saints, present under the form of fragments of bone, made a symmetrical contrast with that other Presence, the flesh of Christ, truly alive and glorious. Therefore, it is not merely the terrestial city which was mirrored in its transient values and mortality, but the glory of the saints, patrons and protectors, surrounding the sacrificed Lamb of the Holy City. We know that it was customary at the time, if there were no relics, to place a page from the Gospels or a consecrated Host into the *mensa* of the altar. This stems from and reinforces that which as already been said.

Some misapplications of this consequence of the incarnation became the target of the Reformers. They dispensed not only with the

Eucharistic Sacrifice and the Real Presence, but with everything suggesting the presence of God in this world.[47] This is why the Churches emerging from the Reformation have no real liturgy in the true sense: liturgy was viewed as a screen hiding the purity of prayer and could only be a parasite in our relationship with Christ. The Catholic response was triumphantly baroque, bathed in golden light, displaying the fundamental optimism of the Counter-Reformation which set about creating a place of honour for Catholicism in the West. A typical expression of this mentality is to be found in a commentary on the texts of the Council of Trent: *"It is necessary that the truth, conqueror of lies and heresy, should declare its triumph so that its adversaries, witnesses to such revelation and happiness in the Church, should be filled with regret at their own weakness and defeat, and be confounded or sufficiently overcome by shame to revert to finer feelings."* [48] But from now on everything said about this subject had to take possible reactions into account.[49] The defence of Catholic truth led to the exaltation of the Real Presence and the Priesthood, relegating the faithful to the status of enthralled spectators (is this always non-participation?) in a sacred performance where nothing was spared that might contribute to the exaltation of the King of Kings.[50] Monstrance and tabernacle, *Quarant' Ore* and solemn Exposition vied to outdo each other in splendour, while Communion was generally distributed outside of Mass, the exact opposite of the reformed practice.

A positive aspect of the gulf between traditional Roman liturgy and the spirit of the times, was that the efforts to replace it hardly ever got off the ground, with the exception of a few ineffective and marginal experiments, like, for example, those inspired by Jansenism.[51] In France, Dom Gueranger was from the first a determined adversary of Neo-Gallican liturgy, so much so that from 1860, most French dioceses went back to the Roman liturgy. Our century has been distinguished by the liturgical movement. Perhaps we do not take into account sufficiently the revolution it represented in the liturgical life of the Church: even among traditionalists, certain modes of practice which are now commonplace would have been unthinkable less than a century ago. If we are among those saddened witnesses to the abuses stemming from wild interpretations of the last Council, we cannot, in fairness, deny the support it has given to the piety of the faithful.[52]

Conclusion

Intellectual and theological problems, the changes and inevitable short-comings of liturgical expression, are simply the negative side of the greatness of the mystery. Is it not part of the order of things that a tremendous truth such as that of the Eucharist will always be a target for distortion and heresy, for rejection and misunderstanding, but also for triumphs, luminous insights, and radiant revelations?

The humble faithfulness of silent Adoration, as well as the yearly solemnities at which the whole country assists in Catholic lands, tap a mystery that can never be exhausted, capable of reaching out across the centuries to touch the hearts of men of good will. We must, however, remain humble before each new insight, each rediscovery, each clearer understanding. What Father de Lubac said about theology also applies to liturgical mystery: *"We must not forget that a thaw is not an absolute fresh start. It presupposes that something had been frozen which was previously warm and alive. There is, in effect, a rhythm of the spirit just as there is a rhythm in nature. Both have their death throes and their winters. Only, what makes possible the illusion we seek to combat is that in the rhythm of the spirit, unlike the rhythm of nature, each thaw, each "palingénésie", is considered to be a metamorphosis. Spring succeeds spring, but none is exactly alike. What is reborn does not simply reproduce what died at the end of the last season. It is a flower of another fragrance, a fruit with a different taste. The spirit is more creative than nature... We should, perhaps, beware of a kind of belief which is more proud than enlightened, a certain type of intelligence which resembles a certain type of culture, which both reflect the convictions of the person who embraces it at that moment. A kind of simplistic philosophy, the tenets of which oddly resemble a thesis lately held by Monsieur Brunschvicg (concerning "the ages of the intellect"). The difference between the two only exists in the fact that the certificate marking the achievement of adulthood was conferred upon human reason some centuries too soon ...* [53]

The enhancement of liturgy entails the enrichment of the liturgy. But their flowering is not exactly parallel, although it has many points in common. Reasoned truth can be no other than truth arrived at by prayer.[54] So one follows upon the other. It seems to me that history demonstrates that *lex orandi*, precedes *lex intelligendi*, if not *lex credendi*. We can comprened that faith must first be lived, must be contemplated in its entirity, before it can give life the the body of the Church, which comes first, according to the intuition of the Fathers. For the Eucharist is transmitted by the Church, and would have no being without her.[55] And we know that the Church in her historical dimension as her actualisation of the eternal *hodie* of God, is *the* guarantee of the ineffable Presence eternally at the heart of her Faith.

In this sense, the real object of the liturgy is the Church, as seen as a *communio sanctorum* of all places and of all times. From it, flow the three ontological dimensions through which she is known: the cosmos, history and mystery. The Church opposes a *group* liturgy which *is not universal ("cosmic"), but autonomous within the group.*

33

Such liturgy has no history, its character is derived from an historical emancipation and doing things its own way, even when it makes use of the backcloth of history. It knows nothing of the mystery because everything is explained - and has to be explained! This is why development and participation are equally as alien to it as obedience, which opens up a meaning which leads beyond the explicable.[56]

At the heart of the Church and her liturgy, is the Real Presence of the glorified Christ, who for love of His Father and for men, His brothers, offered Himself as Sacrifice and Food. The central moment of history, the point of no return, is at once outside time and enclosed within it - between Maundy Thursday and Easter morning. Through the Great Prayer of the Church we glimpse something of this Presence across the centuries, and understand enough to continue on our journey to the mountain of the living God, where He will be all in all.

NOTES

1. Bull *Transiturus de hoc mundo*, 11th of August, 1264, DH 846-847.

2. J.H. NICOLAS, *Synthèse dogmatique*, p. 921.

3. For example, Candidus of Fulda:*Panis ergo corpus est Christi quod assumpsit ex corpore Ecclesia sua* (PL 106, 68-69).

4. PL 105, 1154 d. The same idea is found in Alger of Liège (PL180, 791 a).

5. Paschase Radbert (PL 120, 1296)

6. Lanfranc (PL 150, 425a).

7. Alger of Liège: *Universum Christi corpus, totum Dominicum corpus* (PL 180, 847 a-b).

8. H. DE LUBAC, *Corpus mysticum*, p.118 ff.

9. PASCASE RADBERT *De corpore et sanguine Domini*, PL 120, 1267-1350.

10. It is amusing to note that his reasoning is deficient on this point: theological rationalism betrays reason as much as it undermines the faith.

11. Cf the illuminating comments of J.DE MONTCLOS, *Lanfranc et Bérenger*, p. 441 ff. Bérenger attributes excessive powers to human reason, and, in matters of faith, places it above authority, because he sees authority in purely human terms; on the other hand reason,as he understood it, was a reflection of the divinity of man, permitting us to grasp truth in its entirety. he here betrays his Aristolelianism, in that he maintains that reason lows from the senses. His natural inclination therefore leads him to deny any change in the bread in the Eucharist, because of the evidence of the senses which reveal no change at all.

12. J. DE MONTCLOS, *Op. cit.*, p. 440. The importance of this difference is clearly expressed in the following quotation: *The same tendency which was shown by one group, can be applied to the others. The doctrine of the Real Presence, the true and direct presence of Christ under the sacramental appearances, can sometimes seem too lofty for us, sons though we are of the Catholic Church, but liable to be misled by facile arguments. Why not substitute for this the simple doctrine, lacking in mystery and scandal, of a symbolic presence? We would*

retain the same terminology, continue to speak of the "real presence " of Christ during the celebration of the Supper, and of giving the faithful "the Body of Christ". It could be explained, in terms that anyone could understand, that just as we can use bread in a profane way, for nourishment, so we can use it spiritually, to unite us to Christ. In His Body Christ is in Heaven, and nowhere else; on the altar there is only bread, and nothing else. But if you take this bread in faith, and with a desire to unite yourself with Christ, the meaning, the end, the finalisation of the bread are no longer profane: you will have changed them - they have become sacred. Their nature is profane, but, by their use, they have become sacred. And so a transignification, *a* transdestination, *a* transfinalisation *of the bread takes place. If we allow that the true nature of things is found in their use rather than in their essence, then why not call this "tranfinalisation" by the established and traditional name of "transubstantiation"? Thus, by moving away from the Church, we would join those who are currently drawing nearer to her. It's better to advance than to retreat. This would give prominence to another teaching of Our Lord's: "He that is not with me is against me: and he that gathereth not with me scattereth" (Mt. 12:30).* (C.JOURNET. *La présence sacramentelle du Christ*, pp. 26-28).

13. Dz Sch. 700.

14. Cf. J.DUPONT. "Ceci est mon Corps", pp. 1025-1041.

15. Alger talks of *alterum corpus* and *proprium corpus* (PL 180, 794 c) and Rupert of Deutz in his *De divinis officiis; non duo corpora dicuntur, aut sunt* (PL 170,35).

16. PL 149, 1143 c.

17. Dz Sch. 802.

18. For example, the Council of Florence (Dz Sch. 1320-1321).

19. Could this be because he realised that Aristotle's epistemological realism would not be helpful for this pecise question? See note 10.

20. K.G. GOETZ, *Die heutige Abendmahlsfrage in ihrer geschichtlichen Entwicklung*, Leipzig, 1907, pp. 78-97. *The words of the Last Supper: **Hoc est corpus meum** have given rise to the most varied, discordant, and, one could almost say, the most outlandish interpretations. It appears that as soon as the traditional meaning had been rejected along with the doctrine of the Real Presence, a void appeared in which neither study of the text nor the primitive tradition of the Church gave support for one opinion over another. The Lutherans were the first to feel the force of the apologetic argument based one of these diifferences and varieties of interpretation; it was an argument used against them in a different context. Once the obvious meaning is abandoned, it is not clear where one should stop. These variations even imperil the principle of* Sola Scriptura. *This is what the Lutheran Andrew Osiander explained to Zwingli in a letter he sent him in September 1527; " See how you disagree amongst yourselves! Carlstadt understands it as "This is my body, given up for you"; you understand it as "This signifies my body". Oecolampadius understands it as "This is a symbol of my body", another person, whom you count as one of your own, renders it thus: "That which you eat, which becomes your body, is, thanks to your faith, already my body". Another, someone who has betrayed me in the most outrageous maner, by joining your heresy (i.e., Theobald Billikam) interprets it as: This - that is to*

say, this exterior thing - is my body for your souls, as this bread is for your bodies" .
Yet another (Urban Rhegius), *whose name I have forgotten, says: " This - that is to say, bread in general - is my body; it is sustained, it increases , it becomes greater thanks to the bread, as it is written of man: "Thou art dust, and unto dust thou shalt return"* (Conrad Sam). Thus Osiander was aware, even at that early date, of four opinions *which differed from Luther's. which was itself far removed from Catholic doctrine. For Carlstadt, these assaults were centred on the word* **Hoc**: *for Zwingli on the word* **Est**, *whilst for Oecolampadius it was the word* **Corpus** . *According to Billikan, Rhegius and Sam , they concentrated their attacks on the entire phrase, so as to distort its true meaning.* C.L'EBRALY, *La doctrine sacramentaire de Ulrich Zwingli,* Clermont-Ferrand, 1939, p. 70).

21.   Christian Institutes, IV, 17, § 12ff

22.   Op. cit., IV, 17, § 5.

23.   *The sacrament is, in short, an outward sign, desired and instituted by God to help the weakness of our faith, a sign which must be observed so that God can give us, from above, His promised grace.* (Y. CONGAR, *Vraie et fausse réforme e l'Eglise,* Paris, 1969, p. 391).

24.   Op. cit., IV, 17, § 17 and 30.

25.   Transubstantiation seen as a miraculous means by which the Body and Blood of Christ are placed in the Host and in the chalice, a second immolation of Christ in the Eucharist, an exaggerated insistence on its fruits and efficacity, etc.

26.   Dz Sch. 1651.

27.   Dz Sch. 1636.

28.   Dz Sch. 1652.

29. Bellarmine speaks of *adductio (Controv. de Eucharistia* 1,18): the substance of the bread disappears, forced out by that of the Body of Christ. But St Thomas considers this opinion untenable (IIIa, q. 75, a. 2). Suarez maintained a change of substance without annihilation or production (*Replicatio de Eucharistia,* disp. 50, sect.4, 10). The text of the Canon is much simpler: the consecration appears not to change the bread. In reality, everything is changed, except the outward appearances.

30. Dz Sch. 1653.

31.   *In IV Sent.,* IV, dist. XII, p. 1 dub. IV.

32.   Dz Sch. 1320.

33.   Dz Sch. 1654.

34.   Dz Sch. 1656,

35. Cf. J.H. NICHOLAS, Op. cit., p.918.

36.   Here we could cite the decree *Lamentabili* of Saint Pius X, in which the following Modernist proposition is condemned: *Not all that Paul says about the institution of the Eucharist is to be taken literally.* (Dz Sch. 2045).

37.   Likewise Paul VI's *Mysterium Fidei* quotes the Council of Trent on transubstantiation (G. DUMEIGE, *La foi catholique,* 795,3).

38.   Dz Sch. 3840

39.   Dz Sch. 4007 = 3840.

40.   For example: Dz Sch. 1643ff, and especially 1744ff, with the corresponding

Canons.

41. P. BROWN Le culte des saints, son essor et sa fonction dans la chrétienté latine, Paris, 1984, pp. 20, 21 and 59.

42. Cf. J.A. JUNGMANN, *Misarum sollemnia*, p. 119ff.

43. J.A. JUNGMANN, *op. cit.*, p.117.

44. C. MACHEREL AND J. STEINAUER , *L'Eat de Ciel*, p.90.

45. C. MACHEREL AND J. STEINAUER *Op. cit.*, p.91

46. *In the whole history of religions, and hence also here, the number four has symbolised the four quarters of the the world - that is to say, of the universe, the world in which we live. That is why Benediction is given towards the four cardinal points, thereby placing them completely under the protection of the Eucharistic Lord. The four Gospels express the same point.... The beginning stands for all; in a similar way, the breath of the Holy Spirit is added to the four winds, so that He can penetrate them and make them salvific. We proclaim that the world is the locus of God's creative Word, and that matter is subject to the power of His Spirit.... Is it not wonderful to witness here a link between the new bread - that is, the Eucharistic Bread - and daily bread, and so see a mysterious reminder of Him who wished to become Bread for all in our everyday bread? Thus the liturgy opens out on the everyday, onto our daily lives and worldly worries: it goes beyond the enclosure of the Church because it actually embraces Heaven and earth, the present and the future. How we need this saving sign!* (J. RATZINGER, *La célébration de la Foi*, p. 127) One ought to read the three meditations that the author proposes here, taking as their starting point a commentary on the text of the Council of Trent: *The Feast of Corpus Christi should act against the human faculty of forgetfulness; it should make man grateful, and evokes that which we all have in common, that unifying force which engenders the fixed gaze upon the One True Lord.* (Id. p. 123.)

47. By way of example, this is what the Reformer Pierre Viret said at Lausanne: *There is no creature so small which, by its simple existence and perfection, does not show us the power, wisdom and goodness of God, better than all the images in the world. Even a tree, whatever fruit it bears, still witnesses to the power and goodness of God, which it represents not at all; but when it is converted into an image, it is cursed , and bears no fruit, and only serves idolatry and wickedness.* From this he draws the following conclusion: *The true Church of Jesus rejects human inventions and principally the images that God has so much defended.* (*G.BAVAUD, La dispute de Lausanne*, p. 11ff).

48. Dz Sch 1644

49. Cf. J.A.JUNGMANN, *Op Cit.*, p. 183.

50. At the consecration of the cathedral of Salzburg in 1628, a Mass by Benevoli was sung, with two choirs of eight voices and their respective orchestra, making a total of fifty-three voices (J.A.JUNGMANN, *Op Cit.*, p. 191)

51. It is true that, especialy during the XVIIIth century in France, there was a proliferation of neo-Gallican rites. But that does not invalidate our argument: on the one hand, they hardly affected the structure of the liturgy, while, on the other hand, Tradition itself was strengthened, confirming the truth that what is not in conformity with Tradition will not endure...

52. Well before the Council., Pope Pius XII had already taught this in his encyclical *Mediator Dei*, second part, II,3.
53. H. DE LUBAC *Op. cit.*, p. 365ff.
54. Cf. J. RATZINGER, *Op. cit.*, p. 33ff, in the chapter entitled: *"Forme* et contenu de la célébration eucharistique".
55. Cf. Cardinal Ratzinger' s very pertinent remarks in *Un chant nouveau pour le Seigneur*, p. 155ff.
56. Cf. J. RATZINGER, *Op. cit.*, p. 158.

Bibliography

BAVAUD G., *La dispute de Lausanne (1536)*, Fribourg, 1956.

BAVAUD G., *Le réformateur Pierre Viret (1511-1571)* Sa théologie, Geneva, 1986.

DUPONT J., "Ceci est mon Corps", *Nouvelle Revue Théologique* 80 (1958) 1025-1041

FILTHAUT T., *La théologie des Mystères*. Exposé de la controverse, Tournai, 1954.

JOURNET C., *La présence sacramentelle du Christ*, Saint-Maurice (Switzerland) 1987.

JUNGMANN J.A., *Missarum sollemnia*. Explication génétique de la Messe romaine, Paris, 1956.

LUBAC H. DE, *Corpus Mysticum*, L'Eucharistie et l'Eglise au Moyen Age, Paris 1949.

MACHEREL C., STEINAUER J., *L'Etat de Ciel*, Fribourg, 1989.

MONTCLOS J. DE, *Lanfranc et Bérenger*, La controverse eucharistique du XIème siècle, Louvain, 1971.

NICHOLAS J.H., *Synthèse dogmatique*, Fribourg, 1985.

RATZINGER J., *La célébration de la Foi*, Essai sur las théologie du culte divin, Paris 1985.

RATZINGER J., *Un chant nouveau pour le Seigneur*, Paris 1995.

VONIER A., *La clef de la doctrine eucharistique*, Lyons, 1942.

Veneration of the Eucharist
in the sixteenth century Anglican Reformation

Michael Davies (England)

Michael Davies, president of the Una Voce international organisation, taught for 30 years. He is the author of 12 books dealing with liturgical questions, in particular from a historical perspective. He has published several works on the Anglican reformation and delivers many lectures in the context of the association of which he is president, to which Cardinal Ratzinger recently sent the following message: "The Una Voce international federation has played an important role in the safeguard and usage of the 1962 editions of the Roman Missal in conformity with the directives of the Holy See. For this precious service, I express my gratitude to the members of the federation and accord them my blessing."

The sixteenth-century Protestant Reformers in continental Europe wished to change the existing religion. Mgr Philip Hughes, the greatest British Catholic historian of this century, writes, concerning these so-called Reformers who were really revolutionaries, that:

> The mania to ensure that all future history should date from their own reconstruction of the primitive glory as they imagined this, characterized these revolutionaries as it has characterised all the rest, the social and political rebels as truly as the religious.[i]

Most of the leading Reformers had been priests and it is not surprising that they sensed that it was the Mass that mattered: that it was against the Mass rather than the Papacy that the brunt of their attack must be launched.[ii] This point is stressed by the German historian Dr. J. Lortz:

> For the Catholic Church it was not the attack on the papacy that was the most fateful event which happened during the Reformation, but the emptying out from her mysteries of the objective source of power.[iii]

All the Reformers denied that the Mass is a sacrifice and, with the exception of Luther, they also rejected the substantial presence of Christ in the consecrated elements. The highest form of Protestant belief and yet far removed from the Catholic doctrine was the theory of consubstantiation, as put forward by Luther. The lowest was the symbolistic view put forward by Zwingli, according to which the bread and wine merely "represent" Christ's Body and Blood. Zwingli and Calvin both taught that the Body and Blood of Christ are not contained objectively in the sacrament and therefore they cannot be offered by the priest. The concept of an Eucharistic oblation was quite logically bound up for them with what they described as "bread worship", which they never tired of denouncing.[iv]

Henry VIII
Supreme Head in earth of the Church of England

King Henry VIII of England did not wish to change the existing religion, but to change his existing wife. Had the pope granted King Henry's request to annul his marriage with Catherine of Aragon there would have been no Protestant Reformation in England. The dispensation of Julius II which had enabled Henry to marry the widow of his brother Arthur, who had died at the age of fifteen without consummating his marriage, was perfectly valid, quite unbreakable in canon law, and therefore the annulment could not be granted.

In 1531 Henry chose the compliant Thomas Cranmer, who would obey him without question, as the new Archbishop of Canterbury. Not wishing to antagonize Henry more than was necessary, Pope Clement VII agreed to the appointment. While in Europe on the King's behalf in 1532, Cranmer, who by then was a convinced Protestant, married secretly the niece of Andreas Osiander, a Lutheran minister. Henry would certainly have had him executed had he learned of the marriage or his Protestantism. Henry married his pregnant mistress Anne Boleyn on 25th January 1533. Cranmer obliged his royal patron by declaring the marriage to Catherine of Aragon invalid and the marriage to Ann Boleyn valid. On 11 July 1533 Pope Clement VII excommunicated Henry and all who had taken part in the proceedings of Cranmer's court.

In November 1534 Parliament passed the Act of Supremacy appointing Henry as "the only Supreme Head in earth of the Church of England called *Anglicana Ecclesia*." Refusal to take the oath was made high treason punishable by death. All the English bishops submitted to the King, with the exception of the Bishop of Rochester, St. John Fisher. The saint's scathing comment regarding his fellow bishops will never be forgotten. "The fort is betrayed even of them that should have defended it." Sir Thomas More also died rather than accept the Act, as did a small number of Carthusian monks.

Henry had broken away from Rome, but he would not allow the Church of which he was the head to break away from Roman doctrine. Between 1536 and 1539 he suppressed the monasteries and seized their land and goods, but this was done for financial and not religious reasons. Where the Mass was concerned the king was particularly conservative, and he made no change but for the removal of any prayer for the Pope or any commemoration of St. Thomas Becket.

Despite the breach with Rome, the dissolution of the monasteries, and such measures as the abrogation of certain holy days, what took place in England under Henry VIII was in no way comparable to the Protestant Reformation in continental Europe. Hilaire Belloc is correct in stating that what took place under Henry VIII should be described as "The Schism". He writes:

> It was not an heretical movement in the common use of the term heretical, that is, it did not combat any of the main doctrines such as were being combatted so violently upon the continent of Europe. It did, indeed, deny the authority of the Pope, but it not only did not deny but fiercely affirmed transubstantiation, the Mass, the whole of the sacramental system. We may put it simply by saying that to the ordinary man, in his daily life and weekly religious duties, things seemed to go on exactly as they had before.[v]

The Accession of Edward VI

Henry VIII died in January 1547 and was succeeded by the sickly nine year old boy King Edward VI, the son of Henry's third wife Jane Seymour, who was no more than a puppet of his Protestant dominated Council. Protestants who had hidden their true beliefs during the reign of Henry proclaimed them without fear now that there was nothing to fear from proclaiming them. Their aim was to obliterate the Catholic faith from the face of the land, and the principal means that they adopted to achieve this objective was to destroy the immemorial Latin Mass and replace it with a vernacular Protestant Communion service. The repudiation of the Pope had given Cranmer no satisfaction while popery remained, and by popery he and his fellow Reformers meant the Mass. It was the Mass that mattered not simply to Catholics but to Protestants. Cranmer hated the Mass as if it had been a living enemy. He attacked as the roots of popery, "the popish doctrine of transubstantiation, of the real presence of Christ's flesh and blood in the sacrament of the altar (as they call it), and the sacrifice and oblation of Christ made by the priest for the salvation of the quick and the dead."[vi] The hatred of the Reformers for the Mass can be illustrated perfectly by quoting John Hooper, Bishop of Gloucester:

> I believe that the holy Supper of the Lord is not a sacrifice, but only a remembrance and commemoration of this holy sacrifice of Jesus Christ. Therefore it ought not to be worshipped as God, neither as Christ therein contained; who must be worshipped in faith only, without all corruptible elements. Likewise I believe and confess that the popish Mass is an invention and ordinance of man, a sacrifice of Antichrist, and a forsaking of the sacrifice of Jesus Christ, that is to say, of his death and passion; and that it is a stinking and infected sepulchre, which hideth and covereth the merit of the blood of Christ; and therefore ought the Mass to be abolished and the holy supper of the Lord to be restored and set in his perfection again.[vii]

Despite his hatred of the Mass Cranmer decided to adopt a cautious approach even though, under Edward VI, the Protestants possessed effective political control over the kingdom. Cranmer realized that the Mass must be phased out over a period of years to avoid provoking armed rebellion. Father Francis Clark, in the most authoritative study of the Eucharistic doctrines of the Protestant Reformers yet undertaken, writes:

> In the earlier and critical period Cranmer and his friends saw that it was wisest to introduce the Reformation by stages, gradually preparing men's minds for more radical courses to come. At times compulsion or intimidation was necessary in order to quell opposition, but their general policy was first to neutralise the conservative mass of the people, to deprive them of their Catholic-minded leaders, and then accustom them by degrees to the new religious system.[viii]

The Vernacular and Audibility

Parts of the unchanged Mass were sometimes celebrated in the vernacular even before the imposition of the new services in 1549 and this was, in itself, "indeed a revolution".[ix] It changed the entire ethos of the Mass, and proved to be an effective instrument for revolutionary change as it accustomed the people to the idea that radical changes could be made in the way that they worshipped. By 12 May 1548, it was possible to have a totally English Mass at Westminster, including the consecration.[x] As well as insisting upon the vernacular, the Reformers demanded that, in dramatic contrast with the Latin Mass, the whole service should be audible to the congregation.

Communion under Both Kinds

One of Cranmer's first important innovations was to impose the practice of Communion under both kinds for the laity at the end of 1547. Many Catholics both in England and abroad made the mistake of conceding this change without opposition for the sake of peace on the grounds that it was simply a matter of discipline. Cardinal Gasquet commented that: "The great advantage secured to the innovators by the adoption of Communion under both kinds in England was the opportunity it afforded them of effecting a break with the ancient missal."[xi] Every such break with tradition lessened the impact of those to follow, so that when changes that were not simply matters of discipline were introduced the possibility of effective resistance was considerably lessened.

The Book of Common Prayer - 1549

On 21 January 1549 the First Act of Uniformity imposed Cranmer's First Book of Common Prayer from Whitsunday (9 June) in place of all the traditional Latin liturgical books, and implemented his long-held objective of replacing the Catholic Mass with a Protestant Communion service. Cranmer entitled his new Communion Service "The Supper of the Lorde and the Holy Communion, commonly called the Masse". This title is an accurate description of the new service which was clearly intended to be a Protestant "commemoration" of the Lord's Supper, but contained nothing specifically heretical, and could be interpreted as a Mass.[xii]ESR, p. 182.[xiii] The word "Masse" was dropped from the title of Cranmer's service in the 1552 Prayer book, which marked the final stage of his liturgical revolution, the imposition of a service that could be interpreted as nothing but a Protestant commemoration.

The 1549 Prayer Book expressed its Protestant ethos principally by what it rejected from the traditional Latin Mass. Father Clark explains that:

> The liturgy of the 1549 Book of Common Prayer has been exhaustively studied, and there is wide agreement that its most significant difference in comparison with the Latin rite which it replaced is the omission of sacrificial language.[xiv]

The new service was entirely audible, entirely in English, and Communion was given under both kinds. The *Judica me*, with its reference to the priest going to "the altar of God", and the *Confiteor* were both abolished.[xv] The confession of sins to Our Lady and the saints and angels, and the request for their intercession, was obviously incompatible with the Protestant doctrine of justification. Like Luther Cranmer swept away the entire Offertory rite which was replete with references to sacrifice and the Real Presence. The *Orate fratres* and the Secret Prayer are abolished. Luther abolished the Canon of the Mass completely, but Cranmer contented himself with removing prayers which affirmed specifically sacrifice and the Real Presence. Despite the fact that the words of Consecration had been codified by the Council of Florence, Cranmer did not hesitate to make changes even here.[xvi] The words "which is given for you, do this in remembrance of Me" (*quod pro vobis tradetur, hoc facite in meam commemorationem*), are added to the consecration of the bread, and the words *Mysterium Fidei* are removed from the consecration of the wine. No elevation was permitted in order to exclude any possibility of adoration. The specifically sacrificial *Placeat tibi* before the final blessing was abominated and removed by all the Reformers.

A Cultural Disaster

The change from a totally Latin to a totally vernacular liturgy involved a cultural disaster of cataclysmic proportions as it cut the Catholic people off completely from the entire musical liturgical heritage of western Christendom which was entirely Latin. An Act of Parliament, reinforced by a royal proclamation, ordered the calling in for destruction of all the old "superstitious" Mass books, which the recalcitrant continued to use; the reforming bishops diligently searched out survivals of "popish superstition" in the liturgy; churches were denuded of their vestments, and texts aimed against the Real Presence and the Mass were painted on the walls."[xvii]

The devastation unleashed by the Reformation upon the cultural heritage of the people of England and Wales has been assessed eloquently by Professor J.J. Scarisbrick:

> Between 1536 and 1553 there was destruction and plunder in England of beautiful, sacred, irreplaceable things on a scale probably not witnessed before or since...By the end, thousands of altars had gone, countless stained glass windows, statues and wall paintings had disappeared, numerous libraries and choirs had been dispersed. Thousands of chalices, pyxes, crosses and the like had been sold or "defaced" ...and an untold number of precious vestments either stripped or seized.[xviii]

Altars Replaced by Tables

The replacement of altars by tables was another step directly in line with the liturgical policies of the continental Reformers. Calvin taught that since Christ has accomplished His sacrifice once and for all, God "hath given us a table at which we are to feast, not an altar upon which any victim is to be offered: he hath not consecrated priests to offer sacrifices, but ministers to distribute the sacred banquet."[xix]

After 1549 all the stone altars upon which the Sacrifice of the Mass had been offered for centuries were destroyed and replaced with wooden tables covered with a cloth of linen placed in the chancel.[xx] On 24 November 1550, the King's Council sent a letter to Ridley, the Bishop of London, explaining that:

> First, the form of a table shall more move the simple from the superstitious opinions of the Popish mass unto the right use of the Lord's Supper. For the use of an altar is to make sacrifice upon it: the use of a table is to serve for men to eat upon.[xxi]

The consecrated altars of the Christian sacrifice were cast out and destroyed throughout the land. It is possible to speak without exaggeration of a hatred of the Mass by the apostate priests and bishops who carried out this sacrilegious destruction.[xxii] Bridgett, p. 63.[xxiii] In many ancient churches and cathedrals in England the altar slab was made into a paving stone, or even the step upon which worshippers trod as they entered the church for the new vernacular service. In Cambridgeshire alone more than thirty such altar slabs thus placed to be trampled upon can still be identified.[xxiv]

The Book of Common Prayer - 1552

In 1552 Cranmer imposed his Second Prayer book in which a number of ambiguities contained in the 1549 rite had been excised to leave what no one could see as other than what it was intended to be, a Protestant Communion Service. Cranmer invited a number of the most extreme continental Protestants to England and sought their advice. The most influential of them was the German ex-Dominican Martin Bucer. Bucer rejected any Eucharistic presence of Christ in or under the forms of bread and wine. He fulminated against the sacrifice of the mass, "stuffed full of abominations, which we cannot sufficiently detest: bread worship also (*artolatreia*) laden with endless insult to God, in which bread while its species remained intact was taken for Christ himself, was adored..."[xxv] Cranmer invited him to compile a critique of the 1549 Prayer Book. It was written in Latin and is known as the *Censura*. At least two thirds of his criticisms were acted upon in the compilation of the 1552 prayer Book, a dramatic confirmation of the extent of his influence upon Cranmer.[xxvi]

Bucer censured several aspects of the Communion rite which he feared could lead to its being interpreted in a Catholic sense. He was particularly insistent that the bread should not be placed on the communicant's tongue but in his hand:

> I have no doubt that the usage of not putting these sacraments in the hands of the faithful has been introduced out of a double superstition, firstly the false honour they wished to show to this sacrament, and secondly the wicked arrogance of priests claiming a greater holiness than that of the people of Christ, by virtue of the oil of consecration. The Lord undoubtedly gave these, his sacred symbols, into the hands of the apostles, and no one who has read the records of the ancients can be in any doubt that this was the usage observed by the Churches until the advent of the tyranny of the Roman Antichrist.
> As, therefore, every superstition of the Roman Antichrist is to be detested, and the simplicity of Christ, and the Apostles, and the ancient Churches is to be recalled, I should wish that pastors and teachers of the people should be commanded that each is faithfully to teach his people that it is superstitious and wicked to think that the hands of those who truly believe in Christ are less pure than their mouths, or that the hands of ministers are holier than the hands of the laity, so that it would be wicked, or less fitting, as was formerly

wrongly believed by the ordinary folk, for the Laity to receive these sacraments in the hand: and therefore that the indications of this wicked belief be removed, as that ministers may handle the sacraments, but not allow the laity to do so, and instead put the sacraments into the mouth -- which is not only foreign to what was instituted by the Lord but offensive to human reason...

Although for a time concession can be made to some whose faith is weak, by giving them the sacraments in the mouth when they so desire, if they are carefully taught they will soon conform themselves to the rest of the Church and take the sacraments in the hand.[xxvii]

Bucer's objection to the traditional manner of giving Holy Communion is, therefore, twofold. It perpetuates the belief that there is some essential difference between a priest and a layman, and between the bread and wine used in Communion and ordinary bread and wine. His solution was the imposition of Communion in the hand as an option in the initial stages, but backed by a propaganda campaign designed to bring about speedy conformity.

Signs of the Cross

Signs of the Cross were regarded by the Reformers as conducive to superstition and they removed them from the liturgy. There were twenty-six signs of the cross in the Canon of the Sarum and other pre-reformation English and Welsh Missals. Cranmer reduced them to two in the 1549 Communion Service. Even this concession to tradition evoked the wrath of Martin Bucer who, in his *Censura*, expressed the hope that "the little black crosses which are printed in the book at this point might be withdrawn."[xxviii] Cranmer removed them from his 1552 Prayer Book.

Kneeling for Communion

Despite his implementation of most of Bucer's censures in his 1552 Prayer Book, Cranmer was to be the recipient of a particularly virulent attack by a particularly virulent Reformer, John Knox, for retaining the tradition of kneeling for Communion. The problem was overcome with a typically Cranmerian compromise. The communicants continued to kneel, but the notorious Black Rubric,* was added to the 1552 Communion Service. It reads as follows:

Lest yet the same kneeling might be thought or taken otherwise, we do declare that it is not meant thereby, that any adoration is done, or ought to be done, either unto the Sacramental bread or wine there bodily received, or unto any real and essential presence there being of Christ's natural flesh and blood. For as concerning the Sacramental bread and wine, they remain still in their very natural substances, and therefore may not be adored, for that were idolatry to be abhorred of all faithful christians. And as concerning the natural body and blood of our saviour, Christ, they are in heaven and not here. For it is against

46

the truth of Christ's true natural body, to be more places than in one, at one time.

It is interesting to note the correspondence between this rubric and the doctrines anathematized in two canons of the Thirteenth Session of the Council of Trent in the preceding year, 1551. There can be no doubt that the phrasing of the Black Rubric constituted an explicit repudiation of Canons 1 and 6 of this session.[xxix]

*The expression "Black Rubric" dates only from the 19th century, when the practice of printing the Book of Common Prayer with red rubrics was introduced, and the fact that the Declaration was not really a rubric was marked by printing it in black. In modern two-colour reprints of the Book of Common Prayer it will be found printed in red.

Cranmer was taking careful note of the teaching of Trent at this time, and in March 1552 he wrote to Calvin:

Our adversaries are now holding their councils at Trent for the establishment of their errors...They are, as I am informed, making decrees respecting the worship of the host; wherefore we ought to leave no stone unturned, not only that we may guard others against this idolatry, but also that we may ourselves come to an agreement upon the doctrine of this sacrament.[xxx]

Cranmer's response to the Council of Trent can be found in the Forty-two Articles of 1553 which were basically his work.[xxxi] A passage in article XXIX is illuminating, both with reference to the Black Rubric and to the Thirteenth Session of the Council of Trent. Its relevant section reads:

Transubstantiation, or the change of the substance of bread and wine into the substance of Christ's body and blood, cannot be proved by holy writ, but is repugnant to the plain words of Scripture, and hath given occasion to many superstitions. Forasmuch as the truth of man's nature requireth, that the body of one and the selfsame man cannot be at one time in diverse places, but must needs be in some one certain place: Therefore the body of Christ cannot be present at one time in many, and diverse places.   And because (as holy Scripture doth teach) Christ was taken up into heaven, and there shall continue unto the end of the world, a faithful man ought not, either to believe, or openly to confess the real, and bodily presence (as they term it) of Christ's flesh and blood, in the Sacrament of the Lord's Supper. The Sacrament of the Lord's Supper was not commanded by Christ's ordinance to be kept, carried about, lifted up, nor worshipped.[xxxii]

The question of the veneration of the Eucharist in the Anglican liturgy was thus made absolutely clear in the 1552 Prayer Book it was regarded as an abomination and totally prohibited. The bread and wine distributed in Holy Communion were considered to be no different from the bread and wine used in ordinary meals. The Lord's Supper itself was a meal, no more than a meal, and most certainly not a sacrifice which is why the altars of sacrifice were destroyed and replaced by tables for the Supper.

The Restoration of the Mass

Cranmer's liturgical revolution was so bitterly resented by the ordinary faithful that most of them could be induced to attend the new services only by the threat of legal sanctions.[xxxiii] The profound Catholicity of the English people was made clear when Edward VI died in 1553, and Mary, the devoutly Catholic daughter of Catherine or Aragon came to the throne determined to restore the Catholic faith cost what it may. The Protestant Professor Bindoff notes that soon after her accession to the throne "the Mass was being celebrated in London churches not by commandment but of the people's devotion, and news was coming in of its unopposed revival throughout the country."[xxxiv] Statues, crucifixes, altars, vestments, and sacred vessels were brought out from their hiding places and restored with joy to the churches which had been the pride of the faithful from time immemorial.

The restoration of the Catholic faith under Mary Tudor, in union with the Pope once more, and the restoration of the traditional Latin Mass were welcomed with enthusiasm by at least 99 per cent of the people of England and Wales. Protestantism imposed upon them from above had captured the allegiance of less than one per cent of the population.[xxxv]

Lex Orandi, Lex Credendi

Queen Mary died on 17 November 1558 while Mass was being celebrated in her bed-chamber. No day had passed in her adult life without her hearing Mass. Elizabeth was crowned as a Catholic and promised to reign as a Catholic, but broke her word almost immediately and reverted to Protestantism as this gave her religious as well as political control over her subjects.

The *new* liturgy destroyed the *old* faith when it was imposed once more in the reign of Elizabeth, with such stringent penalties that only a handful of the most fervent Catholics refused to attend the new service despite its evidently uncatholic nature. The six year imposition of Protestantism in the reign of Edward VI hardly affected the faith of the English people, but under Elizabeth they were forced to assist at the Protestant service for decade after decade after decade (Elizabeth reigned until 1603). The official Protestant Communion Service was celebrated upon a table facing the north and not the east. It was celebrated entirely in the vernacular with all the prayers audible to the congregation. Communion was given under both kinds and, in the form of bread, in the hand. The service did not contain one word, one gesture, one rubric to indicate that the bread and wine received in Communion differed in any way from the bread and wine received in an ordinary meal, that any sacrifice was offered but one of praise and thanksgiving, and that the man presiding at the service possessed any powers denied to the congregation. Most of the faithful went reluctantly at first to the new English service, but as the years passed the law *lex orandi, lex credendi* imposed itself as it inevitably will. As you pray, so shall you believe. The people were forced to worship as Protestants and they became Protestants.

Mgr. Hughes remarked with good reason that:

> It is still hard for a Catholic to grasp the fact that these theories and rites were, in a very great measure at least, the accomplishment of men who were priests, who had not only received the Catholic sacraments, but had said Mass; and who had now come to be satisfied with this, and without any sign of regret that the old could not be.[xxxvi]

He also states explicitly that Catholicism in England was destroyed by the liturgical reform of Thomas Cranmer, reimposed in the reign of Elizabeth:

> Once these new sacramental rites, for example, had become the habit of the English people the substance of the doctrinal reformation, victorious now in northern Europe, would have transformed England also. All but insensibly , as the years went by, the beliefs enshrined in the old, and now disused, rites, and kept alive by these rites in men's minds and affections, would disappear without the need of any systematic missionary effort to preach them down.[xxxvii]

There was, however, a faithful remnant which refused to compromise. Above all, it was the young men who went to seminaries in Europe who preserved the Faith in Britain, They returned to give the Mass to the people and only too often to give their lives for the Mass, the traditional Latin Mass which is found in the Missal of St. Pius V. The victors had taken possession of the churches in which the immemorial Mass had been celebrated for centuries, but the faithful remnant possessed the Mass, and it was the Mass that mattered.

NOTES

[i] P. Hughes, *The Reformation in England* (London, 1950), vol. II, p. 158.

[ii] F. Clark, *Eucharistic Sacrifice and the Reformation* (Oxford 1967), p. 107.

iii   J. Lorz, *Die Reformation in Deutschland*, vol. II (Freiburg-im-Breisgau. 1941), p. 229.

iv   Op. cit. note 2, pp. 111-12.

v   G. Constant, *The Reformation in England* (London, 1934), p. viii.

vi   T. Cranmer, *Works* (Cambridge, 1844), vol. I, p. 6.

vii   J. Hooper, *Later Writings*, (Cambridge, 1852), p. 32.

viii Op. cit., note 2, p. 194.

ix   Op. cit., note 1, p. 113.

x   F. Gasquet & H. Bishop, *Edward VI and the Book of Common Prayer* (London, 1890), p. 102.

xi   Ibid, p. 79.

xii   This ambiguity is stressed by Fr. Francis Clark:

> The first Prayer book of Edward VI could not be convicted of overt heresy, for it was adroitly framed and contained no express denial of pre_Reformation doctrine. It was, as on Anglican scholar puts it, "an ingenious essay in ambiguity", purposely worded in such a manner that the more conservative could place their construction upon it and reconcile their consciences to using it, while the Reformers would interpret it in their own sense and would recognize it as an instrument for furthering the next stage of the religious revolution (Op. cit., note 2, p. 182).

xiii

xiv   Ibid., p. 183.

xv   E.C. Messenger, *The Reformation, the Mass, and the Priesthood* (London, 1936), vol. I. A detailed comparison of the reforms of Luther and Cranmer is provided in Chapter VII of this book.

xvi   H. Denzinger, *Enchiridion Symbolorum (Editio* 31), No. 715.

xvii Op. cit., note 2, p. 187.

xviii J.J. Scarisbrick, *The Reformation and the English People* (Oxford 1984), pp. 85 & 87.

xix   J. Calvin, *Institutes of the Christian Religion*, Book IV, xviii, n. 12 (London, 1838), vol. II, p. 526.

xx   Op. cit., note 1, p. 120-121.

xxi   Op. cit., note 6, vol. II (Cambridge, 1846), pp. 524-5.

xxii   Their attitude is well exemplified by the instructions issued by Edmund Grindal, Archbishop of York, to his churchwardens in 1571, during the reign of Elizabeth I. He not only insisted upon the destruction or defacement of any object that could evoke memories of the Mass, and the removal of all the altars restored during the reign of Mary Tudor, but commanded that every trace of their ever having existed be removed:

> The churchwardens shall see that in their churches and chapels all altars be utterly taken down, and clear removed even unto the foundation, and the place where they stood paved, and the wall whereunto they joined whited over, and made uniform with the rest, so as no breach or rupture appear. And that the altar stones be broken, defaced, and bestowed to some common use.
>
> That the churchwardens and ministers shall see that antiphoners, massbooks, grailes, portesses, processionals, manuals, legendaries, and all other books of late belonging to their church or chapel, which served for the superstitious Latin service, be utterly defaced, rent and abolished. And that all vestments, albs, tunicles, stoles, phanons (maniples), pixes, paxes, hand-bells, sacring-bells, censers, chrismatories, crosses, candlesticks, holy-water stocks or vats, images and all other relics and monuments of superstition and idolatry be utterly defaced, broken, and destroyed.
>
> That they shall half-yearly present to the ordinary (bishop) the names of all such persons that be favourers of the Romish and foreign power, hearers or sayers of Masses or of any Latin service...receivers of any vagabond popish priests or other notorious mislikers of true religion.

xxiii   (T.E. Bridgett, *A History of the Eucharist in Great Britain* (London, 1908), p. 63.).

xxiv   Ibid. p. 65.

xxv   E.C. Whitaker, *Martin Bucer and the Book of Common Prayer* (London, 1974), p. 58. This book contains the complete text of the *Censura* in Latin and English.

xxvi   Op. cit., note 2, p. 123.

xxvii   Op. cit., note 23, pp. 34-6.

xxviii   Ibid., p. 60.

xxix   *Canon 1.* If anyone denies that the Body and Blood, together with the soul and divinity, of our Lord Jesus Christ and, therefore, the whole of Christ is truly, really, and substantially contained in the Sacrament of the most Holy Eucharist, but says that Christ is present in the Sacrament only as a sign or figure, or by His power: let him be anathema. (Denzinger, 883.)

Canon 6. If anyone says that Christ, the only begotten Son of God, is not to be adored in the holy Sacrament of the Eucharist with the worship of latria, including the external worship, and that the Sacrament, therefore, is not to be honoured with extraordinary festive celebrations nor solemnly carried from place to place in processions according to the praiseworthy universal rite and custom of the holy Church; or that the Sacrament is not to be publicly exposed for the people's adoration, and that those who adore it are idolaters: let him be anathema. (Denzinger, 888.)

xxx   Op. cit., note 20, pp. 432-3.

xxxi   E.C. Gibson, *The Thirty-Nine Articles of the Church of England* (London, 1898), p. 12.

xxxii   Ibid., pp. 83-4.

xxxiii   Mgr. Philip Hughes writes:

The new Act of 1552 began by lamenting that, notwithstanding "the very godly order set forth by the authority of Parliament for common prayer in the mother tongue," something "very comfortable to all good people" desiring to live a Christian life, "a great number of people in divers parts of this realm . . . refuse to come to their parish churches and other places where common prayer . . . is used". So failure to attend the services on Sundays and holy days, "there to abide orderly and soberly during the time of the common prayer" was now made an offence... Moreover, a new offence is created: anyone who is present at services of prayer, "administration of sacraments, making of ministers in the churches" or any rite at all otherwise done than is set forth in the Prayer Book, shall upon conviction go to prison for six months on the first offence, for a year on the second, and for life on the third. Such are the first penalties to be enacted in England *for the new crime of hearing Mass, or of receiving the sacraments as they had been received ever since St. Augustine came to convert the English, nearly a thousand years before* Op. cit., note 1, p. 126). (My emphasis).

xxxiv   S.T. Bindoff, *Tudor England* (London, 1952), p. 168.

xxxv   Op. cit., note 1, vol. III, p. 50.

The Protestant historian Owen Chadwick writes: "The Reformation in England had captured the genuine allegiance only of a few instructed theologians and some educated merchants and other members of the middle class, particularly in London, and was supported for less unmixed motives by noble potentates." (Owen Chadwick, *The Reformation* (London, 1973), pp. 122-3.

xxxvi   Op. cit., note 1, vol. III, p. 89.

xxxvii   Op. cit., note 20, p. 111

History of the Rite of Distributing Communion

Father Martin Lugmayr (Germany)

Father Martin Lugmayr, born the 9th April 1965, is a member of the priestly fraternity of Saint Peter. Ordained priest in 1989 by His Eminence the Cardinal Mayer, he has a degree in theology. Professor in dogmatics and exegesis at the Fraternity of Saint Peter seminary at Wigratzbad, he is also superior, in Vienna, of the house of Saint Leopold.

1. Foreword

The historian can attempt to portray the events of the past, classify them within a greater context and try to identify their causes. He is only able to comprehend or interpret these events if he has some interest in a specific area, understands the inner relationships, and is able to accept or interpret them.[1] Anyone who is, politically, totally disinterested, will only be able to write an history of England or France with difficulty. Anyone who rejects the possibility that miracles do occur, denies himself access to the history of Israel, Our Lord Jesus Christ, or the Church: not as an historian but as a bad philosopher. What conclusions can be drawn from these considerations for the purposes of our theme? The history of the communion rite cannot be considered from a purely historical perspective. As, on the one hand, there is the Blessed Sacrament and, on the other, man, an understanding of the rite that leads to the sacramentally present Lord with the faithful, must consider both the mysteries of eucharistic faith as well as circumstances connected with the relationship between God and man and its symbolic expression.

2. The Witness of the New Testament

There is no detailed account in the Scriptures of the manner and kind in which Holy Communion was received but we can, however, make some interesting observations.

We can deduce from the words of Christ, "Take ye and eat, this is my body" (Matt. 26,26) that "take" would exclude "receive" - something a subsequent ritual would have needed to take into account.[2] Here, the following can be said: firstly, Luke emphasises that the Lord gave His body to the disciples (Lk. 22,19). Secondly, the limitations of translation into the vernacular become obvious if we quote the inspired original text. The concept *"lambánein"*,

53

etymologically, means "touch, take hold of" but nevertheless can be expanded according to two meanings: an active meaning in the sense of *take, bring into ones area of disposability*, and a passive meaning in the sense of *receive, acquire*. Above all, the latter is emphasised in the New Testament whenever the relationship between God and man is mentioned.[3] We are clearly recipients (vide Cor. I, 4,7). Theologically speaking, it is inconceivable that man should be able to dispose of the body of Christ. As a consequence it is perfectly clear that the rite must do justice to this principle: thus *"lábete"* is to be understood in the sense of "receive".

The Hebrew word *"lkh"*, corresponding to *"lambánein"*, means "take, take hold of, take to oneself" but can also mean "accept, receive".[4] This also applies to Syriac, another major language related to the language known by the Lord. The term *nsb* means, according to its root, "take", but it often means "receive" and this is evidenced in the description of Holy Communion given by St. Ephraem the Syrian.[5]

Confirmation of our thesis is to be found in early Christian literature. Origen stresses that Christ *gives* His body and blood, "when you go up with him to celebrate the Passover he will give you the chalice of the new covenant as well as the Bread of the Blessing, he will give you His own body and His own blood.[6] Again, St. Justin stresses that Christ alone *gave* His body and blood to the apostles, "as the apostles reported in their records, called gospels, they were instructed as follows: Jesus took the bread, gave thanks and said, do this in memory of Me, this is My body, and in the same manner took the chalice and said this is My blood and that He alone gave it to the apostles."[7]

Incidentally, it can be seen from Jn. 13.26 that the Lord gave Judas the dipped bread in the mouth (but what this refers to is not totally unequivocal from the source).

We can seen from the letter to the Corinthians that all those obviously living in mortal sin were excluded from Communion (1 Cor. 5,6 - 13). Furthermore, the so-called secret sinners had to abstain from Communion lest they be guilty of the body and blood of the Lord (1 Cor. 11, 27). Such a forceful warning - the non-observance of which would entail God's punishment (1 Cor. 11,30 et seq) - must correspond to rites which would, firstly, have made possible a non-communion and, secondly, taken into account the required reverence and spiritual awe. This is all the more valid if one stresses, as does C.D.F Moule, that "the only explicit reference in the New Testament to preparation for the Lord's Supper is in terms of *judgment*".[8]

3. The Communion Rite in History
3.1 The Place for Distributing Communion

The sanctuary was separated from the remainder of the church although the organisation of the boundaries changed during the course of history. The clergy received Holy Communion at the altar and the faithful at the railing.[9] That the laity received communion at the altar was mentioned at the council of Laodicea in the 4th century whereby women were explicitly not allowed to approach.[10] Only in Gaul do we find communion being distributed before the altar as a long-established tradition.[11] During the Carolingian period the norms of the universal church also gained acceptance in Gaul.[12] Subsequently, the laity were sometimes given communion at a side altar and, when the rood screen[13] came into fashion, this was mostly before the Holy Cross Altar which was set up in front of the screen.[14] From the 13th century two acolytes spread a white linen cloth before the communicants kneeling before the altar[15], in the 16th century this cloth was spread on a bench which was set up between the sanctuary and the rest of the church nave. This was the origin of our communion rail.

3.2 The Method of Distributing Communion
3.2.1 Historical Overview[16]
From the 3rd century there is evidence that the Eucharistic Body of Our Lord was also being given to the laity in the hand in various provinces of the Church.

In regard to Alexandria and the Egyptian diocese we may quote Clement of Alexandria (+ before 216/7)[17] and Dionysus of Alexandria (+ 264/5)[18], for Palestine we have St. Cyril of Jerusalem (+ 386)[19]. In Syria there are texts from Aphraates (+ shortly after 345)[20], Ephraem the Syrian (+ 373)[21], John Chrysostom (+ 407)[22] and probably Kyrillonas[23] as well. For the 5th century we may, for example, mention Theodore of Cyrus (+ circa 466)[24]. Amongst the Cappadocians we could mention St. Basil the Great (+ 379)[25] and Gregory of Nazianzus (+ 390)[26]. In the East there are later witnesses as in the case of Anastasius Sinaita (+ after 700)[27] and John of Damascus (+ circa 750)[28]. In North Africa the usage mentioned[29] is evidenced by Tertullian (+ after 220)[30], Cyprian (+ 258)[31], Augustine (+ 430)[32] in two polemic treatises[33] and Quodvultdeus (+ circa 453)[34]. According to a letter handed down by Eusebius[35], this was done in Rome and Italy by Pope Cornelius (251/3), Ambrose (+ 397)[36] in his description of man after his creation[37], Gaudentius of Brescia (+ after 406)[38], Petrus Chrysologus (+ 450)[39] and Cassiodor (+ circa 580)[40]. In Spain there are apposite quotes in the acts of the synods of Saragossa (380)[41] and Toledo (400)[42]. In Gaul, Caesar of Arles (+ 542)[43] mentions in his sermons this manner of distributing communion.[44] The Venerable Bede (+ 735) also bears witness to this in England.[45].

55

After 800, this manner of receiving communion is only recorded as a privilege of the clergy.[46] Due to the risk of desecration by Jews and heretics the synod of Cordoba in 839 refused the unreasonable request put by the Casians to receive Holy Communion in the hand *more levitarum*.[47] Regino of Prüm[48] in his "De synodalibus causis", written in 906[49], attributed the following canon regarding the duties of the priest to a synod of Rouen:

"He should not give (communion) in the hand to either a layman or a woman but only on the tongue with the words *May the body and blood of the Lord serve to forgive you your sins and lead you to everlasting life*. If anyone should violate this provision he is to be removed from the altar as he has shown contempt for almighty God and refused to honour Him"[50]. Although even today the existence of this synod is disputed[51], we can allow it as canonical evidence of significance insofar as such a threat of punishment presumes that the opposite, that is communion on the tongue, was the norm.

Communion on the tongue is also attested as the sole method allowed in the Missa Illyrica[52], and also in the Byzantine liturgy.[53]

There are already witnesses for communion on the tongue such as St. Gregory the Great (+ 604)[54] and also reports on giving communion to the sick.   According to Mario Righetti in the 6th century, communion on the tongue seems already to have become more widespread than was once assumed.[55] According to Klaus Gamber, the abolition of communion in the hand had already occurred from the 5/6th century onwards.[56]

Obviously, communion in the hand was impossible where Holy Communion was distributed *per intinctionem* (by intinction in the Precious Blood), a custom which was certainly rejected by the Synod of Braga in 675[57], but was then initially used more frequently in communion for the sick[58] until finally, towards the end of the 8th century, it found greater acceptance in the parishes. At the same time, there is evidence of communion being distributed in the East both by intinction in the precious blood as well as by the aid of a spoon.

Although permitted for the laity, John of Avranches (+ 1079) stresses that the priest may not receive Holy Communion by intinction in the Precious Blood, "not on the basis of any authority but on the basis of the dire need which comes from the fear that some of Christ's blood could be spilt"[59].

So that not one drop of the Precious Blood should fall to the ground when the priest held Holy Communion to the recipient's mouth, a cloth was held under the chin.[60] At Cluny, a plain golden dish was used for this purpose and was held by an acolyte under the priest's hand when the priest dipped pieces of the Host in the chalice held by the sub-deacon and then carried them to the mouth of the communicant.[61] This liturgical tool can be seen as a predecessor of our communion paten.

Up to the 12th century the Precious Blood was also given to the laity (unless it was given by inctinction). Solemn distribution was the responsibility of the deacon. Either the consecration chalice or a special chalice for distributing the sacrament was used (this is still the custom in Ethiopia and East Syria).

Let us now examine in greater depth the rite of distribution under the first kind.

3.2.2. The Rite of Distributing the Body of the Lord

For more than one thousand years there was no form of communion in the hand for the laity in the Catholic Church in either the West or East, or in those communities with apostolic succession. This changed with the encyclical "Memoriale Domini" published in 1969[62]. Wilful disobedience, primarily in Holland, paid off: Rome allowed the so-called "communion in the hand"[63]. Initially, this was deemed a concession for those few countries in which it had been practised as a matter of disobedience - the time-honoured form of the rite was to remain the norm for the Church worldwide - it made a triumphant entry into the Latin rite area, and hand communion was frequently forced on the faithful.[64] The apologists for hand communion asserted, and still assert, that this was merely a revival of an ancient practice. We shall now examine this assertion.

Before receiving Holy Communion, the faithful adored the Almighty with great reverence. St. Augustine taught that, "As he has been transformed into this flesh, and this flesh he has given us to eat, let none eat this flesh if they have not first exalted it. This is how the footstool of the Lord is adored[65] and not only do we not sin when we adore it, we sin when we do not.[66] Regarding the communion of the Precious Blood, Saint Cyril of Jerusalem says that communion should be with "bowing in adoration and reverence, and saying Amen" (Cat. Most. 5.19)[67].

If one were even farther away from the place where communion was distributed, the hands were clearly stretched out towards heaven[68] and then one placed in the other.[69] The faithful were not allowed to bring any other vessel in which to receive the Body of the Lord; the hands, held in the shape of a cross, were all that was allowed.[70] The fathers of the Church never tired of warning that there should be no lack of deep respect, and careful consideration of God's condescension. Saint John Chrysostom preached, "And is it not wonderful when you are standing with the Seraphim, that God allows you to touch what the Seraphim do not dare to touch? 'It is said that one of the Seraphim was sent to me and he had fiery coals which he had taken from the altar with tongs (Is. 6.6). That altar is a type and a picture of this altar; that fire is a picture of this spiritual fire. But the Seraphim did not dare to touch with the hand (ápsasthai) but with the tongs, but you receive it in the hand (lambáneis). If you now examine the present gifts according to their value, they are to be valued much more highly than those which the Seraphim took"[71].

The hands must be free of all sin. Tertullian records lamentable cases, "Religious zeal can only be expressed tearfully for what follows: we are speaking of a Christian who comes from the idols to church, from the hostile workshops into the house of God, someone who raises his hands to God the Father - hands with which he has created idols, who worships with these same hands which, outside, are raised against God. Someone who holds out these hands to the body of the Lord, hands which have made sacrifices to the demons? But even that is not enough. It is bad enough that they receive from other hands what they then pollute but that these hands then give to others what they have polluted. The makers of idols are called into the church community. What a sin! The Jews laid hands on Jesus once: but these people harm his Body every day. Such hands must be cut off! They should now see whether *"if thy hand offends thee, cut it off"* was only meant metaphorically. Which hands should sooner be cut off if not those which offend the Lord's body?[72]

Gregory of Nazianzus also speaks out against women who conduct themselves in a seductive manner, "Do not the hands, when reaching out for the mystic supper, recoil in horror because with them you painted that lamentable beauty (on your face)?"[73]

Later texts mention first washing the hands and covering women's hands. For example, Caesar of Arles says, "What I last said to you is neither difficult nor laborious, I am speaking of that which I have often seen you do. All men wash their hands if they wish to take communion and all women hold out a pure linen cloth on which they receive the Lord's body. What I want to say to you, brothers, is not difficult; as men cleanse their hands with water, so should they cleanse their consciences with alms, and as women hold out a linen cloth on which they receive the Lord's body, they should come with a chaste body and a pure heart so that they may receive Christ's sacraments with a clear conscience. I ask you brothers, would anyone put his clothing in a box which is full of filth? And if no valuable clothing would be put in it, with what brazen effrontery will Christ's Eucharist be received by a soul stained with the filth of sin."[74] In another sermon he said, "If we blush and are afraid to touch the Eucharist with dirty hands, we must be even more afraid of receiving this same Eucharist with a soul stained with sin."[75]

The synod of Auxerre strongly prescribed the covering of women's hands, "A woman is not allowed to receive the Eucharist with hands uncovered".[76]

Finally, the hands of men were also covered - and this can be substantiated by pictorial representations[77] and engravings on silver patens.[78] We should also mention that from 350 there are illustrations of covered hands in pictures of the feeding of the five thousand. We see here the influence of the liturgy.[79]

Particular care should be paid to the question into which hand the Host is to be placed. In the last of his mystagogic catecheses[80] held at Easter towards the end of his life (he died at Eastertide in 387), St. Cyril of Jerusalem instructed the newly baptised as to the manner in which the Blessed Sacrament was to be received.

"When you go to Holy Communion, do not come with flat hands outstretched or the fingers spread out, but make the left hand act as a throne for the right hand which is to receive the King. Take the Body of Christ in the hollow of the (right) hand and say 'Amen'. Hallow carefully your eyes through contact with the Sacred Body and then receive the Host - taking care that you lose none of it because if you lose any of it, it will be as if you had lost one of your own limbs. But tell me, if someone gave you gold dust, would you not take hold of it with the greatest care and make sure that you lost none of it? Would you then not be even more careful with that which is even more precious than gold and precious stones, taking care that not even a tiny crumb is lost?"[81]

At first glance we might think this is a description of today's practice of communion in the hand but on closer inspection we see a distinct difference.

The right hand must be placed over the left hand and not the other way about as is the case today. A small detail? Nothing of the kind! At that time, as today, the majority of people were right-handed and it would not have occurred to any of them to accept or take a present, a valuable gift, with the left hand.[82] According to the description by St. Cyril of Jerusalem, it would have been unthinkable for the faithful to take hold of the Lord's body and carry it to the mouth. Otto Nussbaum comes to the same conclusion, "Above all, it is my opinion that, given the pronounced preference for the right hand throughout the entire early church and in the liturgy, it is inconceivable that the left hand would have been allowed to touch the Eucharistic bread and carry it to the mouth - given that the left hand was always regarded as the lesser in value, as a symbol for what is bad, and therefore inapposite and unsuitable for the ritual service. In my opinion one would more likely take the Host directly with the mouth from the right hand. The kiss of the meal before receipt speaks for this, as does - in particular - the comparison of this kiss with licking the Lord."[83]

Thus the right hand served in the manner of a communion paten from which, bending low, the Host, together with any crumbs, was taken into the mouth.

We should examine in even greater detail Nussbaum's aforementioned argument as many have asserted that such an idiosyncratic custom as the hallowing of the eyes, should have been recorded in the texts by John of Jerusalem, Cyril's successor. But it can be shown that this related to a custom which was widespread at the time of St. Cyril. Aphrahat speaks of specific communion rites in a dissertation on humility which was written before 337AD at the latest: "Your tongue should love silence as it licks the wounds of the Lord. Your lips should consider before parting that with them you are kissing the Son of the King with them".[84] In a commentary on Ri 7.5 he speaks of licking with the tongue.[85]

In instruction 20,8 Aphrahat speaks of the hallowing of the eyes, "The poor man at the door is a symbol of our Saviour (vide Lk. 16,20 et seq). Imploringly, he asked to receive fruits from them (his people) in order to give them to the one who had sent him. But nobody gave him anything (vide Mk. 12,2.6). It says that the dogs came and licked his wounds. The dogs that came were, in fact, the peoples who licked the wounds of our Saviour (vide Mt. 7,6; 15,26 et seq). They took his Body and laid him on their eyes."[86]

There is a text in the writings of St. John Chrysostom, the wording of which is strikingly similar to the wording of St. Cyril of Jerusalem, although it cannot, with certainty, be attributed to the former.[87]

As F. J. Dölger rightly observed, Cyril, pseudo-Chrysostom and Aphrahat complement each other as the latter mentions the hallowing of the lips and the tongue which, certainly, is also meant by Cyril.[88] Theodore of Cyprus also speaks of this kiss of the Lord's Body.[89]

How do we visualise this applying to the senses? As already stated, the body of the Lord was certainly not taken in the left hand. A text by St. John Damascene can help us further. "We approach Him with burning desire and, with our hands held in the shape of a cross, accept the body of the crucified Lord. And after laying on our eyes, lips and forehead, we enjoy (metalábomen) the heavenly coals so that the fire of our desire, which also receives the fire from the coals, consumes our sins, lifts up our hearts and we become wholly inflamed and hallowed by participating in the heavenly fire."[90] This ceremony is performed by a prayerful lowering of the head.

With this application of the senses, particular care must be given to ensuring that not a particle is lost. Because of this danger and, as we may assume, due to improper and blasphemous misuse, this custom vanished.[91]

It was certainly not without good reason that the council of Toledo in the year 400 issued the following canon, "If anyone does not consume the Host when received from the priest he shall be excommunicated as sacrilegious."[92]

In summing up we may say that the right hand served, not as a hand that took, but as a type of communion paten from which the mouth accepted the Lord's body.

But even later, after the blessing of the senses had been discontinued, it was still relatively easy on receiving communion to take away the Lord's body undetected. Towards the end of the 7th century the canons, drawn up by Jacob of Edessa[93] in reply to a question addressed to Jacob by the presbyter, Addai Philoponus, stated:

"As there are, in fact, those who take away particles of the Host and sew them together into a kind of magic band and bind them into a pouch, or hang them on their persons as amulets, or place them in their beds and in the walls of their houses, I would like to ask if it is seemly that this should happen or, if unseemly, what punishment should be given those persons who do such things?" This brought forth the following reply:

"Those, however, who commit such sacrilege with the sacraments of the Body and Blood of Jesus Christ, sacraments worthy of being adored, by using them and treating them just like any other ordinary objects - although in themselves objects worthy of veneration by Christians - hanging them about their necks together with the cross or the bones of the saints and consecrated objects, or placing them in their beds or in the walls of their houses for protection, or in vineyards or gardens or parks, using them just for the protection of material objects, fail to take into consideration that these holy sacraments are the only food for the souls of those who carry the cross as a sign of Christ: they are the leaven and pledge of the resurrection of the dead and life everlasting. If they are clerics they should be removed from office and excluded from communion for a period of three years and be penitents for this period. If they are laity they should be excluded from communion for a period of four years and be penitents for this period."[94]

Let us once again turn our attention to Saint Cyril of Jerusalem. In addition to a detailed description of the communion rite we have an urgent warning to take care for the smallest particles, even crumbs, so that they are not lost. They are more precious than gold and precious stones. What faith in the real presence!

St. Cyril is not the only witness we could call on: approximately 150 years before his birth, Tertullian (160-220) wrote in his work "On the soldiers' crowns": "The sacrament of the Eucharist ... we also receive at early morning meetings and from the hand of none other than the superior (i.e. the priest and bishops). (...) Indeed it alarms us if anything from our chalice or our bread falls onto the ground", De cor. Mil. 3.4.[95]

Origen (185-245), who elsewhere often stresses spiritualising interpretations[96], describes the bearing of the faithful before the Blessed Sacrament in the following manner: "You know, those of you that are used to participating in the sacred mysteries, how concerned you are when you receive the body of the Lord to ensure with all care and reverence that not the smallest particle falls to the ground, and nothing of the consecrated gift is scattered. You believe that you commit a sin should anything fall to the ground through carelessness -

and you are correct in this belief of yours", In Ex. Hom. 13,3[97]. This means not allowing even the merest fragment to fall to the ground. In this regard carelessness is a sin. What could be clearer than that?

4. Summary

There was no rite of communion in the hand as practised today. Strictly speaking, the texts discussed above relate not to communion in the hand but what is a communion patristic on the tongue where the right hand acts as a paten. This is confirmed by the deacon's communion rite in the Byzantine liturgy: he takes up the Body of the Lord with the mouth from the right hand whilst bowing low.

By bowing low with the body held in reverential composure it was demonstrated clearly that a human being is, in this case, the recipient and not some one who takes and gives himself the Host. Even in the case of house communion, which was permitted from time to time, this was observed.[98] Today, the deacon in Byzantine liturgy still communicates in the manner described by St. Cyril (without the blessing of the senses). Cardinal Ratzinger once wrote something fundamental on the essence of the sacramental encounter of the creature with the eternal God that becomes manifest here:

"And for that reason, too, it is a part of the basic structure of the sacrament that it is *received* and that no one can serve himself. No one can baptise himself, no one can ordain himself priest, and no one can absolve himself from his own sins. It is on account of this encounter structure that perfect contrition, by its very nature, cannot remain spiritual, but requires the encounter form of a sacrament. For that reason it is not merely a violation of the external requirements of canon law if one passes around the Host himself and takes it himself, but it is also a violation of the innermost structure of the Sacrament. That in only this Sacrament the priest is allowed to give himself the holy gift points to the 'mysterium tremendum' to which he is exposed in the Eucharist: he acts 'in persona Christi' and so at the same time represents Him *and* remains a sinful person, who lives wholly by receiving His gift.[99]

Furthermore, the early church was concerned from the beginning to ensure that not a single particle was lost. In theory, this care is still observed today.[100] An encyclical dating from 1973 states, "Since the encyclical 'Memoriale Domini', published three years ago, several bishops' conferences asked the Holy See to allow those distributing communion to place the Host in the hands of the faithful. As this encyclical reminds us, 'the provisions of the Church and the writings of the fathers offer rich proof that the greatest reverence and the utmost prudence was, and is, to be applied vis-à-vis the Holy Eucharist').[101] Particularly with this type of communion certain matters have to be carefully considered - as demanded by experience itself. There must be unremitting care and attention present, especially with regard to the question of particles which may have fallen off the Host. This refers to those distributing communion as well as the faithful, whenever the Host is placed in the hand of the communicant.[102]

Shortly before that, the Congregation for the Propagation of the Faith, in a declaration regarding various doubts, held firm that the Real Presence, the actual presence of Christ also extends, in fact, to small particles which have fallen from a consecrated Host and therefore the provisions regarding the cleansing of the paten and the chalice are to be observed.[103]

Is "the greatest reverence and the utmost prudence" applied to the Holy Eucharist today as the fathers once did? Is "continual care and attention" present - in particular with regard to the particles"? Anyone who wants to see and has eyes to see with knows how these questions must be answered. It is not a question of a few excesses or misuses here and there; an obvious carelessness has become the norm, leading to the conclusion that there is a lack of reverence and deficient belief in the Real Presence. All the dangers listed in the encyclical "Memoriale Domini", namely reduced reverence, profaning the sacrament and adulterating the faith[104] have occurred and continue to occur.

Why did all the particular churches banish all rites of communion in the hand? Not, as many think, because the shape and type of the Host has changed. Jungmann, for instance, sees a reason in the change to unleavened bread.[105] This cannot be correct for the reason that there was no such change in the East: normally unleavened bread was always used. If one asserts, as Nussbaum does[106], that the change in communion practice was due to a change in the form of the Host (to flat wafers), there must be some positive reason: in the East the form has not changed! Why, therefore, was there a change in all rites?

"The real reason is rather to be found in the fact that there were bad experiences with communion in the hand for the laity. (...) It will be the same experiences that we are having today and will increasingly have: from deficient reverence on receiving the Host to the direct misuse of the Host to superstitious, even satanic purposes (satanic mass!)[107] Klaus Gamber wrote these lines in 1970 and all his prophecies have come to pass.

Reverence and faith, and striving to create for these an ever more perfect expression in the rite was the spirit of the early church, the spirit of the fathers. Communion on the tongue is the fruit of this loving endeavour. The encyclical "Memoriale Domini" stresses that communion on the tongue should be preserved, "not only because it is based on the custom handed down over many centuries, but because it reveals visibly the reverence of the faithful towards the Host"[108]. It is "effectively ensured by communion on the tongue that Holy

Communion is distributed with due reverence, decorum and dignity and that all danger of desecrating the Host is removed and in which 'in a unique manner, substantial and continuing, Christ, whole and undivided is present with God and man[109] and that, finally, care is scrupulously maintained against that which the Church has always warned against regarding the particles of the consecrated Host".[110]

NOTES

1. "The word "inter-pretation" takes us to the heart of the matter. Every interpretation demands an inter', an intermediation' and an 'interpolation', the actual presence of the interpreter. Pure objectivity is an absurd abstraction. The non-participant has no experience, because participation is a prerequisite for knowledge", J. Ratzinger. *"Schriftauslegung im Widerstreit. Zur Frage nach Grundlagen und Weg der Exegese heute*, in *Schriftauslegung im Widerstreit,* published by J. Ratzinger, Herder, Freiburg I. Br., 1989, 15 - 44, here 23.

2. In point of fact the Congregation for the Propagation of the Faith in a letter written in French accompanying the encyclical "Memoriale Domini" allowed the Faithful to take the Host direct from the ciborium ("On pourra cependant adopter aussi une manière plus simple, en laissant le fidèle prendre directement l'hostie dans le vase sacré, AAS 61 [1969] 547). Four years later, on 21 June 1973 to be precise, this concession was deleted from the agreement "De sacra communione et cultu mysteri eucharistici extra Missam" (vide EDIL., I, no. 3082)

3. Vide ThWBNT, IV, Art., *lambáno* (Delling), 5f.

4. Vide H. Seebass, ThWBAT, IV, 590

5. Vide Pierre Yousif, *L'Eucharistie chez Saint Éphraim de Nisibe,* Orientalia Christiana Analecta 224, Roma, 1984, 298

6. *Hom. XIX. In Jer.,* GCS, Origen III, 13, p. 169, line 30 et seq

7. Apologia, I, 66

8. "The only explicit reference in the New Testament to preparation for the Lord's Supper is in *judgemental* terms", C.F.D. Moule, *The judgement theme in the sacraments,* in *The Background of the New Testament and its Eschatology, Studies in honour of C.H. Dodd,* University Press, Cambridge, 1956, 456

9. Augustine warns those who may not receive Holy Communion because of some sin not to approach "so that they may not be turned away from the altar rails (*de cancellis*)" (serm. 392.5; PL 39, 1712).

10. Council of Laodicea, ca. 44, Mansi II, 571

11. Without limitation the synod of Tours (567) in canon 4 (Mansi IX, 793): "Ut laici secus altare, quo sancta mysteria celebrantur, inter clericos tam ad vigilias, quam ad missas, stare penitus non praesumant: sed pars illa, quae a cancellis versus altare dividitur, choris tantum psallentium pateat

clericorum. Ad orandum vero et communicandum, laicis et feminis, sicut mos est, pateant sancta sanctorum" (The laity may not presume to stand by the altar where the sacred mysteries are celebrated during vigils and the celebration of mass by the clergy: also, the area between the choir rails and altar is available only to the choir and the clergy singing the psalms. For prayer and communion the Blessed Sacrament should be open to the laity and women, as is the custom).

12. In Spain the IV council of Toledo had already decided by 633 (Mansi X, 624) "ut sacerdos et levita ante altare communicent, in choro clerus, extra chorum populus" (that priests and deacon receive Holy Communion in the clergy chancel beyond the people's chancel).

13. For its history and significance vide Klaus Gamber, *Die Funktion des gotischen Lettners aufgezeigt am einstigen "Lectorium" des Regensburger Domes,* in *Sancta Sanctorum. Studien zur liturgischen Ausstattung der Kirche, vor allem des Alterraums,* Friedrich Pustet, Regensburg 1981, 109-119.

14. Vide J. A. Jungmann, *Missarum Sollemnia,* II Herder, Vienna 1948, 454 et seq.

15. That such a cloth has to be spread out before the communicant can be seen in an instruction dated 26.3.1929 (AS 21 [1929] 638) .

16. There is a valuable compilation in Otto Nussbaum's *Die Handkommunion,* Publisher J.P. Bachem, Cologne 1969, 9 et seq.

17. Strom, 1,I,5 (GCS Clem. 2.18 et seq, Stählin)

18. Eusebius, h.e. 7,9,4; GCS Euseb 2,2,648

19. Cat. Myst., 5,21; FC 7,162

20. Hom. 7,21 and hom. 20,8

21. Hymns of faith, 10,8; 10,15 CSCO 154/155; Seq II,2 vide *Naqpayata (= Supplement des Mystères chaldéen),* Mossoul 1901.

22. In Math. Hom. 82,4 (PG 58,743); In illud: Vidi Dominum, hom 6,3 (PG 56, 138 et seq)

23. A rogation liturgy for the feast of All Saints in the year 396 against the locust plague, BKV 6,14: "With one word Your will created us and I became a mother; with one drop of Your mercy heal my children and drive away my pain! If the suffering soul whom Your vestments covered was healed by your cloak how much more will be granted me who take hold of Your entire body. Help and healing come to me!" In my opinion it cannot be concluded with absolute certainty that this is communion in the hand as the person speaking is not an individual but the Church of the City of Constantinople which, after the invasion by the Huns, is once again by a divine judgment.

24. In Cant. 1,2 (PG 81,35)

25. Ep. 93, PG 32,484 et seq.

26. Adv. Mulieres 299 et seq., PG 37,906

27. Oratio de St. Synaxi, PG 89,832

28. De fide 4,13: PG 94,1149

29. A passage in the Passio Perpetuae 4,9 quoted by Nussbaum is, in my opinion, too vague for the purposes of being quotable as evidence (it relates to a vision of future martyrdom).

30. De idol. 7,1; CCSL 2,1106

31. Ep. 58,9; CSEL 3,2,665; D lapsis 22, CSEL 3,1,253 et seq; De lapsis 26, 3,13,256

32. Vide Wunibald Roetzer, *Des Heiligen Augustinus Schriften als liturgeschichtliche Quelle,* Munich 1930, 131-135

33. Contra ep. Parm. 2,7,13, CSEL 51,58; Contra lit. Petil. 2,23,53, CSEL 52,51 et seq
34. De tempore barbarico II, IV, 1-2; CCSL 60,475
35. Hist. eccl., VI,43,18
36. For a more precise presentation of the order of the Mass in Milan vide Josef Schmitz, *Gottesdienst im altchristlichen Mailand,* Peter Hanstein Verlag, Cologne-Bonn 1975
37. Exameron VI,9,69; CSEL 32, 257
38. Tract. paschal. 2 in Ex 31; CSEL 68,31
39. Sermo 33, PL 52,295 et seq; Sermo 34, PL 52,297
40. Hist. eccl. Tripart. 9,30; PL 69,1145
41. Can. 3; Mansi 3,634
42. Can. 14; Mansi 3,1000
43. Vide Karl Berg, *Cäsarius von Arles, Ein Bischof des sechsten Jahrhunderts erschliesst das liturgische Leben seiner Zeit* (Dissertatio ad lauream in facultate Theologica Pontificae Universitatis Gregorianae Urbis, Romae 1935/1944/1946), Kulturverlag, Salzburg 1994
44. Sermo 44,6 CCSL 103,199; Sermo 227,5, CCSL 104,899 et seq
45. De tabernaculo et vasis eius, I,III, c.14; PL 91,498
46. Vide Nussbaum, *Die Handkommunion,* op cit, 25
47. Vide C.J. Hefele, Conciliengeschichte, IV, 2 edition, Freiburg 1879,99
48. We referred to Paul Fournier's canonistic work, *L'oeuvre canonique de Réginon de Prüm,* in *Mélange de droit canonique,* Vol. 2, Scientia Verlag Aalen 1983, 333 et seq
49. Edited by F.G.A. Wasserschleben, Leipzig, 1840
50. "Nulli autem laico aut feminae Eucharistiam in manibus ponat, sed tantum in ore eius cum his verbis ponat: *Corpus Domini et Sanguis prosit tibi ad remissionem et ad vitam aeternam.* Si quis haec transgressus fuerit, quia Deum omnipotentem contemnit, et quantum in ipso est inhonorat, ab altari removeatur", Wasserschleben, op cit, 102 et seq.
51. "Even now it has never been clarified whether or not this alleged council actually took place", Schöningh, Paderborn 1986, 204. The synod is dated either 650 or 688/9.
52. Missa Illyrica, PL 138,1333
53. The Emperor certainly received Holy Communion in the hand but this was not, nevertheless, exceptional as he was a member of the clergy.
54. Pope Gregory told of the healing of a dumb and disabled person by Pope Agapitus I (535-536), who first freed the disabled man from his lameness. "Cumque ei Dominicum corpus ei in os mitteret, illa diu muta ad loquendum lingua soluta est. Mirati omnes flere prae gaudio coeperunt, eorumque mentes illico metus et reverentia invasit, cum videlicet cernerent quid Agapitus facere in virtute Domini ex adiutorio Petri potuisset" (And when he placed the Body of the Lord in his mouth his tongue, so long chained, started to speak. Everyone marvelled and began to weep for joy and they were inwardly gripped by fear and reverence as they realised what Agapitus was capable of doing in the name of the Lord and with the help of Peter.), Dial. Lib III; PL 77,224.
55. Vide his *Manuale di Storia Liturgica,* III, Ancora, Milan 1966, 516
56. Klaus Gamber, *Ritus Modernus, Gesammelte Aufsätze zur Liturgiereform,* Friedrich Pustet, Regensburg 1972, 50

57. Illud vero quod pro complemento communionis intinctam tradunt eucharistiam populis, nec hoc prolatum ex evangelio testimonium recipit, ubi apostolis corpus suum et sanguinem commandavit; seorsum enim panis, et seorsum calicis commendatio memoratur" (As to the point that for the perfection of Holy Communion a Host [dipped into the Holy Blood] may be used, it can be said that this has not been confirmed by gospel witnesses. When the Lord entrusted his Body and Blood to the apostles it was, in fact, recorded that he offered the [transformed] bread and the chalice separately), Mansi XI, 155.

58. Towards the end of the 10th century we find in the case of Burchard of Worms (+ 1025) a point which prescribes the safekeeping of sacred Hosts which have previously been dipped in the Precious Blood, precisely for the purpose of Holy Communion: "Ut omnis presbyter habeat pixidem, aut vas tanto sacramento dignum, ubi corpus Dominicum diligenter recondatur, ad viaticum recedentibus a saeculo. Quae tantum sacra oblatio intincta debet esse in sanguine Christi, ut veraciter presbyter possit dicere infirmo, corpus et sanguis Domini proficiat tibe, etc. Semperque sit super altare obserata propter mures et nefarios homines, et de septimo in septimum diem semper mutetur, id est, illa a presybtero sumatur, et alia, quae eodem die consecrata est, in locum eius subrogetur, ne forte diutius reservata, mucida, quod absit, fiat" (Every priest should have a pyx or some other container worthy of such a great sacrament where the body of the Lord is carefully laid and stored ready to be taken to the dying. This holy sacrifice must, however, be dipped in the blood of Christ so that the priest may truly say, *"Receive the body and blood of the Lord ... etc"*. And it should be always be locked away over the altar away from mice and godless men and every seventh day it shall be consumed by the priest and replaced by another Host, consecrated on the same day, so that it will not become stale through overlong storage which is to be avoided). "Decretorum liber quintus" PL 140, 754

59. Joannis Abricensis Episcopi liber "De officiis ecclesiaticis": "Si autem opus non fuerit (pro viatico), tertiam (particulam hostiae), aut unus ministrorum accipiat. Non autem intincto pane, sed iuxta definitionem Toletani concilii seorsum corpore, seorsum sanguine, sacerdos communicet, excepto populo, quem intincto pane, non auctoritate, sed summa necessitate timoris sanguinis Christi effusionis permittitur communicare", PL 147,37.

60. In the Coptic liturgy every communicant holds a covering, which he is given by the minister, under his chin.

61. Vide Udalrici, Consuet. Clun. II,30; PL 149,721

62. AAS 61 (1969) 541-545

63. For a more precise textual analysis vide Georg May, *Mund- oder Handkommunion*. 2nd edition., Schmid-Fehr. (no year quoted)

64. Examples are to be found in May, *Mund- oder Handkommunion*, op cit 75 et seq

65. Augustine refers in Psalm 98.5 (*Et adorate sabellum pedum eius - worship at his foot stool*) to the flesh of Christ.

66. Et quia in ipsa carne hic ambulavit, et ipsam carnem nobis manducandam ad salutem dedit: nemo autem illam carnem manducat, nisi prius adoraverit; inventum est quemadmodum adoretur tale scabellum pedum Domini, et non solum non peccemus adorando, sed peccamus non adorando", Enarr, in Psalm 98.9; CSEL 39, 1385

67. A few examples from a later period for worship before receiving Holy Communion; in the rules of the Order laid down by Saint Columba, (+615) provision is made for bowing three times before receiving Holy Communion, elsewhere one kissed the ground, the *Consuetudines* of Cluny, drawn up in 1080, called for genuflection. Vide Jungmann, *Missarum Sollemnia*, II, op cit, 458

68. Vide the apostles communion in the Russano codex dating from the 6th century.

69. Augustine, for example, speaks of the "manibus coniunctis", the "hands joined together", in *Contra ep. Parma*, 2,7,13, CSEL 51,58: "sed interim attendant utrum saltem Optatus habuerit aliquam maculam aut aliquod vitium; non usque adeo caeci sunt, ut et istius vitam omnino immaculatam et omni vitio carentam fuisse respondeant, cur ergo accedebat offerre dona deo et ab eo ceteri coniunctis manibus accipiebant, quod maculosus et vitiosus obtulerat?" (but, inter alia, you should pay attention as to whether Optatus has, at the least, some blemish or error as they are not yet so blind that they would reply that his life was free of all blemish or error. Why, therefore, did he offer up gifts to God, and why did they receive from him with hands joined together that what he had brought which was stained and imperfect?).

70. Vide the II Synod of Trull (692), can. 101, Mansi II, 985 et seq. If anyone wishes to receive Holy Communion, "he should hold his hands according to the image of the cross and so approach to receive the Blessed Sacrament. Anybody who, instead of the hand, present some receptacle made of gold or some other material so as to receive a perfect communion shall, therewith, under no circumstances be admitted by us as they prefer an inanimate object (which is inferior to man) to the image of God." Although Trullanum II was not recognised by Pope Sergius as a number of anti-Roman canons were adopted, John VIII accepted their resolutions (in 878?), insofar as they did not contradict Roman teaching and practice (vide K. Baus, LThK2, 10,381 et seq).

71. In illud: Vidi Dominum, hom. 6,3: PG 56,138 et seq

72. De idolatria, c7, CCSL 2,1106: "Ad hanc partem zelus fidei perorabit ingemens: Christianum ab idolis in ecclesiam venire, de adversaria officina in domum dei venire, attollere ad deum patrem manus matres idolorum, his manibus adorare, quae foris adversus deum adotantur, eas manus admovere corpori domini, quae daemoniis corpora conferunt? Nec hoc sufficit. Parum sit, si ab aliis manibus accipiant quod contaminent, sed etiam ipsae tradunt aliis quod contaminaverunt. Adleguntur in ordinem ecclesiasticum artifices idolorum. Pro scelus! Semel Iudiaei Christo manus intulerunt, isti quotidie corpus eius lacessunt. O manus praecidende! Viderint iam, an per similitudinem dictum sit: *si te manus tua scandalizat, amputa eam.* Quae magis amputandae, quam in quibus domini corpus scandalizur?"

73. Adv. mulieres 299 et seq., PG 37,906

74. Sermo 227,5, CCSL 104,899 et seq "Ad extremum, fratres carisisimi, non est grave nec laboriosum quod suggero: hoc dico, quod vos frequenter facere aspicio. Omnes viri, quando communicare desiderant, lavant manus suas et omnes mulieres nitida exhibitent linteamina, ubi corpus Christi accipiant. Non est grave quid dico, fratres: quomodo viri lavant aqua manus suas, sic de elemosinis lavent conscientias suas; similiter et mulieres, quomodo

nitidum exhibitent linteolum, ubi corpus Christi accipiant, sic corpus castum et cor mundum exhibeant, ut cum bona conscientia Christi sacramenta suscipiant. Rogo vos, fratres, numquid est aliquis, qui in arca sordibus plena velit mittere vestem suam? Et si in arca sordibus plena vestis non mittitur pretiosa, qua fronte in anima quae peccatorum sordibus inquinatur Christi eucharistia suscipitur?"

75. "Et si erubescimus ac timemus eucharistiam manibus sordidis tangere, plus debemus timere ipsam eucharisticam intus in anima polluta suscipere". Sermo 44,6, CCSL 103,199

76. Synod of Auxerre (between 561 and 605), can. 36: "Non licet mulieri nuda manu eucharistiam accipere", Mansi 9,915

77. For example the apostles' communion in the Codex of Rossano dating from the 6th century.

78. On the Dumbarton Oaks paten one can see clearly that the apostles received communion with covered hands. (Illustration in LCI,1,174 et seq).

79. Dom Gabriel M. Brasó offers an exhaustive study on the theme of covered hands in his *La velació de les mans. Recull d'un tema d'arqueologia cristiana*, in *Liturgica I, Cardinali I A. Schuster in memoriam*, Montserrat 1956, 311-386.

80. Traditionally, the five Jerusalem mystagogic catecheses were traced back to St. Cyril of Jerusalem. It was only after an essay by W.J. Swaans (1942) they were attributed by a number of people to a successor of Cyril, namely John of Jerusalem. The oldest manuscript, the Codex Monacensis 394 dating from the 10th century, names, in point of fact, John as the author. In Ottobonianus 86, which is almost as old, the name of Cyril has been added by another hand. But we are in possession of other manuscripts, Coisilianus 277 (11th century), Bodleianus Roe 25 (11th century), Vindobonensis 55 (11th century?), Marcianus II.35 (12th century?) and Ottoboniamus 220 (16/17 centuries), which quote Cyril as the author. Eustratius of Constantinople (+ 582) quotes the mystagogic catecheses and gives Cyril as the author. According to Auguste Piédagnel (vide SC 126,33 et seq) other objections of a liturgical and theological nature are not convincing. Differences between the 18 catecheses and the mystagogic catecheses can be explained by arcane discipline and subsequent extended theological knowledge. Even if John did, possibly, revise the texts to some extent, we would not be in a position to dismiss Cyril. In any event they bear witness to liturgical practices towards the end of the 4th century.

81. Cat. Myst. 5,21. The Greek text can be found in a critical edition, for example in the "Fontes Christiani", volume 7, p. 162. The German translation mentioned above is guided by constant reference to the original text both in the German version by Röwekamp (for the volume mentioned of the FC) and also the text by F.J. Dölger which he published in "Antike und Christentum", Volume III, Münster in Westfalen., Aschendorff 1932, 235 et seq.

82. Vide ThWBNT II, 37 et seq and IX, 415 regarding preferment of the right hand in antiquity and in holy scripture.

83. Otto Nussbaum, *Die Handkommunion*, op cit, 18 et seq.

84. Aphrahat, *Unterweisungen*, 9,10; translated and introduced by Peter Bruns, FC5/1, 265

85. In encyclical 7.21 he speaks of those whom Gideon was to select according to God's following command: "He who licks water like a dog should join the

battle" (Rule 7,5); "Of all the animals which were created at the same time as man, there is none which so loves his master as the dog which also keeps guard day and night. Even if he is beaten by his master he will still not desert him. And if he goes hunting with his master and a powerful lion meets his master he will give up his life for his master. And those who were selected from the water were that brave. They follow their master like dogs and gave up their lives for him, valiantly fighting his battle. They keep watch day and night and bark like dogs when they ponder the law night and day (Ps. 1,2). They love our Lord and lick his wounds when they receive his body and turn their eyes to him and lick him with their tongues as a dog licks his master. Those who do not ponder the law are called 'dumb dogs which cannot bark; all who do not fast with joy are called greedy dogs who cannot satisfy themselves' (Is. 56,10 et seq). "FC 5/1, p. 229 et seq.

86. Aphrahat, *Unterweisungen,* 20.8; FC 5/2, page 465
87. ""When you go to Holy Communion, do not come with arms outstretched, but make the left hand act as a throne for the right whereby the right is likewise curved as a preparation to receive the King. Take the Body of Christ with great fear so that not one particle (*tis margarites*) falls from your hand and you should thereby damage one of your own limbs. Similarly, approach the chalice without stretching out your hands upwards when you say the "Amen". As long as there is some moisture on your lips touch your eyes and your forehead with your hands and thus the remaining senses shall be healed. And then day Thank God for having honoured you with such a great mystery. Ecologa 47, PG 63,898.
88. F.J. Dölger, *Das Segnen der Sinne mit der Eucharistie,* "Antike und Christentum", Volume III, Münster in Westfalen., Aschendorff 1932, 231-244, here page 237. In the article quoted there are other witnesses for the blessing of the senses.
89. In Cant. 1,2 (PG 81,53). At the point "Osculetur me osculis suis": "but there is no earthbound and earthy meaning which may be confused with the word "kisses". We should consider that at the mystical time (*en tô mustikô kairô*) we receive the limbs of the bridegroom, kiss and embrace them and lay our eyes on the heart. It is similar with a bridal embrace. We believe that we are fully with him. We embrace and kiss him and, in the words of scripture, love casts out fear."
90. St. John Damascene, de fide 4,13; PG 94,119
91. "In Germany, there was a custom common from the 14th century, which reminds us of the blessing of the senses with the Host, which was customary one thousand years earlier. After the ablution of the fingers, one touched ones eyes with the fingers and spoke the words *Lutum fecit Dominus ex sputo et linivit oculos meos et abii et vidi et credidi Deo* (John 9,11). This was a custom which could easily become superstitious and irreverent, and it subsequently fell into disuse" , Jungmann, *Missarum Sollemnia*, II. 508
92. "Si quis autem acceptam a sacerdote eucharistiam non sumpserit, velut sacrilegus propellatur". Can. 14: Mansi 3,1000
93. Born circa 633, died in 708 in the Monastery of Tel'eda. Despite his monophysitic views he was a much admired Syriac author.
94. C. Kayser, Die Canones Jacob's von Edessa (Leipzig 1886) 13,14, quoted by F.J. Dölger, *Die Eucharistie als Reiseschutz. Die Eucharistie in den Händen*

der Laien, Antike und Christentum, Volume 5, 2nd edition, Publisher, Aschendorff, Münster 1974, 241

95. De corona militum c.3, CCSL 2,1043; "Eucharistiae sacramentum (...) etiam antelucanis coetibus nec de aliorum manu quam praesidentium sumimus (...) Calicis aut panis etiam nostri aliquid decuti in terram anxie patimur".

96. Vide Werner Schütz, *Der christliche Gottesdienst bei Origenes*, Calwer Verlag, Stuttgart 1984, 156 - 172

97. PG 12,391; SC 321, p. 384, 69-72

98. Basil the Great, ep. 93, PG 32,484 et seq: "We take communion four times each week, on the Lord's day, the fourth day, Friday and Saturday and also on those other days dedicated to a Saint. That in times of persecution, anyone may be compelled to receive communion by his own hand in the absence of a priest or a deacon, is by no means a momentous affair. It is, in essence, superfluous to mention it as it is confirmed by various facts due to its long usage All the inhabitants, in fact, take communion at home and receive it from each other when no priest is present. In Alexandria and Egypt all those initiated amongst the population (*'ekastos kal tôn en laô teloúnton*) will usually take communion at home and, if they wish, participate on their own initiative. If, in fact, the priest's sacrifice is celebrated and the sacrificial victim distributed, he who receives at the same time the sacrificial offering as a whole and then partakes of it on individual days believes, correctly, that he has shared in the sacrifice and received it from him who gave it. Even in the Church, the priest gives a share and he who receives it holds it with full powers (*met' exousías 'apá*ses) and thus carries it with his own hand to his mouth. It is the same whether one receives one share from the priest or whether he receives several shares at the same time." Otto Nussbaum notes that the corresponding receptacle for house communion was normally such that one took the Lord's body with the mouth, vide *Die Handkommunion* op cit 21.
But because of the misuses, the superior of the Monastery of Atripe, Schenute (+ 466), highly respected by the Egyptian Christians, was compelled "with all force to object to members of the community taking Hosts home with them from the celebration of the last supper. The priest or deacon should not give even as much as a mustard seed to any person asking for this favour'", Leipoldt, Schenute of Atripe and the rise of Egyptian national monasticism = TU NF X,1 (Leipzig 1903) 184 vide also p. 31; quoted by F.J. Dölger, *Die Eucharistie als Reiseschutz*, op cit 240 et seq.

99. *Kirche, Ökumene, Politik*, Johannes Verlag, Einsiedeln 1987, 19.

100. In the case of the orthodox churches the warning words of St. Cyril of Jerusalem stating that not even the smallest particle of the Body and Blood of Christ should be lost, continued to be taken seriously. Not only theoretically but also in practice, as evidenced by the utterly diverse security measures. Vide Karl Christian Felmy, *Customs and practices surrounding Holy Communion in the Eastern Orthodox Churches*, in *Bread of Heaven, Customs and practices surrounding Holy Communion*, edited by Charles Caspers, Gerald Rouwhorst, Kok Pharos Publishing House, Kampen, 1995, 41 - 59, here 47 et seq.

101. Encyclical "Memoriale Domini", 29 May 1969; AAS 61 (1969) 542

102. Encyclical "Immensae caritatis" dated 29.1.1973, AAS 65 (1973) 264-271, here 270

103. Declaration of 2 May 1972, Notitiae 8 (1972) 227
104. Vide AAS 61 (1969) 544
105. Vide *Missarium Sollemnia,* II, op cit, 463
106. *Die Handkommunion*, op cit., 28
107. Klaus Gamber, *Ritus Modernus,* op cit, 52
108. AAS 61 (1969) 543
109. Encyclical "Eucharisticum mysterium, n. 9 AAS 59 (1967) 547
110. "Memoriale Domini", AAS 61 (1969) 543

Homily delivered at the Opening Mass of the Colloquium on 9th October, 1996.

Bishop Georges Lagrange (France)

"Heal the sick and say to them, 'The Kingdom of God has come near to you."

Here then is the primary task of those whom Christ sends: to announce that in the Son of God made man the Kingdom of God is made close to us, comes to us.

It is not we ourselves who by our own strength can hoist ourselves up into the Kingdom of heaven; the Kingdom comes to us, the Heavenly Jerusalem descends to us. It is the Father's envoy who has come down from Heaven, Who hgas been made man for us: *descendit de caelis . . et homo factus est.*

That is what we must proclaim; this message which does not have its origin in any human heart; it is a Revelation from God. It is not something we can discover or find out for ourselves; we must hear it, learn it, become disciples, be initiated. And this initiation is made at the same time both by preaching and catechesis and also by the sacraments which indeed we call the sacraments of initiation: Baptism, Confirmation and the Eucharist: the Eucharist which is the goal of them all, "the centre and summit of the Christian life," as Vatican II declares.

This brings us to one of the central problems of Christian Liturgy. In the Liturgy it is always Christ who is the chief celebrant and it is always His mystery which is being celebrated. As Fr. Clement reminded us, "The Liturgy is the vehicle of the Mystery." But if someone has not been initiated into the Mystery of Christ, then to him the Liturgy is a sealed-up fountain. He is lost. He does not understand anything. And then one is tempted to think that the Liturgy is badly constructed, that it ought to be changed, changed indeed so as to fall into line with our tastes, our wants, our preoccupations. To want to make people assist at Mass who are not evangelised, who have not been initiateed into the Mystery of Christ, is to put these people off the Mass, make them not want to come again - unless the Mass is so constructed that it is no longer centred on the Mystery of Christ, in which case it is the initiated, not the evangelised who are lost.

The Liturgy and faith in Christ and His Mystery are thus indissolubly linked together. As Saint Paul says in the epistle to the Romans, "How can they call upon the Lord if they have not first believed in Him?" And how can they believe in Him without having heard His Word? And how can they hear His Word if no one proclaims it? But how can it be proclaimed if no one is sent to do so? As the Scripture says, 'How beautiful are the feet of them that proclaim the Good News!' And yet not all have given to that Good News the obedience of faith. As Isaiah says, "Lord who believed us when we spoke? And so it is that faith comes from hearing; and what we hear is the proclamation of the word of Christ." (Rom. X, 14-15)

Gestures Accompanying the Words of Consecration in the History of the *Ordo Missae*

Father Cassian Folsom OSB (United States)

Father Folsom is a monk at Saint Meinrad Abbey in the state of Indiana (United States). He was ordained priest in 1984 and obtained his doctorate in liturgy at the Saint Anselm Pontifical Institute in 1989 with a thesis on the liturgical preachings of Saint Leo the Great. After having been professor of liturgical and sacramental theology at Saint Meinrad theology school, he has been professor at the Saint Anselm Pontifical Institute of Liturgy since 1993.

The abbey of Le Barroux has a postcard which depicts the elevation of the chalice at the conventual Mass. This gesture is surrounded by various signs of reverence: the priest holding thumbs and index fingers together, the monk ringing the tower bell, the acolytes holding a torch in their right hand, and the thurifer incensing the Precious Blood. The scene on this postcard -- which also serves as the cover of a book on the liturgy -- includes the whole complex of reverential gestures which accompany the words of consecration in the Mass. It is these gestures which are the subject of this study.

Introduction

Gestures of reverence at this particular moment of the Mass did not spring full-blown out of nowhere, but have their own history and development. The gradual formation of this complex of gestures can be traced by making a chronological study of the *Ordo Missae* and the *Ritus servandus in celebratione Missae*.[i] Further information about these gestures can be gleaned from indirect sources: theological or historical writings which happen to describe the consecration of the Mass. This conference, however, limits itself to a study of the direct sources: the *Ordines Missae* themselves in the course of their historical development.

The texts are as follows:

1. The *Ordo Missae* known as *Paratus*: late twelfth century, beginning of thirteenth century
2. The *Ordo Missae* known as *Indutus planeta*: 1243
3. The *Ordo Missae* of the Roman Missal of 1474, *editio princeps*
4. The *Ordo Missae* of John Burckard: ca. 1500 (which is much more detailed than a normal *Ordo Missae*; it belongs to the literary genre which would later be called *Ritus servandus in celebratione Missae*)

5. The *Ritus servandus in celebratione Missae* found at the beginning of the Roman Missal of 1570
6. The *Ordo Missae* of the Roman Missal of 1570
7. The *Ordo Missae* of 1965
8. The *Ritus servandus in celebratione Missae* of 1965
9. The *Variationes in Ordinem Missae Inducendae* of 1967
10. The *Ordo Missae* of 1970.

This conference will be a commentary on these texts, in order to answer the question: How have the gestures of reverence which accompany the words of consecration changed and developed in the course of the centuries? In the conclusion we will be in a position to address the question: What do these changes mean?

In order to follow the argument more easily, a copy of these ten texts has been provided.

I.   *Paratus*: **late twelfth century,**
     beginning of thirteenth century

The *Ordo Missae "Paratus"* -- which takes its title from the first rubric after the vesting prayers, *Paratus autem intrat ad altare* -- is in the tradition of the Rhein-type Ordo. While its origins are obscure, it is firmly in place by the end of the twelfth century in the usage of the Roman Curia. It is the first *Ordo Missae* of the Roman tradition to indicate special gestures to accompany the words of consecration.

Two different editions of the text are presented here: the first one taken from a single manuscript, *Ottobonianus latinus* 356 of the Vatican Library; the second one a composite text including variants from a dozen or so different manuscripts.

Ottobonianus latinus 356, according to the research of Stephen Van Dijk, represents the urban reform of Cardinal Orsini (later Pope Nicholas III) in the third quarter of the thirteenth century.[ii] Note the rubric just before the *Qui pridie*: *Hic accipiens hostiam, reverenter levet eam iunctis manibus*. Aside from the adverb *reverenter*, which indicates an attitude of reverence, it is important to notice the verbs *levet* (used for taking the host into the priest's hands) and *elevet* (used for taking the chalice into his hands). According to Peter Browe, it is necessary to distinguish between two kinds of elevation at this point in history: a more ancient elevation of the host and chalice as part of the priest's gesture of taking the Eucharistic elements into his hands, and a thirteenth-century development by which the host was elevated (and later the chalice as well) after the words of consecration in order to show the consecrated species to the people.[iii] In the manuscript in question there is no indication of this more recent elevation. Nor is

76

there any genuflection indicated. The *Ordo* provides the words, but is short on gestures.

The composite edition of *Paratus* shows that the manuscript tradition is by no means unanimous concerning these gestures. In the far left column, some manuscripts give only the words of the canon, with no gestures of reverence whatsoever. In the middle column, the abbreviation *So* indicates *Ottobonianus latinus* 356, which we have already seen. In the far right column one manuscript, *Mm* (Santa Maria Maggiore BB.ii.15), a later, revised *ordo* of the papal court, tells quite a different story.[iv] In this manuscript, and this one only, we find the newer gesture of elevation for the sake of *showing* and, curiously enough, the gesture of elevation for both the host and the chalice. However, the manuscript in question probably represents some outside influence, since these gestures do not find their way into Roman liturgical books for quite some time. It is axiomatic that the Roman tradition, being extremely conservative, is reluctant to accept new developments even though they may be quite widespread elsewhere.

In the *Paratus* tradition, therefore (excluding the manuscript from Santa Maria Maggiore), aside from the priest reverently taking the host into his hands, there are no precise gestures of reverence accompanying the words of consecration.

II.   *Indutus planeta:*[V] 1243

When Haymo of Faversham, the fourth Minister General of the Franciscans, compiled his *Ordo Missae* in 1243, his intention was to include not only the words of the priest but also the gestures, thereby supplying the many lacunae of the *Ordo Missae "Paratus"*. Haymo's description, therefore, is an Order of Action and Speech (*Ordo agendorum et dicendorum*) for use of the priest in private Masses or weekday conventual Masses, according to the custom of the Roman Church. This is an important witness to the development of the *Ordo Missae*, and the increasing attention given to rubrical directives.

For the consecration of the host, we see the priest's gesture of taking the host into his hands and raising it: *accipit hostiam...et parum elevans*. After the words of consecration over the host, a medium bow is indicated for adoring the Body of the Lord: *adorato corpore domini cum mediocri inclinatione*. The elevation follows, *reverenter*, so that the consecrated host can be seen by all the people. Note, however, that there is no bow or genuflection after showing the Body of the Lord.

For the consecration of the wine, we find the same gesture of taking the Eucharistic species, in this case the chalice, and raising it: *calicem accipit...et parum elevat*. However, there is no showing of the chalice to the people. This is because the Precious Blood within the chalice could not actually be seen, and therefore was not the object of the same devotion as was given to the consecrated host. In fact, it took several centuries before the showing of the chalice as a parallel gesture to the showing of the host became widespread.

Indutus planeta is the first document to mention that after the consecration the priest must hold his thumbs and index fingers together.[vi] The rubric comes after the consecration of the chalice, however, and not after the consecration of the host.

III.   *Missale Romanum, Editio princeps* 1474

The first printed edition of the Roman Missal gives precious little information about gestures of reverence accompanying the words of consecration. This does not mean that in actual practice such gestures were necessarily absent, but simply that the rubrical directives for these gestures had not yet found their way into the liturgical books.

In the *editio princeps* there are rubrics indicating that the priest takes the host into his hands (*hic accipiat hostiam in manibus*), and likewise the chalice (*hic...levet calicem*), but that is all. The indications of *Indutus planeta* are not incorporated, and even the adverb *reverenter* of *Paratus*, referring to the manner in which the priest takes the host into his hands, is missing. Since the *editio princeps* is an immediate source for the Pian Missal of 1570, this scarcity of information is somewhat surprising.[vii] In terms of the physical layout of the text, it should be noted that the words of consecration are set in upper case letters.

IV.   *Ordo Missae Ioannis Burckardi,* ca. 1500

The lack of rubrical directives in the *editio princeps* points to an underlying problem of the time period: liturgical anarchy.[viii] John Burckard, master of ceremonies under several popes, prefaces his detailed description of the ceremonies of the Mass with this comment:

> Engaged from my youth in the sacred ceremonies, when I saw that not a few priests in the celebration of Mass frequently imitated many abuses, and diverse rites and unsuitable gestures, I thought it unworthy that there is no definite norm transmitted to the priests by the holy Roman Church, Mother and Teacher of all the churches, to be universally observed in the celebration of the

Mass. Therefore, I have gathered these ceremonies together and published them; they are taken from the various decrees of the holy fathers, which the Supreme Pontiffs have instituted for the above mentioned celebration. And when I recently reviewed the collection of the same, I discovered that more ceremonies had been omitted than handed on. I added, therefore, what was necessary, and as much as I was able, completed the work.[ix]

The *Ordo* of Burckard, therefore, intends to be as complete as possible, and for that reason is an extremely valuable source for this study. The gestures of reverence accompanying the words of consecration are highly developed and organized into a unified complex of ritual action:

Consecration of the host

1. At the *Hanc igitur*, the altar server lights the torch, which he holds in his right hand, and kneels behind the celebrant.

2. Just before the *Qui pridie*, the priest wipes his thumbs and fingers on the corporal.

3. Just before the words of consecration, he uncovers the ciborium if there is one (called a *calix* or *vas*).

4. He places both elbows on the altar, and bows his head, so as to pronounce the words of consecration *distincte, secrete* and *reverenter*.

5. After the consecration of the host, following the lead of Haymo of Faversham, Burckard indicates that the priest must hold thumbs and index fingers together from this point until after communion unless, of course, he is touching or holding the host.

6. The priest genuflects in adoration. (This gesture is parallel to the medium bow of *Indutus planeta*).

7. The elevation of the host follows, as high as he can comfortably do so, so as to reverently show the Body of Christ to the people for their adoration.

8. Meanwhile, lest the priest's gesture of elevation be hindered by the constraints of his vestments, the minister raises the edge of the chasuble to assist him.

9.   After the elevation, the priest places the consecrated host back on the corporal *veneranter*.

10.   Again, he genuflects all the way to the ground, and venerates the host a second time. The *Ordo* of Burckard is the first document to indicate a double genuflection: this gesture of reverence will remain until 1967.

11.   The priest replaces the cover of the ciborium.

Consecration of the chalice

1.   Next the celebrant takes the pall off the chalice.

2.   He rubs his thumbs and index fingers together over the lip of the chalice, lest there should be any particle of the consecrated host clinging to his fingers.

3.   There are explicit directions as to how to hold the chalice for the blessing and the words of consecration.

4.   Again, the priest places both elbows on the altar, bows his head, and pronounces the words of consecration *secrete, distincte* and *reverenter*.

5.   He genuflects in adoration.

6.   The elevation of the chalice follows -- again, as high as the priest can comfortably do so -- to show it to the people for their adoration. This is the first Roman *Ordo Missae* in which the elevation of the chalice is parallel to the elevation of the host, and the gestures of reverence for the Precious Blood are parallel to the gestures of reverence for the Body of Christ.

7.   During the elevation, the minister helps the priest with the chasuble, as before.

8.   After the elevation, the priest places the chalice back on the corporal *reverenter* (the parallel indication for the consecration of the host is *veneranter*).

9.   He covers the chalice with the pall.

10.   Genuflecting a second time, the priest venerates the sacrament again.

11.   The altar server extinguishes the torch, and returns it to its place.

The thoroughness of Burckard's rubrics and the authority of his position as papal Master of Ceremonies assured his description of the Mass ceremonies a place of great prominence. After the Council of Trent, when those charged with the reform of the Roman Missal began their work, the *Ordo Missae* of John Burckard became their point of reference.

V.   *Ritus servandus in celebratione Missae* 1570 (VIII:4-8; IX:1)

The state of liturgical anarchy which prevailed in 1500 had not improved much by 1570. For that reason, detailed rubrics were the order of the day, obligatory and universally prescribed . The literary genre of the *Ordo Missae*, however, does not allow for extremely detailed instructions. For that reason, an introductory document was inserted at the beginning of the Roman Missal, called *Ritus servandus in celebratione Missae*. This text is based upon the ceremonial directives of Burckard, and in many cases, follows the text of Burckard word for word.

Concerning the gestures of reverence which accompany the words of consecration, only a few slight changes from the *Ordo Missae* of Burckard are to be observed.

1.   During the elevation, the priest should keep his eyes fixed on the host or the chalice (*et intentis in [hostiam] oculis, quod et in elevatione calicis facit*, VIII:5)

2.   There are directions for the ringing of the bells. The altar server, shortly before the Consecration (although the precise moment is not mentioned) should alert the faithful by the ringing of the bell (VIII:6). This gesture, while appearing in the *Ritus servandus* for the first time, is by no means new. There is already evidence from the thirteenth century, when Pope Gregory IX in 1239 ordered that a bell be rung before the consecration of the Body of the Lord.[x]

After the Consecration, the server rings the bell three times for each elevation, or he may ring the bell continuously until the priest places the consecrated host or chalice back on the corporal.

3.   There are also provisions for degrees of solemnity. During a solemn Mass, in addition to the other gestures of reverence, the Blessed Sacrament is to receive the honor of incense. The thurifer

81

kneels on the Epistle side, and for each elevation, incenses the consecrated host or chalice three times. This gestures applies also to sung Masses in which incense is used (VIII:8).

4.   In the directives of Burckard, the torches were to be extinguished immediately after the consecration of the Precious Blood. Here, the same principle is operative, but with the further clarification that if the faithful will be going to communion, the torches remain lit until then (VIII,8).

VI.   *Ordo Missae* 1570

The *editio princeps* of 1474 has often been mentioned as the immediate ancestor of the *Missale Romanum* of 1570, although the question of precisely which edition or editions were used by the post-Tridentine liturgical commission is somewhat more complicated.   In any case, while the *editio princeps* was certainly faithful to the ancient traditions of the Roman Church, the *Ordo Missae* contained therein was too sparse, too lean to respond to the pressing need of the day for precise and complete rubrical directives.   Recourse was had, therefore, to the work of John Burckard.   In this way, the *Ordo Missae* of 1570 filled in the lacunae of the *editio princeps*, while leaving the wealth of rubrical detail to the *Ritus servandus*, as has already been shown.

The *Ordo Missae*, therefore, distills the entire complex of ritual gestures into a few brief indications.

1.   The words of consecration are pronounced over the host *distincte* and *attente;* over the chalice *attente* and *continuate.*

2.   There is a genuflection both before and after each elevation: each time the rubric says: *genuflexus adorat.*

3.   After the consecration of the Body of Christ, the thumbs and index fingers of the priest are to remain joined until the ablution after Communion.

The rubrics do not pretend to be complete, but serve to jog the memory of the priest. For more detailed information about his part, and the part played by the other sacred ministers, the *Ritus servandus* is to be consulted. This is the situation that obtained until the Second Vatican Council.

VII.   *Ordo Missae* 1965

In the Conciliar document *Sacrosanctum Concilium* (1963), paragraph #50 is dedicated to the *Ordo Missae*. It reads:

> The Order of Mass is to be revised in a way that will bring out more clearly the intrinsic nature and purpose of its several parts, as also the connection between them, and will more readily achieve the devout, active participation of the faithful.

> For this purpose the rites are to be simplified, due care being taken to preserve their substance; elements that, with the passage of time, came to be duplicated or were added with but little advantage are now to be discarded; other elements that have suffered injury through accident of history are now, as may seem useful or necessary, to be restored to the vigor they had in the tradition of the Fathers.

The difficulty with this paragraph, of course, is its interpretation and application. In fact, how to interpret not only this paragraph but all of *Sacrosanctum Concilium* soon became a pressing issue. Precisely in order to interpret the conciliar text, *Inter Oecumenici*, the first instruction on the orderly carrying out of the Constitution on the Liturgy, was prepared by the *Consilium*, and published in September of 1964.[xi] There was some debate, however, about how to interpret this Instruction. According to Cardinal Antonelli, then secretary of the Congregation of Rites, the Instruction "is a text of law, not autonomous, but one which is based upon another text [i.e. *Sacrosanctum Concilium*], the concrete application of which it intends to determine... By its very nature, the Instruction can not be contrary to or go beyond the Constitution."[xii] On the other hand, the position of the *Consilium* was that the Instruction was basically a transitional document, until such time as the definitive changes could be put into effect.[xiii] In fact, as the present papal Master of Ceremonies, Pietro Marini, makes clear, with the publication of *Inter Oecumenici*, it was the *Consilium* and its interpretation which gained the upper hand.[xiv]

As a result of the changes introduced by *Inter Oecumenici*, and prompted by the request of various publishing houses for more specific information about how these changes were to be incorporated into the liturgical books,[xv] the *Consilium* published a revised *Ordo Missae* and *Ritus servandus* in January of 1965.

However, neither in paragraph #48 of *Inter Oecumenici*, which deals with the *Ordo Missae*, nor in the 1965 revised *Ordo Missae* itself, is there any mention of the gestures accompanying the words of consecration. The text of the 1965 *Ordo Missae* at this point (paragraphs #37-38) is identical to that of the 1570 *Missale Romanum*. The rubrics for the gestures which accompany the words of consecration remain exactly the same.

VIII. *Ritus servandus in celebratione Missae*, 1965

Since the genre of the *Ritus servandus* is different than that of the *Ordo Missae*, more of the 1965 changes were able to be incorporated into former than into the latter. The paragraphs which deal with the consecration (#65-70), show the following modifications in the text of the 1570 *Ritus servandus*.

65. The word *pyx* is used instead of *calix* or *vas* to describe the ciborium containing the small hosts for the faithful. (Cf. also #67).

66. The words of consecration continue to be spoken *distincte* and *reverenter* but no longer *secreto*. This applies to the consecration of the chalice as well (#68).
For the elevation of the host, the rubrics *quantum commode potest* and *in altum* are omitted. The height of the elevation, therefore, is no longer specified. This applies to the elevation of the chalice as well (#68).

67. The possible ways of ringing the bells are no longer specified (i.e. three short rings or one continuous ring). The rubric simply says: *iuxta cuiusque loci consuetudinem.*

67. The gesture of assisting the priest with his chasuble is omitted at both elevations.

69. The movements of the deacon and subdeacon at a solemn Mass are modified. This pertains in particular to the deacon, who is to stand behind the celebrant unless his assistance is needed beside him.

70. Instead of torches (*intorticia*) the text uses the word candles (*cerei*). These candles are not extinguished after the elevation of the chalice, since the communion of the faithful is presupposed.

Marini comments on the nature of these changes, saying:

> Certainly the rite of 1965 reproduced the letter of the text of John Burckard, which had been the base upon which the liturgical commission established by Pius V had elaborated the *Ritus servandus*. But in spirit, the *Ritus servandus* of 1570 could no longer be found in that of 1965...[xvi]

IX. *Variationes in Ordinem Missae Inducendae*, 1967

Just as the first Instruction on the orderly carrying out of the Constitution on the Liturgy, *Inter Oecumenici*, was followed by modifications in the *Ordo Missae* in 1965, so also the second such Instruction, *Tres abhinc annos*,[xvii] was followed by further modifications in the *Ordo Missae* in 1967.   As the document itself explains, this was in response to the requests of various bishops for further changes:

> At least for the moment, not every proposal can be sanctioned. Others, however, do seem worthy putting into effect immediately, because pastoral considerations commend them and they seem to offer no hindrance to the definitive reform of the liturgy yet to come. Further, they seem advantageous for the gradual introduction of that reform and are feasible simply by altering rubrics, not the existing liturgical books (*Tres abhinc annos*, Introduction).

As in the case of *Inter Oecumenici*, this Instruction likewise is understood as a transitional step toward the definitive reform of the liturgical books themselves. Paragraphs #7-16 deal with changes in the *Ordo Missae*; paragraphs #7,10 and 12 deal directly with the consecration of the Mass. Since the changes in this document are rather significant, it is useful to examining these paragraphs before going on to study the 1967 *Ordo Missae*.

7.   In this paragraph, the number of the priest's genuflections during Mass are greatly reduced, probably because they were judged to be "unnecessary duplications" (cf. SC 50). At the time of the consecration, the celebrant now genuflects only once after each elevation.

10.　"In Masses celebrated with a congregation, even when not concelebrated, the celebrant may say the canon aloud..."

12.　"After the consecration, the celebrant need not join thumb and forefinger; should any particle of the host have remained on his fingers, he rubs his fingers together over the paten."

The Instruction includes a long footnote to paragraph 12, reporting a query made of the Sacred Congregation of Rites concerning this gesture, along with the reply given.

> Query: In view of the permission provided in the Second Instruction not to join the thumbs and index fingers after the consecration, may the ablution of the fingers over the chalice be omitted?

> Reply: The permission not to join the thumbs and index fingers after the consecration presupposes that no particle of the host has remained on the fingers or, if it has, that it is shaken off the fingers onto the paten. If, therefore, these points are carefully observed, it does not seem to exceed or contravene the spirit of the law to omit the ablution of the fingers over the chalice (the ablution to be consumed afterward by the priest). For in these cases there is no reason for the ablution of the fingers, even as there is no reason for joining the fingers, that is, no danger that any particle of the host will be lost or profaned. Hygienic reasons also recommend this solution, especially after the distribution of communion: *Notitiae* 3 (1967) 304, n.108.

The answer to the query is revealing, for it shows that the basic reason for doing away with the gesture of holding thumbs and index fingers together was a practical one: if any particle of the consecrated host might have clung to the fingers of the priest, it would have already been brushed off into the chalice. The gesture therefore had no practical usefulness. What the reformers overlooked, however, was the symbolic power of this gesture: once consecrated hands touched the sacred host, they could not touch anything else until they were purified. Furthermore, when in subsequent years various kinds of unleavened bread were used which because of their consistency resulted in more crumbs, the danger of having loose particles of the consecrated host remained a real one.

Because of the changes indicated in the second Instruction, a revised version of the *Ordo Missae* was needed once again. The edition of the 1967 *Variationes* published in *Notitiae* has two parallel columns, the left column showing the *Vetus Ordo Missae*, the right column showing the *Novus Ordo Missae*.   The section dealing with the consecration is paragraphs #37-38, indicating the following changes:

1. During the *Qui pridie* and the *Simili modo*, the blessing over host and chalice is omitted, just as the multiple signs of the cross had been omitted elsewhere in the canon.

2. The genuflection before showing the Body of Christ or the Blood of Christ to the people has been omitted.   Only the genuflection after showing the consecrated species remains.

3. In the 1967 *Ordo*, the consecrated host is placed back on the paten, not the corporal.

4. The rubric about the priest keeping his thumbs and forefingers together has been omitted.   A new rubric says instead: *Post consecrationem, celebranti licet pollices et indices non coniungere*.

The 1965 *Ordo Missae/Ritus servandus* and the 1967 *Variationes* were all provisional documents.   With the publication of the 1970 *Missale Romanum* and its *Ordo Missae*, substantial changes were introduced which had not been possible prior to the new editions of the liturgical books.

X.   *Ordo Missae* 1970

In the 1970 *Missale Romanum*, there is no longer any *Ritus servandus in celebratione Missae*; this has been replaced by the *Institutio generalis Missalis Romani*.   Paragraph #109 of the IGMR speaks in a general way about the rubrics for the consecration, indicating simply that when the priest says the Eucharistic Prayer, he should follow the rubrics given for each of them.   It was necessary to be very general in order to accommodate the specific differences for the four Eucharistic Prayers contained in the 1970 and 1975 editions.   The same paragraph #109 gives directions for the ringing of the bell, repeating the indications given in *Ritus servandus* 1965, #67, only this time making them optional.[xviii]

Each section of the new *Ordo Missae* is numbered; the sections dealing with the consecration in the Roman Canon are #91-93.   The more noteworthy changes are as follows:

1.   The *Qui pridie* is preceded by a general rubric: "In the formulas which follow, the words of the Lord are to be pronounced distinctly and clearly, as the nature of these words requires."[xix]   This rubric was

inserted at the insistence of Pope Paul VI. After the experiments with the *Novus Ordo* which took place in January 1968, Pope Paul wrote to Fr. Bugnini with his observations, including the comment:

> As already noted, the words of consecration are not to be recited simply as a narrative but with the special, conscious emphasis given them by a celebrant who knows he is speaking and acting "in the person of Christ".[xx]

In communicating the Pope's wishes to the Consilium, Bugnini summarized this point as follows:

> In all the Eucharistic Prayers there should be a rubric before the consecration reminding the priest that the words of consecration are not to be uttered "in the manner of a narrative" but "clearly and distinctly as required by their nature".[xxi]

2. After the words *qui, pridie quam pateretur*, there is a rubric, which says: *accipit panem*. Up until and including the 1967 *Ordo*, the rubric had read *accipit hostiam*. Although the words spoken by the priest are *accepit panem in sanctas ac venerabiles manus suas*, the rubrics up until this time had always used the word *hostia* instead of *panis*, the understanding being that this was not ordinary bread, but bread that would become the sacred victim.

3. The manner in which the priest takes the host or the chalice into his hands is now different. The 1965/1967 *Ordo Missae* and the 1965 *Ritus servandus* describe these gesture according to the tradition of John Burckard: elbows on the altar, host held with the thumb and index fingers of both hands, chalice held in both hands, etc. In the *novus Ordo*, those specific details are omitted, to be replaced by the general rubric: *eumque parum elevatum super altare tenens*.

4. The 1970 rubrics omit the bowing of the head (*caput inclinat*) at the words *tibi gratias agens*.

5. The sequence of word and gesture is now changed. Up until now, the priest's gesture of placing his elbows on the altar in preparation for the words of consecration came <u>after</u> *accipite et manducate ex hoc omnes*. Now the gesture is different (*parum se inclinat*) and it comes <u>before</u> *accipite et manducate ex hoc omnes*. The effect is to change the focus from the very words themselves, to the larger institution narrative.

6.   This shift of emphasis is further demonstrated by a change in which words are capitalized (or set in larger type-face) and which words are not.

1962: HOC EST ENIM CORPUS MEUM

1970: ACCIPITE ET MANDUCATE EX HOC OMNES: HOC EST ENIM CORPUS MEUM, QUOD PRO VOBIS TRADETUR.

This applies to the consecration of the chalice as well:

1962: HIC EST ENIM CALIX SANGUINIS MEI, NOVI ET AETERNI TESTAMENTI: MYSTERIUM FIDEI: QUI PRO VOBIS ET PRO MULTI EFFUNDETER IN REMISSIONEM PECCATORUM.

1970: ACCIPITE ET BIBITE EX EO OMNES. HIC EST ENIM CALIX SANGUINIS MEI, NOVI ET AETERNI TESTAMENTI: QUI PRO VOBIS ET PRO MULTI EFFUNDETER IN REMISSIONEM PECCATORUM. HOC FACITE IN MEAM COMMEMORATIONEM.

7.   Up until the 1967 *Ordo*, the words of consecration were spoken directly (that is, physically) over the elements. There is no indication of such a gesture in the *novus Ordo*, unless it is implicitly indicated by the rubric: *parum se inclinat.*

8.   In the consecration formula for the host, the words *quod pro vobis tradetur* have been added. This addition was originally made in the new Eucharistic Prayers, and then to standardize them all, the addition was carried over to the Roman Canon as well.[xxii]

9.   There is only one genuflection after each consecration, as per the 1967 *Ordo.*

10.   The rubric *detecto calice* has been omitted, the presupposition being that the pall is no longer used. In IGMR #103, speaking of the role of the deacon, the text reads: *et palla pro opportunitate cooperit.* The pall, therefore, is optional.

11.   The words *mysterium fidei* have been removed from the consecration formula for the chalice, and added as an acclamation after the completion of the entire consecration of both elements.

12.   The phrase *Haec quotiescumqe feceritis, in mei memoriam facietis* has been replaced with *Hoc facite in meam commemorationem.*[xxiii]

It is clear from comparing the sources that, in respect to the previous tradition extending back to the thirteenth century, the *Ordo Missae* of 1970 has significantly reduced the gestures of reverence accompanying the words of consecration.

Conclusion

Our study of the *Ordo Missae* has revealed three basic stages in the history of the gestures of reverence accompanying the words of consecration: 1) the development of these gestures from the thirteenth to the fifteenth centuries, 2) the fixing of these gestures in the sixteenth century, and 3) the reduction of these gestures in the late twentieth century. In each of these three stages, the gestures are directly related to theology and piety.

Stage 1: In the late twelfth / early thirteenth centuries, the desire of popular piety to venerate the consecrated host and the uncertainty as to the proper moment to do so, gave rise to the practice of elevating the host after the words of consecration. The development of the scholastic understanding of transubstantiation gave a strong theological foundation to this gesture of reverence. (The parallel gesture of elevating the chalice was a later development).

Stage 2: The extreme variety in liturgical practice if not outright chaos of the fourteenth and fifteenth centuries, prompted John Burckard, papal master of ceremonies, to compile a detailed description of the Mass ceremonies around the year 1500. Those charged with a reform of the *Missale Romanum* after the Council of Trent incorporated the work of Burckard into the *Ordo Missae* and *Ritus servandus in celebratione Missae* in order to correct abuses and counter Protestant denials of the Real Presence of Christ in the Mass. The prescription and standardization of the gestures of reverence accompanying the words of consecration built a protective wall around this sacred moment of the Mass, and reinforced Catholic Eucharistic theology.

Stage 3: The modification and reduction of these gestures in the 1970 *Ordo Missae* would appear to correspond to important shifts in contemporary understandings in the fields of anthropology and theology.[xxiv] Anthropologically, an Enlightenment view of man as a primarily intellectual and rational being now predominates. In this view, man does not need symbolic gesture or repetition: these things are primitive and not worthy of modern man. Theologically, transubstantiation is rejected as an inadequate explanation of the mystery of the Eucharist.[xxv]   With the emphasis on the entire Eucharistic action and the down-playing of the moment of transubstantiation, rubrical changes were also made, reflecting the new theological presuppositions.   While it is true that any one theological explanation does not exhaust the depths of the mystery, the abrupt theological shift had serious consequences and opened the door to many abuses.   In certain countries, substantial majorities of the Catholic faithful no longer believe in the Real Presence of Christ in the Eucharist.   To be sure, the reduction of gestures of reverence at the moment of consecration is not the only explanation of this confusion and loss of faith, but if we accept the axiom that liturgical practice influences belief, then it seems logical to conclude that these liturgical changes have contributed to a lack of reverence and a corresponding loss of the sense of the sacred.

Fr. Cassian Folsom, O.S.B.
July 11, 1996

NOTES

[i]___   The term *Ordo Missae* in its most primitive sense refers to a collection of personal prayers for the use of the celebrant, in order to foster his devotion during the celebration of Mass.   Such prayers were designed for those places in the structure of the Mass which did not already have prescribed prayers of their own: in particular, during the introductory, offertory and communion rites.   Bonifas Luykx distinguishes three basic stages in the development of the *Ordo Missae*: the Apology-type, the Frankish type and the Rhein-type: B. Luykx, "Der Ursprung der gleichbleibenden Teile der heiligen Messe", *Liturgie und Münchtum* 26 (1960) 72-119.   For a good summary, cf. B. Baroffio and F. Dell'Oro, "L'*Ordo Missae* di Warmondo d'Ivrea", *Studi Medievali* 16 (1975/II) 801-806.   The term *Ordinarium Missae* was first used in the thirteenth-century, to mean simply the unchanging parts of the Mass, for by this time the specific order of prayers and rubrics had become fairly well established (cf. Luykx, p.72).   In this paper, no distinction is being made between these two terms.

[ii]___   According to Van Dijk, in the thirteenth century there were four liturgical traditions existing in Rome side by side: that of the papal court, the Lateran basilica, the urban or presbyteral tradition represented by St. Peter's, and the reform of Orsini, which attempted to combine elements of the papal and urban traditions.   While Van Dijk argues that *Ottobonianus latinus* 356 (along with *Codex* 100 of the library of Avignon) belongs to the Orsini reform, M. Andrieu maintains that this manuscript represents the usages of the papal chapel itself. For the debate between these two scholars, cf. the following (in chronological order):
1.   Andrieu, M., "Le missel de la chapelle papale à la fin du XIII siècle", *Miscellanea F. Ehrle*, vol. 2, Studi e Testi 38, Roma 1924, 348-376.

2.	Van Dijk, S., "Three Manuscripts of a Liturgical Reform by John Cajetan Orsini (Nicholas III)", *Scriptorium* 6 (1952) 213-42.
3.	Andrieu, M., "L'Authenticité du *Missel de la chapelle papale*", *Scriptorium* 9 (1955) 17-34.
4.	Van Dijk, S., "The Legend of *the Missal of the Papal Chapel* and the Fact of Cardinal Orsini's Reform", *Sacris Erudiri* 8 (1956) 76-142.
5.	Van Dijk, S., "The Authentic Missal of the Papal Chapel", *Scriptorium* 14 (1960) 257-314.

Until a closer study is made of these two texts (a critical edition of which is now in preparation), the question remains open.

iii___	Peter Browe, *Die Verehrung der Eucharistie im Mittelalter*, Rome: Herder, 1967, pp.29-33. According to Browe, the gesture of elevating the host for the sake of showing it to the people -- which we find in the synodal legislation of the Parisian Bishop Odo of Sully (1196-1208) -- was not concerned so much with the theological question of the precise moment of transubstantiation, but rather was a response to the pastoral problem of people venerating the host before the words of consecration. In order to prevent this abuse, Odo ordered that the priest should elevate the host after the words of consecration in such a way that the people could see it clearly; thus they would not be confused about the proper moment for manifesting their devotion.

iv___	For a description of this manuscript, cf. S. Van Dijk, "The Authentic Missal of the Papal Chapel," *Scriptorium* 14 (1960) 257-314. Van Dijk places the date of the manuscript in the third quarter of the thirteenth century (p.269), with additions made in the mid-fifteenth century (p.288). Cf. also S. Van Dijk and J. H. Walker, *The Origins of the Modern Roman Liturgy: the liturgy of the papal court and the Franciscan order in the thirteenth century*, London 1960, pp.158-165.

v___	This *Ordo* gets its name from the opening rubric: *indutus planeta, sacerdos stet ante gradum altaris*. Cf. Stephen J. P. Van Dijk, *Sources of the Modern Roman Liturgy: The Ordinals by Haymo of Faversham and Related Documents (1243-1307)*, vol.2, Leiden 1963, p.3.

vi___	*Nota quod ab hoc loco usque ad ultimam purificationem manuum sacerdotis iungendus est index cum pollice, preterquam in signationibus et cum tangitur corpus domini* (Van Dijk, *Sources of the Modern Roman Liturgy*, p.11).

vii___	A. Frutaz has shown that the actual Missal used by Cardinal Sirleto in preparing the revision of the Roman Missal for the post-Tridentine commission entrusted with that charge, was not the *editio princeps* of 1474, but a Venetian edition of 1497. Cf. A. P. Frutaz, "Contributo alla storia della riforma del Messale promulgato da san Pio V nel 1570," *Problemi di vita religiosa in Italia nel cinquecento*, Padova 1960, 187-214. It would be interesting to examine the *Ordo Missae* of this 1497 Missal to see if it differs from that of the *editio princeps*.

viii___	I am not speaking of legitimate liturgical diversity here, but of liturgical abuse. Cf. *Abusus, qui circa venerandum missae sacrificium evenire solent, partim a patribus deputatis animadversi, partim ex multorum praelatorum dictis et scriptis excerpti* (8 augusti 1562), in *Concilium Tridentium: Diariorum Actorum, Epistularum, Tractatuum*, vol.8, Freiburg-Breisgau 1919, pp.916-921.

ix____ Versatus ab adolescentia circa sacras Cerimonias Reverendissime domine: cum viderim complures presbiteros in celebratione Missarum: multas abusiones: et diversos ritus: et gestus inconvenientes frequenter imitari indignum existimavi: non esse a sancta Romana ecclesia: omnium ecclesiarum Matre et Magistra traditum sacerdotibus certum modum: qui in celebratione huiusmodi universalter observaretur. Collegi propterea alias in unum et in publicum tradidi: ex diversis decretis sanctorum patrum: que Summi Pontifices pro celebratione predicta instituerunt. Et cum nuper collecta huiusmodi reviderem comperi plura esse omissa quam tradita. Addidi igitur que occurrebant: et prout potui complevi opus... *Ordo Missae Ioannis Burckardi* in J. Wickham Legg, *Tracts on the Mass*, Henry Bradshaw Society 27, London 1904, pp.121-122.

x____ *...ante corpus domini cum idem conficitur.* Cf. S. Van Dijk, *The Ordinal of the Papal Court from Innocent III to Boniface VIII and Related Documents*, Spicilegium Friburgense 22, Fribourg 1975, p.513, n.1.

xi____ Latin text of *Inter Oecumenici* (September 26, 1964): AAS 56 (1964) 877-900; English text: International Commission on English in the Liturgy, *Documents on the Liturgy, 1963-1979*, Collegeville 1982, pp.88-110.

xii____ Giampietro, N., *Il Cardinale Giuseppe Ferdinando Antonelli e gli sviluppi della riforma liturgica dal 1948 al 1970*, Diss. Pontificio Istituto Liturgico, Roma 1996, pp.211-212.

xiii____ Bugnini describes the situation regarding changes in the Mass: "Some would have preferred to see the rite completely revised. The Consilium was of this opinion at the beginning, and it had even prepared a draft. But this idea was then rejected when it was realized that the disadvantages would outweigh the advantages, both in regard to the rite, the rubrics, the habits and education of the clergy, and in relation to the reform, which might be jeopardized by such a complete revision. There was unanimous agreement at this point that there should instead be a careful revision of the *Ordo Missae* so as to include in it whatever could be introduced without difficulty. A. Bugnini, *The Reform of the Liturgy: 1948-1975*, Collegeville 1990, 114.

xiv____ P. Marini, "L'Istruzione *Inter Oecumenici*, una svolta decisiva (luglio-ottobre 1964)", *Ephemerides Liturgicae* 108 (1994) 214.

xv____ Cf. P. Marini, "Il *Consilium* in piena attività in un clima favorevole (ottobre 1964-marzo 1965)", *Ephemerides Liturgicae* 109 (1995) 115-116.

xvi____ P. Marini, "Il *Consilium* in piena attività in un clima favorevole (ottobre 1964-marzo 1965)", *Ephemerides Liturgicae* 109 (1995) 119-120.

xvii____ Latin text of *Tres abhinc annos* (May 4, 1967): AAS 59 (1967) 442-448; cf. also *Notitiae* 3 (1967) 169-194. English text: International Commission on English in the Liturgy, *Documents on the Liturgy, 1963-1979*, Collegeville 1982, pp.135-140.

xviii____ Paulo ante consecrationem, minister, pro opportunitate, campanulae signo fideles monet. Item pulsat capanulam ad unamquamque ostensionem, iuxta cuiusque loci consuetudinem (IGMR 109).

xix____ *In formulis quae sequuntur, verba Domini proferantur distincte et aperte, prouti natura eorundem verborum requirit* (MR 1970/1975, #91).

xx____ Bugnini, *The Reform of the Liturgy*, p.365.

xxi___ Bugnini, *The Reform of the Liturgy*, p.370.

xxii___ For more information, cf. Bugnini, *The Reform of the Liturgy*, pp.381-382). On Oct. 24, 1968, a file was sent to Pope Paul VI by the secretariat of the Consilium reporting on the group's 11th general meeting. Among other things, the report included a statement on the Lord's words in the formula of consecration. Bugnini wrote: "As we look forward to the publication of the revised Order of Mass, which will necessarily contain all four Eucharistic Prayers, it seems advisable to accede to the request from many quarters that the Lord's words in the two formulas of consecration be made the same in all the Canons and in every celebration. This uniformity will help the celebrant, especially in concelebration, where it will ensure an unhesitating and dignified enunciation of these formulas that are at the heart of the Mass" (p.382)
    "In order to achieve this uniformity it is necessary:
a)   to add the words "which will be given up for you" to the formula for the consecration of the bread in the Roman Canon;
b)   and to remove the words "They mystery of faith" from the formula for the consecration of the wine" (p.382).
Bugnini reports: "These changes were made without opposition..." (p.382).

xxiii___ In the same report of October 24, 1968, Pope Paul VI was asked to approve "the substitution, in the Roman Canon, of *Do this in memory of me* for *As often as you do this, you will do it in memory of me*. The latter of these two is liturgical, that is, it is found as such only in the liturgical tradition and not in the biblical sources. The second is found as such in Luke (22:19) and in Paul (1 Cor 11:24). The second text seemed preferable as being easier and at the same time more biblical. The change was approved unanimously by the Consilium" (Bugnini, *The Reform of the Liturgy*, pp.382-383).

xxiv___ The theories put forward here can be debated, of course. In proposing these explanations, I am not calling into question the good intentions of the reformers. Rather, I am simply trying to understand the broader philosophical and theological context of the times in order to grasp more clearly what happened, and why.

xxv___ One has only to recall Pope Paul VI's encyclical *Mysterium Fidei*, written before the close of the Council (1965), in response to this very problem.

Concerning Exposition of the Blessed Sacrament

Father Christian-Philippe Chanut (France)

Father Christian Chanut, born near Bordeaux in 1948, has been parish priest of Saulx-les-Chartreux, about 20 km south of Paris in the Evry diocese, since 1979, the year of his priestly ordination. After studies in modern languages and literature and in law, he specialised in modern history. After joining Saint Sulpice seminary, he specialised in teaching XVIIIth century history; since then, besides his pastoral activities, he lectures as a historian, in various religious houses including the seminary of the Fraternity of Saint Peter.

"Such a cult, which is directed in consequence to the Trinity of Father, Son and Holy Spirit, accompanies and pervades above all the celebration of the Eucharistic liturgy. But it should also fill our sanctuaries, even outside the hours of Mass. Since it was instituted by love, and renders Christ present sacramentally, it is indeed worthy of thanksgiving and worship."

(John Paul II: Letter on the Mystery and worship of the Holy Eucharist, No. 3).

As everyone knows, Benediction of the Blessed Sacrament is a devotional exercise which consists in exposing the consecrated Host upon the altar, where it is then honoured by hymns, prayers and liturgical actions; at the end of these, the priest blesses the faithful with the consecrated Host, before replacing it in the tabernacle.

Since this liturgy of Eucharistic exposition is of a relatively late date, it is naturally an object of contention for those who cherish the chimerical plan of returning Christian worship to its primitive purity. It may be noted in passing, that these lovers of primitive purity do not hesitate to invent rites, and new gestures totally unknown to ancient Christianity (handshakes, open hands raised waist high, acclamations, the waving of cloths, etc.) As a matter of fact, behind this alleged concern to renew contact with the usages of the Apostolic age, lies hardly concealed a grave questioning of Eucharistic faith. The *Cathechism of the Catholic Church*, promulgated by John Paul II on 11 October 1992, summarily dismissed these pretensions, whose aim was the abolition of any Eucharistic worship outside the Mass. Making a resumé from Paul VI, the *Cathechism of the Catholic Church* says: *"The Catholic Church has given and continues to give the cult of adoration which is due to the sacrament of the Eucharist, not only during the Mass, but also outside its celebration: by using the greatest care in preserving consecrated Hosts, in presenting them to the people for their solemn veneration, and in carrying them in procession."* [1] This present account of Eucharistic

95

exposition will be simply one of history (scarcely at all enlivened with pastoral reflections), and will discuss in succession, the adoration of the real and substantial Presence of the Lord, during the celebration of Mass, of the Eucharistic reserve, and of expositions of the Blessed Sacrament.

Adoration of the real and substantial Presence of the Lord in the Eucharist

Whatever the official texts may prescribe, the adoration of the real and substantial Presence of the Lord in the Eucharist, is nowadays commonly reduced to almost nothing, or is even non-existant, for the attitudes and gestures of adoration are set aside as inconvenient anachronisms. In fact, adoration came much before reservation in the tabernacle. Thus Origen,[2] who proclaimed adorable the mystery of the Eucharist, invited the faithful *to humble themselves* before the Lord, Who is hidden under these veils; Saint Cyril of Jerusalem[3] ordered a bow when approaching the chalice *"as a sign of adoration and veneration"*; Saint Ambrose[4] professed that *"we still adore today the flesh of our Redemption, and we adore it in the mysteries which He instituted, and which are celebrated each day upon our altars;"* Saint Augustine ordered that *"no one should eat the flesh of Jesus Christ without having adored it; and far from it being that we sin in adoring it, not to adore it would be to sin."* [5]

Progressively, if I may so put it, the faithful of the ancient communities manifested spontaneously their interior adoration of the Real Presence of the Lord in the Eucharist, by gestures which -- experience has taught us -- produce what they signify, in the hearts of those who make them. Whilst it is probable that the first Christians were content to remain standing upright during the celebration of Mass, there appeared, after their time, without it being either a general custom or obligatory, at first the inclination, then the genuflection spoken of by Saint Epiphanius,[6] Saint Jerome,[7] in the *Apostolic Constitutions* [8] and all sorts of Patristic writings.

Doubtless there will be occasion to speak of this again elsewhere, but the heart of the question being asked today, is to know whether the gestures of adoration, in particular the genuflection, better aid or not the faith of the people in the Real Presence: in view of the opposite experience, imposed during the last thirty years by the liturgical terrorists, has faith in the Real Presence been thereby strengthened? Unhappily, it seems not, since Eucharistic heresies have become current coin, and the mounting flow of adoration has been brusquely cut off, even if, one can see, here and there, that happily it is being resumed, without this being, however, a general movement. The old mania of wishing, at any price, to rediscover the usages of the first Christian period, counting as nothing the pious contributions of the later centuries, is absolutely contrary to the Tradition of the Church and, far from being a forward move, is a regression both in piety as well as in faith, since one is the expression of the other. If a person who is accustomed to prostrate himself on both knees, is obliged to do no more than incline his head, the mystery is depreciated in his eyes, to the profit of his own elevation and, in doing this, far from familiarising him with the Real Presence, the natural vehicle of his devotion is taken away. Let it be said in passing, that the same thing happens concerning the manner of communicating and for the transport of the Eucharist. It must, at last, be understood that these three things are intimately linked and, to favour one to the detriment of the others destablizes devotion. It once happened that I found myself in a certain religious community where one prostrated oneself to the earth at the consecration, or at an exposition of the Blessed Sacrament, but on approaching or returning from Holy Communion, not the slightest gesture of piety was apparent; little attention was paid to the purification of sacred vessels, and the sacred species were carried about like any ordinary thing. These holy women believed firmly in the Real Presence, which they adored daily, but their manner of proceeding threw Eucharistic piety off balance; as though the Lord were less worthy of adoration on receiving communion than at the elevation, in the tabernacle than in the monstrance. Our fathers were very wise people when they developed the gestures of Eucharistic adoration, which demonstrate faith more surely than does speech, however exact this may be.

The Eucharistic Reservation

If, for the period before the peace of Constantine, we are reduced to conjecture, it is nevertheless probable that the faithful did sometimes take with them to their houses a portion of the sacred species, either to give communion to the sick, or to communicate themselves; St. Basil reported that *"in the town of Alexandria and in the rest of Egypt, the faithful kept the communion at home, and took at divers times what they had received at church, from the hands of the officiant."* [9] It is not rare to find allusions to this domestic usage of the Eucharist, most often inviting the faithful to show respect and act with prudence;[10] this is illustrated by Hippolytus of Rome in the *Apostolic Tradition*, Tertullian in the *Ad uxorem* and in *De oratione*, Novatian in *De spectaculis*, and St. Cyprian in *De lapsis*. Without the total disappearance of the conservation of the Eucharist in private houses, to which St. Jerome, St. Paulinus of Nola and St. Augustine bear witness, it is certain that after the peace of Constantine, one finds being established the rule of permanently reserving the Blessed

97

Sacrament in the *pastaphoria* of the churches, as witnessed at the end of the fourth century, in the *Apostolic Constitutions*. St.John Chrysostom invited the faithful forcefully to come and adore the Real Presence of the Lord: *"The Magi came from the borders of Persia to adore the Child in the stable; and we, who have no need to expose ourselves to the dangers and fatigues of a long journey in order to adore Him in our churches and our tabernacles, we who have only to leave our houses, should we refuse to do this? Is it not the most culpable of negligences, even the blackest and most monstrous ingratitude?"* At that period the Eucharist was not kept in the choirs of churches, but in a particular place, often near the sacristy, the *conditorium* of which the Ambrosian *Ordo* of Berold speaks.[11] Lest one should be tempted to believe that the Eucharist was simply kept in a wall cupboard in the sacristy, it should be enough to refer to the description given by St. Paulinus (353-431) to Sulpicius Severus (historian and hagiographer) of the basilica of St. Felix at Nola.[12] The principal apse was flanked by two subsidiary apses, the *secretaria*, of which the right-hand *secretarium*, the *diaconicon*, sheltered the Eucharist and the sacred vessels. *"This is the spot where the sacred reserve is placed, and from which are taken the holy things which make for the splendour of the cult;"* the *secretarium* on the left, the *prothesis*, contains the sacred books: *"If anyone experiences the holy desire to meditate on the law, he can rest here to consult the holy books."*

The *prothesis* was from that time treated with respect and, to emphasise its majesty, the care of the Real Presence was reserved to the priests: the Council of Laodicea (about 360), the first Council of Vaison (452), and the Council of Agde (506) excluded the subdeacons; the *De Ecclesiasticis Officiis* of St. Isidore of Seville (d. 636), gave the guardianship to deacons. The author of the *Life* of St. Didier of Cahors (d. 655), praises the holy bishop for having taken care that the sacred vessels shone brilliantly, the *sacrarium* was clean and the lamps were lit.[13] In the sixth century, a synod held at Verdun ordered that the Blessed Sacrament should be reserved in a *"prominent and honourable place and, if the resources of the church permitted, there must be a lamp before it, a lighted lamp."* [14] Do not imagine that these different texts, whether they were decisions of councils or synods, constituted new provisions; on the contrary, they were extending to the churches which depended on their authority, usages born of the piety of pastors, with which the faithful were well content.

Wherever the Eucharist was reserved, the Church taught that *"Christ must be adored, for He is the Word of God, and He must be adored with the same adoration in His own flesh."* [15] If it is perhaps hazardous to suppose that perpetual adoration was already performed in the prestigious monastery of Agaune, in 522, it is certain that the fourth canon of the Council of Tours, held in 567, ordered that the doors of the sanctuary should remain open, to allow the faithful to come, whatever the hour, to pray before that altar.

In the Carolingian epoch recluses began to appear who, from their cells joined on to a church, were able to see the tabernacle through the hagioscope (cut through the chancel wall or arch). The most ancient rule for recluses, that of Grimla c, written at the end of the ninth century, prescribed that they should take delight in the spectacle of the Presence.[16] This institution came into being as a reaction against the symbolism of Ratramnus (d. 868), to which was opposed the realism of St. Paschasius Radbertus (c.785 - c.860), who affirmed the identity of the Eucharistic Christ with the historical Christ.[17] The faithful gave the greatest marks of honour to the Real Presence in the tabernacle, *"the adorable Host of the Son of God"*, to speak like the Anglo Saxons of that time, who loved to pray before the altar, even when the church was empty; thus, their King Alfred (871-901), who heard Mass every day and who recited the different hours, went secretly by night to the church to pray before the Blessed Sacrament. The first confraternity of the Blessed Sacrament, whose members proposed to honour Jesus present in the Eucharist, had come into being already in the ninth century at St. Rémi of Laon. The hagiographers tell us that the holy bishop Wulstan of Worcester (d.1095) made frequent visits at night to the Blessed Sacrament, as King Wenceslas (d. 935) of Bohemia had done. King Robert II, the Pious, (d.1031) caused a cart to precede him on which was carried the Blessed Sacrament. He would then adore it beneath a tent put up during halts. St. Louis (d.1270) did the same, even on his crusading ship, and the popes retained this privilege until the time of Benedict XIII (d. 1730).

The time available does not allow us to tell you anything about the vessels and the furniture of the places where the Eucharist was reserved. It should, however, be emphasised that the custom of reserving the Eucharist on the high altar came into being in Carolingian lands towards the eighth century; in the middle of the succeeding century, Leo IV recommended this usage to the Roman clergy. [18] Nevertheless, the tabernacle remained for a long time moveable, and it had to await the Italian Renaissance and the Tridentine reform, for it to be generally located on the altar. St. Charles Borromeo ordered this usage through the Council of Milan in 1565. The holy reserve (the tabernacle), as the Catechism of the Catholic Church concludes, was at first destined to preserve the Eucharist in a worthy manner, so that it could be carried to the sick, and to those absent, outside the Mass. Through the deepening of the Faith in the Real Presence of Christ in His Eucharist, the Church became aware of the sense of silent adoration of the Lord present under the eucharistic species. It is for that reason that the tabernacle should be placed in a particularly worthy place in the church; and this must be constucted in such a way that it underlines and manifests the truth of the Real Presence of Christ in the Blessed Sacrament." [19]

Eucharistic Exposition

Now, in the course of the Middle Ages, in order better to adore the Real Presence by fixing their gaze, the faithful wanted to see, if not the Sacred Host itself, then the sacred vessel which contained it; to make this possible eucharistic cabinets or cupboards were constructed, examples of tabernacles with pierced doors, or with openings contrived in the walls, so that the sacred vessel could be glimpsed. So that the faithful could see this sacred vessel better, it was placed on a stand, which became the ciborium which we know today. Sometimes eucharistic eyes were pierced through the walls of churches, so that at night, it might be possible to distinguish from the outside, if not the ciborium or the tabernacle, at least the light which gave witness to the Lord's Real Presence.

The first Eucharistic exposition, in the way we know it today, that is to say, the elevation at the Consecration, seems to have been instituted to counter the symbolist heresy of Berengar (who died in 1088), who denied the Real Presence of Christ in the Eucharist. Like every other dogmatic error, the heresy of Berengar, which followed on that of the manicheans of Orleans (1022) and of Arras (1035), provoked a double reaction: on the one side, the learned reaction of the theologians (Lanfranc, Guitmond of Aversa, Alger of Liège, Hugh of Saint Victor), who deepened the doctrine in order to refute the objections; on the other, the pious and pragmatic reaction of the people, who gave witness to their faith through appropriate devotional practices. Lanfranc (d. 1089), who was Archbishop of Canterbury, instituted, for Palm Sunday, a procession of the Blessed Sacrament, before which all were to kneel.[20]

On the other hand, the errors of Berengar do not seem to have been at the source of the institution of the rite of elevation after the consecration; nevertheless, indirectly, they contributed strongly to drawing the attention, and consequently the interest of the faithful in the consecrated Host. The *Ancren Riwle* prescribed for recluses, on first rising, to direct their thoughts towards the Holy Eucharist reserved on the high altar and, and having turned towards it, to adore it on their knees, saying: *"Hail! Source of our creation! Hail, Reward awaited and desired!"* [21]

This current of adoration, into which mediaeval piety blossomed, urged the faithful who could not receive sacramental communion to ask for a sight of the Sacred Host. In the *Sentences* of Anselm of Laon, which were written at the beginning of the twelfth century, one can read that this communion is very real although it is

100

only spiritual. At the end of the twelfth century, the request was strong enough to bring into being the rite of elevation in the course of the Mass. It was to give effect to this request, which had become almost general, that there appeared the decree of Eudes de Sully, Bishop of Paris from 1196 to 1208, which laid down that, after the words of consecration, the priest should elevate the Host "*in such a manner that it could be seen by all.*" [22] Eudes de Sully was of the opinion that the contemplation of the Sacred Host constituted "*a noble hommage of faith and adoration, most salutary for the faithful.*" William of Auxerre (1150-1232), professor at the University of Paris, declared that "*the priest raises the Body of Christ so that all the faithful see it, asking for what is useful for their salvation.*" [23] The bishops who, following Eudes of Sully, prescribed the same practice, gave witness to the same concern for piety; thus, the council of Exeter (1287) stated: "*That the Host is to be raised, so that it can be contemplated by all those who are round the altar: the piety of the faithful is both enlivened and the merits of their faith thus increased.*" [24] From the beginning of the thirteenth century, the elevation was widely enough spread, for Pope Honorius III (1216-1227) to sanction the custom, by requiring that the faithful should then bow with respect (1219). At the Elevation at Mass, the faithful formed the habit of saluting the Christ of the Sacrifice with acclamations, or by short formulas of devotion of which there is an example in the *Queste du Saint-Graal* (composed about 1220), where King Mordrain cries out: "*Ave salus mundi Verbum Patris, Hostia vera!*"; in the fourteenth century, this prayer was again proposed for the elevation, in a missal of Chartres.

In the thirteenth century, "*the thought and the cult of the Eucharist became, almost throughout the Church, the object of constant and direct sollicitude,*" [25] for both faithful and theologians. There then began the habitual visits to the Blessed Sacrament for which St. Francis of Assisi (1181-1226) composed the act of adoration.[26] St. Thomas Aquinas (1225-1274), like his master, St. Dominic, passed long periods before the tabernacle, as did Marie d'Oignies (d.1213).[27] The contemplation of the Host was thought of as a spiritual communion at which, according to Peter Lombard (d.1164), "*those who eat spiritually are said to receive the truth of the Body and the Blood.*" [28] William of Auxerre (1150-1232) wrote, that it "*causes a greater love of God.*" [29] Confraternities of the Blessed Sacrment were set up.[30]

This current of contemplation continued and became exaggerated, and into this the sovereign Pontiffs of the sixteenth century tried to bring good order. One recalls that the Lord revealed to St. Gertrude (1255-1303), "*that whilst he who communicates really, receives great advantages for his salvation, nevertheless, he who, through a duty of obedience and holy discretion, deprives himself of receiving this august sacrament corporally, but who, being enflamed with desire and the love of God, communicates spiritually, receives before God much more*

101

abundant fruit." [31]   At the end of the fourteenth century, St. Dorothy of Dantzig (d.1394), who could only communicate a few times a year, arranged her life as mother of a family, in order to go each day to contemplate the Sacred Host, persuaded that she thus received many graces.[32]   In default of receiving the Viaticum, the contemplation of the consecrated Host was equivalent to communion. Thus, St. Juliana of Mont-Cornillon (1193-1258), to whom was due the initiation of Corpus Christi, who herself on her death bed, was not able to receive communion, *"died whilst gazing at the Host with a penetrating look."* [33] This belief was, in the fifteenth century, stressed in the *Tractatus sacerdotalis* of Nicholas de Blony, and in the Ritual of Reims; in the course of the sixteenth century, this spiritual communion as Viaticum was recommended in numerous Rituals, like that of Strasburg (1500), of Rodez (1514), of Schwerin (1521), of Mainz (1551), and of Paris (1574).   Maximilian I of Hapsburg (1459-1519) who, having fallen down a Tyrolean precipice and seeing that he could not receive the Viaticum, desired to be shown the consecrated Host so that he could adore it.[34]

We must now return to St. Juliana of Mont-Cornillon,[35] and the institution of Corpus Christi by Urban IV (1261-1264).   Two years after taking the habit, Sister Juliana received one night a vision of the orb of the moon, radiant with light, but traversed at its diameter by an obscure line; not understanding this vision, she asked for an explanation from some virtuous sisters, who counselled her not to go into this mystery more deeply, but could not stop themselves gossiping about it, to such an extent that visitors came to trouble her with questions. Sister Sapience, Prioress of the convent, knowing of Juliana's devotion to the Eucharist, and her taste for solitude, caused to be built for her an oratory to which she could retire to pray. Since nobody had explained her vision, she resolved to ask the Lord to reveal this mystery to her and in 1210, whilst she slept, a voice said to her: *"The Church Militant is represented by the orb of the moon; the mark which veils a part of it, signifies that it lacks one feast of which God wishes the institution; it is the feast of the most august and most holy Sacrament of the altar. Maundy Thursday, in truth, designates this, but the divers other ceremonies of this day, inhibit the solemnity; another must be established which will be honoured and observed throughout Christendom. And this for three reasons: 1. so that faith in the mysteries of religion, which diminishes and will continue to diminish, if no remedy is brought forward which will strengthen and confirm it in its entirety; 2. so that those men who love and seek truth may be fully instructed therein, and may draw from this source of life strength to advance in the path of virtue; 3. so that the daily irreverences and impieties which are committed against the majesty of this sacrament, may be redressed and expiated by a profound and sincere adoration."* From that time Juliana was occupied in the thought of God alone, Who favoured her with an extraordinary mystical life, the gift of prophecy and the knowledge of hearts.

In 1222, when Sister Sapience died, Juliana was elected prioress of Mont-Cornillon. She had not yet divulged the revelation which she had received and, and when she asked the Lord to deliver her from this mission, she received, on the contrary, an order to act without delay. Hardly knowing how to set about it, she decided to reveal her mission to Eve, a recluse whom she had not long before encouraged, and whom she saw once a year, and to Isabelle, a religious of Huy. They appealed to John of Lausanne, a pious and learned canon of the Church of St. Martin, near which Eve the recluse lived; the canon contacted James Pantaléon, archdeacon of Liège, Hugh of Saint-Cher, provincial of the Dominicans, and the Fathers John and Gerard, all doctors of the University of Paris, who authorised Juliana to get John, a religious of Mont-Cornillon, to compose the office for Corpus Christi. As the clergy of Liège were divided concerning the utility of this feast, Juliana who did not wish to precipitate anything, went off on a pilgrimage to Cologne, Tongres and Maastricht. A favourable movement occurred at Liège but Roger, the new superior at Mont-Cornillon, incited the sisters against their prioress who, with four of her sisters, and thanks to the support of John of Lausanne, was able to take refuge near the church of St. Martin.

Three months later, the bishop of Liège deposed Roger, and gave the office to John (the author of the office), and Juliana resumed her place as prioress. The bishop of Liège, Robert of Thourotte, still hesitated to establish the feast when, on the road to the council of Lyons, God intimated to him His will; on his return to Liège, he established the feast of Corpus Christi in his diocese (synod of 1246). Robert of Thourotte died (16 October 1246), without having been able to celebrate the Feast, but the canons of St. Martin did so in 1247. Under the successor of Robert of Thourotte, Henry of Gueldre, who restored Roger, the persecutions against Juliana began again; accompanied by three faithful women (Agnes, Ozilie and Isdabelle of Huy), she had to retire at first to Robermont, Val-Notre-Dame, then to Namur, near to the church of St. Aubin. Her companions were, however, fearful about her health, which was much weakened. *"Fear nothing"*, she told them, *"I will keep faithful company with you until death, and I will even survive you."* And in fact, two of them (Agnes and Ozilie) died shortly afterwards. Then Juliana retired to the Cistercian Abbey of Salsines. Nevertheless, Hugh of Saint-Cher, who had become cardinal of St. Sabina and papal legate in the Holy Roman Empire, approved the establishment of the feast of Corpus Christi, which he celebrated in 1252, extending it to all the dioceses of his legation.

Soon, Juliana lost at Salsines the one faithful companion who remained to her; another religious of Mont-Cornillon, Ermentrude, was sent to assist her until her death. The persecution struck the nuns of Salsines, and Juliana had to retire to Fosses, situated between the Sambre and the Meuse, where she was attacked by a grave illness; she sent to summon Canon John of Lausanne, but he did not think that he had any need to go, and she found herself in a state of extreme abandonment, which she had, moreover, predicted. The malady grew worse during Lent. On Easter Sunday, in spite of her exhaustion, she wished to go to the church, where she assisted at matins and lauds, and received Holy Communion, remaining in the church until the end of the day. In the evening she returned to her cell, and asked for Extreme Unction, which she received with tears of joy and an admirable presence of mind. On the Wednesday after the Easter Octave, she was much worse: Himana, the abbess of Salsines, who had come when she heard of the danger, wished to spend the night with her, but Juliana invited her to rest, assuring her that she would not die that day. On the Thursday, she asked Ermentrude to recite her office so that she could at least follow it in spirit and heart. On Friday, Himana came to visit her again with some nuns, and all judged that it was the end. Juliana fell asleep in the Lord on 5 April 1258.

Three years later, the old archdeacon of Liège, James Pantaléon, who had since become bishop of Verdun (1253), then patriarch of Jerusalem (1255), then although he was not a cardinal, was elected Pope (29 August 1261). Eve, the recluse of the collegiate church of St. Martin of Liège, wrote to him asking him to institute the Feast of Corpus Christi for the universal Church. Urban IV, no doubt after the eucharistic mirable of Bolsena,[36] published the Bull "Transiturus" on 11 August 1264, at Orvieto: *"We have judged it well to rule that, beyond the reminder which is made daily in the Church of such a great Sacrament, that there should also be made annually a more particular and solemn memorial, assigning for this a particular day, which we wish shall be the Thursday after the Octave of Pentecost."* The Feast was not received in all parts of the Latin Church until the time of Clement V, at the time of the ecumencial Council of Vienne (1311), at which was renewed Urban IV's constitution. It seems that the liturgy of Corpus Christi, at the time of its institution, did not contain an exposition of the Blessed Sacrament, but the Christian people, who had a great desire for it, took advantage of every possible occasion to see the Host. Amongst these occasions, Eucharistic miracles did not go unnoticed, for they were multiplied at this time, either to protect believers, or to respond to doubts or to sacrileges.[37] Thus, ten years before the Feast was solemnly inaugurated by Urban IV, Thomas of Cantimpré[38] gave witness that at Douai on Easter Sunday 1254, a Eucharistic miracle took place at the time of the exposition of the Blessed Sacrament.[39] *"Acquainted of this event by the reports which soon spread, wrote Thomas of Cantimpré, I went to Douai. Having gone to the*

104

house of the Dean of St. Arné, by whom I was particularly known, I begged him to let me see the miracle. He consented, and gave his orders to satisfy me. The box was opened; the people rushed round, and a short time after the box was opened, everyone cried out: ' Here He is, I see Him; here He is, I see my Saviour.' I stood struck with astonishment: I only saw the shape of a very white bread, and yet my conscience did not reproach me with any fault which could stop me seeing, like the others, this sacred Body. Hardly was I occupied with these thoughts, than I saw the face of Jesus Christ in His full age. On His head was a crown of thorns, and two drops of blood flowed from His forehead on to His face at each side of the nose. On the instant I fell on my knees, and weeping, adored. I rose: on the Head was no longer the crown nor the blood: but I saw a man's face, more venerable than anything one could imagine. It was turned towards the right, so that the right eye was scarcely visible. The nose was very long and very straight, the eyebrows arched, the eyes very gentle and lowered: long hair fell shoulder-length. The beard, which the iron had not touched, curled of itself under the chin and, near the charming mouth, it became thinner, leaving on each side of the chin two small spaces without hair, as happens with young men who have let their beards grow after their childhood. The forehead was wide, the cheeks thin, and the head, like the fairly long neck, was a little inclined. Here is the portrait, here the beauty of this most agreeable Face. In the space of an hour, the Saviour was seen plainly, under different forms. Some saw Him stretched on the Cross, others coming to judge men; many, and this was the greatest number, saw Him in the form of a Child."

It is probable that the Eucharistic exposition was accomplished with the ciborium, above which momentarily the Host was raised to be shown to the people, as one can see happened at Douai. However, as the faithful wished to contemplate the sacred species for a longer time, a new sacred vessel was conceived in which to expose the Blessed Sacrament: this was at first called *monstrancia* then *ostensorium*. [*The French have two words here, following the Latin: the English translation for both is now, certainly, only* monstrance. *Translator's note.*] The church of St. Quentin of Hasselt (Belgium) has preserved a monstrance (*monstrancia*) which was offered in 1286 by Edwige, prioress of Herckenrode, to her abbey.[40] At the beginning of the fourteenth century, expositions of the Eucharist were of such wide occurrence that John XXII (1316-1334) ordered, for the Feast of Corpus Christi, a procession of the Blessed Sacrament, of which the first took place that year, starting from the cathedral of Avignon (1318). Before John XXII's decision, apart from the procession which Lanfranc had prescribed for Palm Sunday, almost two and a half centuries earlier, there had already been seen some solemn processions of the Blessed Sacrament, notably at Cologne (1279) and at Worms (1315). The application of the decree of John XXII took place slowly, but the procession is mentioned at the Council of Sens (1320), at that of Tournai (1323), in a manuscript of Chartres (1330) and, doubtless

105

of that epoch, in an *Ordinary* of Rouen. Without a doubt Reims should also be mentioned since the archbishop, Robert de Courtenay (d.1324), bequeathed a monstrance for the procession of the Blessed Sacrament.[41] In most of the other countries the delay lasted until the fifteenth century, when popular pressure became so much greater, that Martin V granted special indulgences for assistance at the procession on the Feast of Corpus Christi.

The exposition of the Blessed Sacrament for purposes of contemplation, in spite of some clerical resistance, spread quickly in reply to pressure from the faithful. In 1328, in the church of St. Fortuné of Todi, the Blessed Sacrament was exposed daily;[42] at the same period, in the house of the Teutonic Knights of Dantzig, blessed Dorothy of Montau (d.1394) went several times a day to adore the Blessed Sacrament exposed in the monstrance;[43] at Munich, a citizen offered a monstrance of transparent crystal for the adoration of the Blessed Sacrament (1395). In the following century, expositions of the Blessed Sacrament were so frequent at Passau, Schwerin, Breslau and Cologne, that the ecclesiastical authorities, in particular Nicholas of Cusa,[44] fearing that habit would destroy piety, tried to limit them to Corpus Christi and its octave. Nothing came of it and, at the pressing demand of the faithful, whose spiritual progress priests noted well, the expositions extended beyond the Feast and its octave.

Whilst the cult of the Eucharist outside Mass was developing, a particular form of public evening prayer around the *Salve Regina* was becoming established. This antiphon, of which the composer is hardly known, was introduced into some of the Offices of the Blessed Virgin by the bishop of Puy, Adhémar of Monteil (1079-1098), and spread very rapidly into popular piety at the time of the Crusade, of which Adhémar was the first (....) About 1221, when certain Dominicans of the convent of Bologna were victims of diabolic possession, their prior, in order to deliver them, caused the *Salve Regina* to be sung each evening at Compline. The effect was so good that the practice spread to other Dominican houses and, from the middle of the thirteenth century, even into parishes, where it gave birth to a kind of popular office. It is known that the king, St. Louis (d. 1270), with his family and his attendants, assisted each evening at such an exercise, which spread abroad widely in France, England, the Low Countries and Italy. The hour was convenient for all, and the execution easy for all, to the extent that this evening prayer became one of the central features of the Christian life. At that time great personages, such as Count Thibaut V of Champagne (1262 in favour of the chapter St. Stephen of Tours), were known to make foundations so that canons, or regulars, might chant the *Salve Regina* after Compline. New confraternities were established to bring together the faithful in the evening, before the altar of the Blessed Virgin, where they sang and prayed (London Bridge in 1334, Bruges at Ypres in 1365, and all over

106

France and Italy up to the sixteenth century).

With the two exercises of worship developing simultaneously, it was not long before there was a desire to bring them together: this happened in particular places in the course of the sixteenth century, and in a general manner at the beginning of the seventeenth. At first, it was usual to bless the faithful with the ciborium [or primitive monstrance: Translator], which was later transformed into the monstrance [as known now: Tr.]. It should be noted, however, that the first description of the service of Benediction of the Blessed Sacrament, such as we know it today, dates from Hildesheim in 1493; doubtless it had already spread, because something similar can be found for the cathedral of Amiens in 1499. The Council of Cologne (1452) already had a text for Benediction. It goes without saying that the rite, not the word, is meant: for that only appeared in the 1660s.

The Council of Trent required that *"the most Holy Sacrament"* should be *honoured "with the fullness of Divine worship [latria];"* [45] in this spirit, devotion to the Blessed Sacrament developed: to the habit of private visits and liturgical benedictions, were added the Forty Hours, perpetual adorations and nocturnal adoration programmes by Confraternities founded to that end.[46] Religious Orders and Congregations were founded or reformed for the adoratiuon of the Blessed Sacrament.[47] The cult of the Eucharist outside the Mass blossomed in the classical epoch, when Benedictions of the Blessed Sacrament commonly took place outside great feasts, and in France in 1682, were definitively regulated according to what the *Roman Ceremonial* of 1600[48] had foreseen. In 1644, all Parisian parishes exposed the Blessed Sacrament and gave Solemn Benediction on the first Thursdays of the month;[49] M. Olier augmented the number of these in the parish of St. Sulpice.[50] This was the period when the worldly devotee described by La Bruère, reserved his place for Benediction.[51] In the chapel of the Château of Versailles, the incontrovertible Duke of Saint-Simon gave witness, that one could see *"all the galleries fringed with ladies at Benediction during the winter, Thursdays and Sundays, at which the King rarely missed assisting."* This devotion continued and grew throughout the eighteenth century and, in many places, Benediction took place daily. After the French Revolution, it was resumed strongly from the start of the nineteenth century, becoming general, before being disapproved of in the sixties, under the pretext of protecting the Mass.

The Second Vatican Council entered into the tradition, although many, having no doubt at their disposition only expurgated texts, used these as the pretext for abolishing the cult of the Blessed Sacrament. For *Presbyterorum ordinis* told priests that *"in order to be able to carry out their ministry faithfully, they should resolve inwardly to converse each day with Christ the Lord, by visits to and personal worship of the Blessed Eucharist."* [52] Paul VI asked *"that in the course of the day, the*

107

faithful should not neglect to pay a visit to the Blessed Sacrament, which should be kept in the church in a most worthy place, with the greatest possible honour, according to liturgical rulings. For a visit is a mark of gratitude towards Christ our Lord present in this place, a token of love and a homage of adoration which is due to Him." [53] John Paul II teaches: *"The Church and the world have a great need of the Eucharistic cult. Jesus awaits us in this sacrament of love. Let us not refuse the time to go and meet Him with adoration, in a contemplation full of faith, and ready to make reparation for the grave faults and offences of the world. May our adoration never cease."* [54]

For our time, it is emphasised with interest that the regulation of the Eucharistic cult outside Mass, is governed by the *Ordo de sacra communione et de cultu eucharistica extra missam*, published in Rome on 21 June 1973, approved and confirmed by the French-speaking bishops on 5 January 1978, and lastly published in French on 2 February 1983. Although it is not universally observed, it is opportune to recall that the new Canon Law (applicable since 1983) recommends, in canon 942, *"that there should be every year a solemn exposition of the Blessed Sacrament,*[55] *during a convenient time, even if not in a continuous manner, so that the local community may meditate more profoundly on the Eucharistic mystery and adore it."* Concerning this, it should be noted that the new Code of Canon Law requires that a *"special lamp"* burn constantly before the Tabernacle of the Holy Reserve *"to indicate and honour the presence of Christ"* (canon 940). Lastly, wherever this is possible, in the judgement of the diocesan bishop, canon 944 desires that a procession of the Blessed Sacrament should be organised, to pass through the streets of the locality, as a *"public witness of veneration of the Holy Eucharist,"* especially on the Feast of Corpus Christi.

Father Christian-Philippe Chanut
Parish Priest of Saulx-les-Chartreux.

NOTES

1 Paul VI: *Mysterium fidei* (3 September 1965).

2 Origen (185-254): Homily XIII on Exodus; homily V on Isaiah.

3 St. Cyril of Jerusalem: *Mystagogical Catecheses* (V 22).

4 St. Ambrose: *De Spiritu Sancto*, III 12.

5 St. Augustine: Commentary on Psalm XCXVIII 9.

6 St. Epiphanius: *Expositio fidei*, XXIV.

7 St. Jerome: *Commentary on Isaiah* XIII 45.

8 *Apostolic Constituions*, VIII 9.

9 Epistle *Ad Caesaream*.

10 A.G. Martimort: *L'Église en prière, introduction à la Liturgie*, (Desclée, Tournai, 1965).

11 *Beroldus sive Ecclesiae Mediolanensis kalendarium et ordines* (Magistretti: Milan, Giavanola, 1894).

12 St. Paulinus of Nola: Epistle XXXII.
13 *Vita sancti Desiderii Cadurcensis*, chapter XII.
14 C. Chardon: *Histoire des sacrements* (Paris 1745).
15 9th canon of the second Council of Constantinople (553).
16 Grimlaïc: *Regula solitariorum.*
17 St. Paschasius Radbertus: *De corpore et sanguine Domini.*
18 Leo IV died in 855.
19 *Catechism of the Catholic Church*, No. 1379.
20 *Decreta pro ordine S. Benedicti.*
21 *Règle des recluses* (translation of G. Meunier, Tours, 1928. Also Early English Text Soc.)
22 *Statuta Ecclesiae Parisiensis* (Paris, 1777).
23 William of Auxerre: *Summa aurea* (Bibliotheque municipale, Besançon, manuscript XLI).
24 Maskell: *Ancient Liturgy of England* (Oxford, 1882).
25 R.P.H. Thurston: *L'Eucharistie et le Saint-Graal* (*Revue du clergé français*; Paris 1908).
26 *We adore Thee, O most holy Lord Jesus Christ, here, as in all churches in the whole world, and we bless Thee, because Thou hast redeemed the world by Thy holy Cross!*
27 Jacques de Vitry: *Vita* de Marie d'Oignies.
28 Peter Lombard: *Sentences* (IV, 9).
29 William of Auxerre: *Summa aurea.*
30 It is said that there existed a confraternity of the Blessed Sacrament at St. Rémi of Laon, in the 9th century; that of St. Godard of Rouen is dated 1120. It appears that that of Avignon goes back to 1226; also for that period, those of Troyes (1264), and of St. Martin of Liège.
31 St. Gertrude: *Revelations*, XXXIX.
32 A. Molien: *Le culte rendu à l'Hostie* (in *Eucharistia*, Paris, 1941).
33 Adhémar d'Alès: *Eucharistie* (Paris 1930).
34 Whilst hunting chamois near Innsbruck, he slipped so badly into a hollow in a steep rock (Martinswald), that it was absolutely impossible, humanly speaking, for him to get out of it. Maximilian took stock of his situation. Resigned to his death, he wrote painfully these few words on a scrap of parchment, which was fortunately on him, and which he let fall to the bottom of the valley, where a number of people had already gathered: *"Since I cannot receive the holy Viaticum, go and fetch a priest, who must bring the Blessed Sacrament and bless me from afar, and I will die consoled."* His desire was granted, and the priest of the village at the foot of the rock came, surrounded by his parishioners and carrying the monstrance, in order to bless the unfortunate prince. He still found means in the rugged rock to kneel to adore his Saviour, and behold, a young man dressed as a Tyrolese, was suddenly at his side, offering him a hand and saying: *"The God that you have adored, sends me to deliver you; follow me."* And, marvellously, sustained by the hand of this celestial guide, the Archduke slowly descended the length of the steep rock, to the stupefaction of the witnesses of this memorable scene.

Everyone wished to know the liberator, but he had disappeared from the sight of all. That monstrance has been piously preserved at the castle of Frazenburg, near Laxenburg.

35 Henri and his wife de Frescinde, living in the village of Rétine, near Liège, died in 1197, leaving two orphans: Agnes (b. 1191) and Juliana (b.1192). The two little girls were placed in the convent of the Augustinian Hospitallers of Mont-Cornillon, a new foundation where the nuns, very faithful to their vow of poverty, took care of lepers and the sick. Situated at the gates of Liège, the monastery of Mont-Cornillon contained a masculine and a feminine community; that of the women had a prioress, but the prior of the men was her superior. Under the authority of Sister Sapience, who instructed them in Christian doctrine and recounted to them the lives of the saints, Agnes and Juliana lived in a small farm dependent on the convent. Juliana, filled with enthusiasm for the religious life, had yet a great attraction towards solitude; she learned the psalter by heart, and gave herself up to such great austerities that Sister Sapience had to bring her back to moderation, teaching her that in the eyes of the Lord, the practice of obedience was worth more than sacrifice. Juliana, having received the religious habit of Mont-Cornillon at fourteen years of age (1207), learned Latin in order better to understand the truths of religion, and became familiar with the writings of the Fathers, especially St. Augustine and St. Bernard.

36 Peter of Prague, celebrating Mass at St. Catherine's tomb, was tormented by doubts about the Real Presence of Christ in the Eucharist. At the fraction of the Host, he no longer saw a white Host but something reddish, like living flesh, from which dripped on to the corporal drops of blood which did not stain his hands. Overwhelmed, he deposed the Host in the chalice, covered it with the veil and carried it to the sacristy. Urban IV, then living at Orvieto, sent bishop James Maltraga and some theologians to Bolsena, amongst whom were perhaps St. Thomas Aquinas and St. Bonaventure.

37 The Host was changed into bleeding flesh at Ferrara (1171), Alatri (1228), Bolsena (1264), Darica (1239), Santarém (1247), Offida (1273), Paris (1290), St. Daniel and San Cugas del Vallès, near Gerona (1297); the wine in the chalice was true blood at St. Ambrose of Florence (1230).

38 Thomas of Cantimpré, born at Lewes near Bruxelles in 1201, died about 1270. Having begun his studies at Liège, he entered the Augustinian Abbey of Cantimpré, near Cambrai (1217), then went to the Dominicans (1232) who sent him to study at Cologne and Paris. He taught theology at Louvain, and was a celebrated preacher in Germany, Switzerland and France, wrote several *Lives* of saints, some Latin poetry, and a moral work full of imagery, based on histories of saints and observations of nature *(Bonum universale de apibus).*

39 *"Douai,"* wrote Thomas of Cantimpré, *"is a large and spacious town, situated on the right side of the road between the noble cities of Arras and Cambrai. In the town, in the church of the Canons of St. Arné, one Easter time, a priest, who had given Communion to the people, saw with alarm that one Host lay on the ground. He knelt down and sought to recover the Body of Jesus Christ; but at*

once, the Host rose of itself into the air, and laid itself on the linen used by the priests to purify their consecrated fingers. The priest cried out, called the canons, and these, gathered at his cry, and saw on the linen a body full of life, in the form of a charming child. The people were soon called, and were admitted to contemplate the prodigy, and all those there, without exception, enjoyed this celestial vision."

40 The bevilled edge of this monstrance is inscribed: "ANNO DOMINI $M^0CC^0LXXX^0VI^0$ FECIT ISTUD VAS FIERI DOMINA HEILEWIGIS DE DIEST PRIORISSA IN HERKENRODE, CUJUS COMMEMORACIO IN PERPETUUM CUM FIDELIBUS HABEATUR."

41 Adhémar d'Alès: *Eucharistie* (Paris, 1930).

42 Ibid.

43 Jean de Marienwerder: the *Septililium.*

44 Decree of Cologne (1452).

45 Session XIII, chapter III.

46 Such as the Confraternity of Langres from 1547, or the famous Blessed Sacrament Company founded in 1630. The Confraternity of the Most Holy Sacrament, was founded at Rome by Paul III's Bull (*Dominus noster Jesus Christus*, 30 Nov.1539), and confirmed by Paul V (Brief of 3 Nov. 1606): it sufficed that a confraternity be canonically erected to share in all the advantages of the Roman Archconfraternity.

47 Fruitless attempt by bishop Sebastian Zamet at Langres (1626), but a marvellous realisation by the Benedictines of the Blessed Sacrament founded in Paris (1652) by Anne of Austria and Mother Mechtilde of the Blessed Sacrament. Many founders of this epoch put adoration of the Blessed Sacrament in the first place of devotion, such as the Franciscan Tertiaries of Picpus (Paris 1594), the Missionaries of the Clergy (Avignon, 1632), the Dominican Sisters of the Perpetual Adoration of the Blessed Sacrament (Lagnes, 1636), the Poor Daughters of the Blessed Sacrament (Rome, 1650), the Religious Sisters of Corpus Domini (Macerata, 1683), the Congregation of the Sisters of the Blessed Sacrament (Romans, 1715), the Religious Sisters of the Congregation of the Blessed Sacrament (Mâcon, 1733), the Congregation of Sisters of the Blessed Sacrament (Autun, 1748), the Order of Religious Sisters of St. Norbert (Coire, 1767), the Priests of the Blessed Sacrament (Mileto, 1780).

48 *Roman Ceremonial,* Clement VIII: *De Adoratione Augustissimi Sacramenti* (Bk.3, cap.4).

49 *Advis à Messieurs de Paris pour le culte du Très Saint Sacrement dans les paroisses* (1644).

50 L'abbé E.-M. Faillon: *Vie de M. Olier* (Paris, 1873).

51 La Bruyère: *Les Caractères* (De la mode, no. 21).

52 *Presbyterorum ordinis,* no. 18.

53 Paul VI, Encyclical *Mysterium Fidei,* 3 September 1965.

54 John Paul II: *Dominicae cenae,* 14 February 1980.

55 No. 86 of the Decree of the Sacred Congregation for the Sacraments and Divine Worship, of 12 September 1983.

The Encyclical *Mediator Dei* of Pius XII

Dr Wolfgang Graf (Germany)

Professor Wolfgang Graf, born in 1943, studied political, theological and historical sciences at Frankfurt, before preparing a political sciences doctorate at Mayence. He was one of the co-founders, in 1989, of the first Initiativkreise katholischer Laien und Priester *("The Initiative Circles of Catholic priests and laymen"). These associations seek to contribute to the spreading and to the defence of Catholic doctrine according to the Magisterium. Circles now exist in ten German dioceses and in two Austrian dioceses. As president of the Initiative Circle in the diocese of Augsburg, Wolfgang Graf is also co-editor of the monthly revue* Der Fels.

1   The Encyclical on the eve of its 50th anniversary

In 1977 the editors of the magazine *Communio* interviewed Cardinal Ratzinger on the subject "Can the liturgy be changed or is it immutable?"[1] The editors were saying, "Consider this: in 1947 we had Pius XII's Encyclical *Mediator Dei* and twenty years later, reform. A silent landslide in the course of twenty years. . ."[2] So the Encyclical appeared to them as an example of a document which evolution within the Church had superseded with uncontrollable rapidity.

Such was the evaluation made 30 years after the Encyclical. How much more, might one claim, is this evaluation justified today, as we approach its fiftieth anniversary?

But this Encyclical is not the only document to which this sort of thing seems to have happened. On the next page, Cardinal Ratzinger himsellf confirms'"here. too, the Council has quite simply been superseded", when asked, "whether there is, indeed, still a Latin rite". At the time of this interview fourteen years had passed since the adoption of the Council's *Constitution on the sacred Liturgy*. It would be no easy task to say which of these two texts will, in the long term, bear more fruit.

In any case it would appear useful to return to the text of Pius XII and consider certain elements of its historical background and some of its effects. This is my intention to day and it would be hard to go further within the restricting confines of an exposition.

2   Reasons why the Encyclical was written

2. 1   The liturgical movement and its objectives

In many ways , the Encyclical *Mediator Dei* can be seen as a reaction to the Liturgical Movement which had been developing since the beginning of the twentieth century, pricipally in France and Germany, but also in neighbouring countries such as Belgium. This movement sought to bring Catholics to participate in a deeper manner in the celebration of the liturgy. This *participation* in the celebration of the liturgy would come from a better *understanding* of the liturgy, a way to this would be a better understanding of the *history* of the liturgy.

There was also a notable tendency to consider as normative what people thought they knew about the primitive Church. In 1970 Josef Andreas Jungmann S. J. , one of the most important figures in this movement, who continued to exercise an active influence after the Council, sought to summarise what has been called the "early Christianity theory"
when he wrote, "It is the community assembled for the Eucharist which presents the holy offerings in the Body and Blood of Christ "[4]

Within this passage one can identify several key concepts: the event, which is called the "Eucharist", the "community" which seems to be the operator, and the presentation of the Body and Blood of Christ "in" the holy offerings. In a wider Catholic context, this text would appear to be dogmatically correct and pass unnoticed.

Certainly this is how many of those who supported the Movement objectively saw it. The "points of rupture" only became evident later. For most commentators, their sense of the Catholic faith, and perhaps for some, concern over the need for an *imprimatur* restricted any deviation from it.

Paradoxically it is in the commentary in the celebrated *Lexikon für Theologie und Kirche* that Jungmann adds a further point for orientation, "Attempts at reform in the 16th century" which in German speaking countries "were taken up again at the beginning of the 18th century"[5]This reference to reformers from the Enlightenment, like Wessenberg, is accompanied by a virulent critique of the post-tridentine era. "The tension between post-tridentine theology and the *Ordo Missae* handed down by ancient tradition had become too great. On the one side there were the still simple ideas gratefully received from the patristic era, which were still satisfied with a simple "we" to designate the presenters of the offerings and ask God to receive and bless them, and on the other side the still-new theory of sacrifice (like the mark of a victim -author's note) which no longer saw anything beyond the process of transsubstantiation"[6]. "It is not only the Latin language which has become foreign to Christian people, it is the whole essential form of the piety of the Roman liturgy". For Jungmann, "popular piety tends more towards secondary mediations than to the mystery of Christ"[7]

Of course, during the pontificate of Pius XII, what was written was more moderate, and we can be sure that many did not share these ideas; however men like Odo Casel, Romano Guardini or Pius Parsch, to name but three other German-speakers, used occasionally ambiguous formulations, which were radicalised by some of their successors.

The ties which developed between different countries also date from the period between the two World Wars. This was when the Burg Rothenfels youth movement became the chosen field for the efforts of Fr. Doncoeur to use the liturgy as a teaching tool, thereby perhaps unintentionally acting as a precursor of those seeking to divert the liturgy to purely anthropocentric ends [8]. The publication of magazines and the foundation of collections of books - one thinks in particular of the foundation of the "Editions du Cerf"imprint in 1932 - allowed the Liturgical Movement to strengthen both its diffusion and organisation.

The seizure of power in 1933 by the National Socialist in Germany did not interrupt the Liturgical Movement at all. On the contrary, as opportunities for action were reduced, or even eliminated, in the political and social fields, in organisations and associations, in journalism and education, activity was transferred, by way of compensation, to the field of internal affairs in the Church - where such obstacles hardly existed - and in particular to the liturgy[9]. The liturgical experiments which took place then at Rothenfels and elsewhere, among which, one may cite, in Germany as well as in France, celebration facing the people and the use of vernacular languages gave rise to counter movements, which with the help of books, also reached the general public[10].

2. 2   The "truce"

However, under the nose of the national-socialist state, almost all parties involved wished to avoid public disputes within the Catholic Church. In contrast to the damaged and divided Protestant churches the Catholic Church in Germany presented a remarkable front to national socialist persecution. The bishops wanted to use every means to maintain this solidarity in the eyes of the world. Even those who were critical of the liturgical experiments desired this solidarity and in particular the homogeneity of the liturgy. It fell to the bishops to defend this homogeneity.

And this is what they tried to do: in 1940 they set up a "Liturgical Department" of the Episcopal Conference, assisted by a

"Liturgical Commission"[11]The chief thinkers of the Liturgical Movement occupied the leading positions in these organisations. The moderator of the Episcopal Conference for liturgical matters was Albert Stohr, bishop of Mainz, a friend of Guardini. The proposal came from Simon Conrad Landesdorfer O. S. B. , bishop of Passau, who collaborated with Stohr in the name of the Episcopal Conference [12]. Already in the previous year, 1939, at a meeting in Fulda, Landesdorfer appeared with Frs. Guardini and Jungmann as the driving forces of the movement.

A long letter from Guardini to bishop Stohr in 1940 is typical of Guardini's estimation of the situation and of the way in which he influenced both bishops and the faithful[13].

In the letters Guardini discusses four areas of error which are important in liturgical matters: liturgism, practicism, dilettantism and conservatism.

For Guardini, *"liturgism* is the tendancy to afford to the liturgy an importance which it does not have"[14]Such an error begins by underestimating what is important, then rediscovering it and finally overvaluing it. This is how the liturgy comes often "to be regarded as constituting Christian, Catholic religious life itself"[15]. Such a religious life might be that of a monastic community, detached from reality but presented as a model community. Such a forced and exaggerated conception is characterised by "purely aesthetic sensibilities and ways of thinking", which in the long run are the opposite of a personal and popular piety and only become more accentuated as it produces disciples [16].

Practicism is for Guardini another error, but in the opposite direction. It wants to "help people absorb new conditions within a Christian perspective; thus it has transferred the essence of pastoral activity to the fields of organisation and education. . In so doing it has often ignored the essence of religious life, its inner meaning and dignity, which should not be subordinated to any other objective. Practicism has sometimes gone so far as to regard as a waste of time such things as prayer, the freely given absorption of man into eternal things, a holy service before the face of God"[17]. The liturgy becomes "something useless and superfluous"which according to the spirit of the age is to be put "in the service of moral actions or other edifying undertakings "[18]"But, by doing this, practicism, misunderstood the first and most important meaning of the liturgy, . . for the more it is without ulterior ends the richer it is in blessings[19]; but practicism "wanted direct, rapid and tangible results"[20]

Dilettantism comes into being when a direction "imposed by the general public forces its way into the conscience"[20] it is then something "of the hour, an important but dangerous point"[22]"Many, filled with good intentions, have attempted to modify divine worship in its liturgical form"[23] but often with disastrous results. "Setting out

115

from the idea that men can only pray in the language of everyday life, they have afforded importance to the German language. Convinced of the importance of liturgical symbols, they have tried to bring them more clearly to the fore and give a popular appearnace to the sacred rites"[24]. In this field there are "grave inadequacies" and so it has sometimes appeared "That those concerned not only did not know Latin but also had no knowledge of German. Furthermore, which was very serious, they associated the issue of liturgy with other issues such as confused ideas about the role of the laity in the Church or the relationship between the ethical and religious etc. "[25]However it should be noted that in his evaluation of dilettantism Guardini does not include disobedience to superiors and the Church's canonical norms.

According to Guardini it is in reaction to these ideas that the representatives of *conservatism* have formulated their reservations. "And they were right on all these points, but themselves succumbed to the danger of rejecting everything they were not used to. "[26] They do no understand that "The elements that are being abandoned by those they criticise originated in that , religiously speaking, most sterile period, the nineteenth century, and that these elements often replaced much of the wealth of the Church's devotional life"[27] For Guardini, "by assimilating popular and private devotions of dubious value to the Mass", the adherents of conservatism separate the sacraments "from their important context so that they become purely external rites"[28]In short, even the conservative forces often do not have a proper conception of what the liturgy really is, many only see "what is there, but without really understanding why it is so. [29]

What matters is to examine the advice which Guardini gives to the bishops on the base of his in essentials exact description of the errors he discerns. Firstly he warns them of the danger of "administrative intervention" - on this matter it is interesting to note that he frequently uses the term "administration" when referring to the Church authorities.

He writes: It is normal that the ecclesiastical administration should intervene against arbitrary innovations which have been sanctioned neither by the ministry nor by the competent authority (he recognises here two possible justifications). On the other hand , it is essential that they do not withdraw their trust from those who have been working for a long time, seriously and in a responsible manner, in these areas and that they are protected against attacks which call into question their convictions and their work[32] Guardini is not content to argue for freedom for the Liturgical Movement, after 1940 he further demands that the bishops should protect its representatives from criticism. He goes on, "More than anything else, work on the liturgy needs time. . We know it is a lot to ask that matters be allowed to remain in suspension. But to achieve something worthwhile, one cannot do otherwise; and what would be far worse than a degree of provisional uncertainty would be measures which would prevent the work begun several decades ago from bearing the fruits which are already beginning to ripen."[33]

Guardini goes so far as to write, "I know enough about theory and practice to be able to give an answer it will be impossible to ignore; but I do not wish to do so. "[34]Whatever may lie behind these words, the bishops allowed the Liturgical Movement, including its most radical supporters, the necessary time to occupy more and more key positions , so that numerous abuses were tolerated as pardonable excesses of zeal.

During the war and the period that followed it, the Liturgical Movement established itself, not only in Germany but also in France. The position of most of the French bishops was identical to that of their German colleagues. In 1943 under the leadership of Dom Beauduin, the Pastoral Liturgical Centre was set up, which was to publish the magazine "La Maison-Dieu", and in association with the publishers "Les editions du Cerf" the series *Lex Orandi*.

2. 3   The genesis of the Encyclical

In this context, how was it that the Encyclical *Mediator Dei* was written?As far as I know we possess no document which throws light on who shared in the draughting of this Encyclical, although we are better informed, for instance on the Encyclical *Quadragesimo Anno* of 1931(35) and *Mit brennender Sorge* of 1937[36] under Pius XII. We do know that in spite of all the burdens weighing on him - the Holy See was at the time situated in the centre of the fascist and national socialist empire- Pius XII was not only concerned with political events and their evaluation in relation to pastoral work and moral theology, but that he followed closely developments in the areas of dogmatic theology and liturgy. He was greatly helped in this by his remarkable knowledge of the situation in Germany and of the German language.

One might wonder if in that troubled period of history the Pope did not have "better things to do", but this would be to misunderstand PiusXII's conception of his task, and it would be out of keeping with the tradition of the Church. Take the year 1794 for example. Just at that particularly critical moment the Church "had nothing better to do "than to occupy itself with an Italian provincial synod held at Pistoia eight years earlier. Its graded condemnations of certain ambiguous phrases [37] were from the point of view of dogma and Church history, an important event which bore witness to genuine pastoral concern at the time, and to which the Encyclical *Mediator Dei* refers.[38]

At the height of the war, in June 1943, the Encyclical on the

Church, *Mystici Corporis*, was published. It was of great importance. Four years later, when Italy was going through a critical period due to the expansion of communism, the Encyclical on the liturgy appeared.

We can be quite sure that its preparation took some account of a letter sent in 1943 by Archbishop Groeber of Freiburg to the German episcopate. In seventeen points Archbishop Groeber criticises erroneous dogmatic positions which relate directly or indirectly to the liturgy, and which are also considered in *Mediator Dei* [39]. Among these positions are errors about the mystical Body of Christ, about the Church, an exaggerated importance given to the element of a meal in the Mass etc.[40] Furthermore exaggerating the importance given to the common priesthood of all believers, to the detriment of the ordained priesthood, is also criticised, a matter of consequence in the area of liturgy when the role of the laity is accented, as is use of the vernacular. On all these points appeal was made to the example of the past, held normative for the present, to justify the criticised position.[41]

In contrast to what Guardini was thinking and saying in 1940, Archbishop Groeber showed clearly how recent practices were replacing valid norms. He also asks the bishops to intervene, in this case against the mentioned errors, and with the express wish that Rome should intervene directly in the process.[42]

Cardinal Bertram, president of the episcopal conference, in fact sent a memorandum to Rome, but it characteristically defended the Liturgical Movement and encouraged liturgical reforms. The reply of Cardinal Maglione, the secretary of state, is relatively open ended and allows the German bishops a certain margin for manoeuvre.[43]

So the bishops continued to grant imprimaturs, so long as the authors took pains not to express openly theories that were too advanced. Cardinal Ratzinger mentions an important work in this category, *Eucharistia: Gestalt und Vollzug* by Joseph Pascher which appeared in 1947 just before the Encyclical. Like Guardini and others before him, Pascher says, "The basic form of the Eucharist is a meal"[44]. But for him the form of a meal in no way excludes the dogmatic concept of sacrifice; on the contrary the elements of sacrifice can very well be seen in the symbolism of the meal.[45]

These attempts at renovation proved all the more promising when supported by arguments based on pastoral considerations. This was also the direction favoured by Dom Lambert Beauduin since the first issue of *La Maison-Dieu* , in which he set out "practical norms for liturgical reforms". Through the intermediary of sympathetic bishops, whilst maintainig the established order, one could hope to obtain success in Rome, particularly with the Congregation of Rites. "We shall have to go one step at a time. . . Go forward patiently. . . get people thinking the right way. . . Stress the moral and practical aspects as well. . . The Church is not afraid to modify its discipline for the good of its children. . . "

These efforts aimed for international co-ordination at their meetings, for instance with German Catholicism, which even immediately after the war was not isolated from the bosom of the Church. Even at that time there were contacts with representatives of different Christian churches, as Fr. Duploye, one of the principal thinkers of the movement would later admit[46] Fr. Duploye tells of an incident on the fringe of a liturgical meeting at Le Thieulin, near Chartres, at which, among others, forty superiors and rectors of seminaries participated. "A few days before the meeting at Le Thieulin I was visited by Fr. Bugnini, an Italian Vincentian, who had asked me to invite him. He listened very attentively for four days without saying a word. When we were back in Paris he said, "I admire what you are doing, but the greatest service I can do you is never to say in Rome one word of what I have just heard"[47].

3   The principal themes of the Encyclical

3. 1   Some basic definitions.

The Encyclical *Mediator Dei*[48] is striking for the profundity of what it affirms. Unlike what is sometimes the case in later magisterial texts, it is characterised by a simple and clear vocabulary. Although it often endeavours to present various themes or even rejected positions in an equitable and nuanced way, it does not contain any "compromise formulas", which might seek a *balance* between incompatible positions at the expense of clarity or even of truth.

For the liturgy Pius XII's starting point is Christ. It is He who is the "Mediator Dei", who is presented here , first of all, as the eternal High Priest; "He wills the worship which He has inaugurated and which He has offered throughout His life on earth to be continued without ceasing. "[49]By this is meant above all what He did on Maundy Thursday and Good Friday. "At the Last Supper with solemn rite and splendour He celebrates the new Pasch and provides for its continuance by the divine institution of the Eucharist; and on the following day, raised up between earth and Heaven, He offers the saving sacrifice of His life "[50]"The priesthood of Jesus Christ is constantly active throughout the ages"[51] affirms the Pope. The reason for this is the presence of Christ. To be exact at about the notions he is speaking about, the Pope repeatedly refers to the doctrine of the mystical Body of Christ, which is the Church. [52]Furthermore the fundamental concepts of his Encyclical of 1943 *Mystici Corporis* are at once both the premises and the foundation of everything he teaches in this Encyclical. Thus he states that "The Church, therefore, has one and the same purpose, office, and function as the Incarnate Word. . ."[53]"Therefore in the whole conduct of the liturgy the Church has her divine Founder present with her. "[54]This presence of Christ is realised in many ways, which Pius XII does not shrink from classifying in order of importance when he says "Christ is present in the august sacrifice of the altar, in the person of his minister and especially under the Eucharistic species; he is present in the Sacraments by his power which He infuses into them as instruments of sanctification; he is present, finally in the prayer and praise that are offered to God, in accordance with his promise, "When two or three are gathered together in my name, I am there in the midst of them". This classification, displeasing to a fair number of people would be modified by what came later. [56]The *Constitution on the Sacred Liturgy* itself on this point makes its own characteristic modifications.[57]

Doubtless in 1947 Pius XII had reasons enough to concern himself with positions which, inspired by Odo Casel's "theology of mysteries" only saw the glorified Christ in the liturgy, and not the "historical" Christ. For the Pope such a separation is unthinkable, "The sacred liturgy puts Christ before us whole and entire, in all the phases of His life. . . . 'What Jesus Christ was yesterday, and is today, He remains for ever.'"[58]

According to Pius XII's definition the liturgy represents "the whole public worship of the Mystical Body of Jesus Christ, Head and members. "[59]In this sense "its object is the Sacrifice, the Sacraments, and the offering of praise to God; its purpose is to unite our souls with Christ and to sanctify them through the divine Redeemer, that Christ may be honoured and through Him and in Him honour be given to the Blessed Trinity."[60] This "trinitarian"perspective is equally a fundamental feature of the Encyclical.

The Pope presents in moving terms the whole range of the effects the liturgy has on human life: it aids and exhorts to sanctity, it enriches us in baptism, strengthens us in confirmation, consoles and reconciles us in confession, gives us strength for marriage, guides us as *viaticum* to the grave, it consecrates and blesses, above all in ordination, and helps the souls in purgatory.[61]

So it can be said that "the whole liturgy contains the Catholic faith, inasmuch as it is a public profession of the faith of the Church. [62] Pius XII is definitely well aware of the link between the *lex orandi* and the *lex credendi*. However the liturgy is not a "sort of touchstone by which to judge which truths are to be held by faith"[63] and which should in some way be tested by ritual. "Indeed if we wanted to state quite clearly and absolutely the relation existing between the faith and the sacred liturgy we could rightly say that 'the law of our faith must establish the law of our prayer'."[63]

However "The summit, we may also say the centre, of the Christian religion, is the Mystery of the Most Holy Eucharist". [64] This is of "primary importance in the liturgy."[65] For this reason we are going to spend more time on this particular aspect in the light of the Encyclical.

3.2   Sacrifice and meal

Reusing the terms of the Council of Trent, Pius XII affirms that in the sacrifice of the Mass "the sacrifice of the Cross is perpetually represented (*repraesentatur*) and, with a difference only in the manner of offering, renewed (*renovatur*)[66]. As the Pope stresses, it is "no mere simple commemoration . . . it is truly and properly the offering of a sacrifice . . . an unbloody immolation."[67]

So it is the same priest, Christ, whom the priest represents, it is the same offering, and the Eucharistic species "symbolize the violent separation of His Body and Blood"[68]: the aims of the sacrifice are the same: glorification of the Heavenly Father, the thanksgiving due to God, and thirdly expiation, propitiation and reconciliation. Certainly Christ redeemed us on Calvary "but this purchase does not take its full effect immediately. . . It is necessary for each member of the human race to get vitally in touch with the sacrifice of the Cross"[69]. This is exactly what happens in the Mass.

It is in this perspective that Pius XII sees the liturgical life of the primitive Church which replaced the Old Testament worship, the "shadow" of the worship given by Christ "Wherever their pastors are able to assemble the faithful, they erect an altar on which they offer the sacrifice, and around which are disposed the other rites . . ."[71]

The Pope does not ignore the fact that the word "Eucharist" means thanksgiving[72]; which does not prevent him, for the sake of greaer clarity, from speaking more often of "sacrifice"or from using equivalent terms.[73]

Moreover, in the Eucharistic sacrifice and in the other Sacraments, their efficacy "is primarily *ex opere operato*"[74]however one may speak of an efficacy *ex opere operantis*, when the efficacy of an action does not depend on the good will of a participant but on the action of the Church: "*ex opere operantis ecclesiae*, inasmuch as the Church is holy and acts in the closest union with her Head."[75]

Pius XII usually uses an unambiguous terminology - for example he speaks of the "transubstantiation of the bread into the Body of Christ". [76]He uses an equal care, though in a more restricted sense, for the term *sacra synaxis*, which is found in the *Novus Ordo Missae*, using it exclusively for the reception of Holy Communion and not for the Sacrifice of the Mass. [77]By so doing he insists on the use the primitive Church made of this term, which Cardinal Ratzinger also stresses: "It   must be   emphasized   again   and again   that the Eucharistic Sacrifice is essentially the unbloody immolation of the

Divine Victim . . . The Communion (*sacra synaxis*) belongs to the integration of the Sacrifice; it is a participation of the Sacrifice by the reception of the Blessed Sacrament".[79]

The Pope thus declares the error of "the sophistical contention that the Mass besides being a sacrifice is also the banquet of a community of brethren: and that the general Communion of the faithful is to be regarded as the culminating point of the whole celebration".[80]

Pius XII then already saw clearly what such conceptions would lead to in our days and explicitly rejected them: this should not be forgotten when people talk, too frequently, of an unbroken continuity between our own age and that of Pius XII.

This theme is linked with the Communion of the faithful. Certainly the Pope recommends the frequent Communion of the laity - after appropriate preparation; he is very clear on this point. [81] He nevertheless emphasizes that it is not the Communion of the faithful but that of the priest which is absoutely indispensable for the validity of the Mass[82]. When Mass is celebrated in the presence of the faithful, they should "when they cannot easily receive Holy Communion in reality" do so "at least by desire".[83]

With the Council of Trent, the Encyclical does encourage the faithful to "receive the Eucharist sacramentally, and so gain more abundant fruit from this Sacrifice". [84] But the Pope adds, in the manner of his predecessor, Benedict XIV (1742), who "in order that it might be more evident that by receiving Holy Communion the faithful take part in the Sacrifice", praised the devotion that prompts the desire of some, not only to communicate when present at Mass, but preferably to receive particles consecrated at the same Mass. [85] Certainly genuine participation in the sacrifice does not depend on it, and there are a number of reasons for receiving Communion outside Mass; however with reference to the words of the Canon *ut quotquot ex hac altaris participatione . . . sumpserimus*[86], the priest should fulfil this wish when so requested by the faithful.

It is not surprising that precisely this passage of the Encyclical is one of the few to be quoted with approval by those authors who otherwise are not at all in agreement with the theology of PiusXII. We shall come back to this point.

3. 3 The priest and the people

Without prejudice to the doctrine of the common priesthood of all the faithful, which Pius XII certainly alludes to in several instances, [87] from the point of view of the nature of worship it is possible to understand Catholic liturgy as it is presented in *Mediator Dei* as a priestly liturgy "conducted primarily by priests in the name of the

Church". [88] Just as by baptism the faithful are separated and distinguished from other people by "an indelible character", [89] "so the Sacrament of Order sets priests in a class apart from all other Christians". [90] In its immutability as an image of the celestial hierarchy, *Ordo* "is imparted to selected individuals by a sort of spiritual birth". [91] They alone have certain powers and are "enabled to perform the lawful acts of religion by which men are sanctified". [92]

Mission in the sense of John 20: 21 originates with God. The Pope stresses that priesthood does not "originate in the Christian community, nor is it derived by delegation from the people". [93] The "priest is God's representative for the people entrusted to his care". It is only through this is that the priest is "vice-regent of the people". [94]

Here too it is essential to see Christ: "The priest acts in the name of the people precisely and only because he represents the person of Our Lord Jesus Christ, considered as Head of all the members and offering Himself for them: that the priest, therefore, approaches the altar as Christ's minister, lower than Christ, but higher than the people; that the people, on the other hand, because it in no way represents the person of the divine Redeemer and is not mediator between itself and God, can in no way possess the priestly right. "[95] All this is certain with the certainty of faith. [96] And this is also the reason why he rejects those views that state that "one and the same grace unites Christ with the members of His mystical Body". [97]

This is also a fitting context to answer the question of the people's participation in the Sacrifice of the Mass. The Pope rejects the view of those who "regard the Eucharistic Sacrifice as a true 'concelebration', and think that it is much better for priests to assist and 'concelebrate' with the people, than to offer the Sacrifice privately when the people are not present."[98]

Pius XII admits that the faithful do present offerings, but "in a different way". [99] This is shown by the *Ordo Missae*, which at numerous places, which the Pope quotes, marks the distinction ". . . my sacrifice and yours"[100], or in the Canon "for whom we offer, or who offer to Thee" or "this offering of us Thy servants, indeed of the whole of Thy household" or "we, Thy servants, indeed the whole of Thy holy people". [101]

What then is the way in which the people presents the Sacrifice? Pius XII begins by citing a number of "remote reasons", [102] which nonetheless have been given prominence by the so-called liturgical reform: the responses of the Christians to the priest's prayers, their offering of bread and wine, or the alms they give to the priest "in order that the priest may offer the Divine Victim for their intentions". [103] He then comes to the deeper reasons: the people offers the Sacrifice "through the priest", they also "offer with him inasmuch as they unite their sentiments of praise, entreaty, expiation and thanksgiving with the sentiments or intention of the priest, in order that those sentiments may be presented to God the Father. . ."[104]

For the same reason the Pope rejects the arguments of those, who already at that time wanted to see modifications in the respective roles of priest and people on the basis of the "social nature" of the Mass: "this Sacrifice, always and everywhere, necessarily and of its very nature, has a public and social character"[105], whether or not the faithful assist at Mass. Furthermore, the simultaneous celebration of Mass at several altars neither alienates the community nor endangers its unity, and "it is in no way necessary that the people should ratify what has been done by the sacred minister".[106]

So to say in this context that the liturgy is only the "assembly of the faithful" would be in the words of Cardinal Ratzinger "in itself a revolution", even if appeal where made to the text about the "two or three" who gather in the name of Christ. For such a definition implies that "It is not the Church that comes before the group, but the group before the Church" and so the group would be the "place from which liturgy originates".[107] Finally, such an understanding leads to a "dogmatisation of the autonomous group" and an "egalitarianism" incompatible with the declared Catholic doctrine about the relation between the priest and the people in the liturgy.

3. 4   Liturgy and piety

Pius XII empasises very clearly that in celebrating the Mass the will of the Founder should be carried out exactly. However, to this external and perceptible celebration, to this "objective piety" there should be added an interior personal "subjective " piety, so that the rite should not become an empty ceremony. Nonetheless "to have their proper effect they require our souls also to be in the right dispositions" and the faithful have to do their part.[109] The Pope mentions a number of means to this end: he praises the use of a missal, the singing of solemn Mass (but only insofar as " they are in exact conformity with the rules of the Church and the rubrical instructions"[110]). He also criticises those who exaggerate the importance of these means, suggesting that they are the only way to celebrate Mass, as for Pius XII, this "is wrong and irrational". The Pope is well aware that many of the faithful cannot use a missal, even in their own language, and that furthermore, spiritual needs are different and can change. He also is of the view that Christians can profit from the Eucharistic Sacrifice in other ways such as by "devoutly meditating" or by "other religious exercises".[111] The Pope thus proves himself to be a better psychologist than the present day pastoral specialists, and he allows a far greater freedom than they do.

Something particularly dear to him is thanksgiving after receiving Holy Communion and after Mass. Here again he criticises those who, "paying more heed to the sound of words than their meaning", consider such thanksgiving pointless as "the Mass itself is a thanksgiving, and also that it comes under the category of private devotions and is not directed to the benefit of the community".[112] He also particularly reminds priests of their duty to say a thanksgiving prayer and of course to prepare themselves in a fitting way.[113]

From this need to give thanks there flows naturally both the offering the faithful make of themselves - certainly accomplished in the Holy Sacrifice, but which should encompass their whole life - and adoration of the Eucharist.

For the Pope, this adoration has existed in the Church "from the beginning", and he refers to such rites of adoration as genuflection and profound inclination as well as the second Council of Constantinople [115] and St Augustine, whom he quotes: "no one eats that Flesh without having first adored it . . . far from sinning by adoring it, we sin by not adoring it".[116] This adoration is required in the case of the Eucharist, because, unlike other Sacraments, "it not only causes grace, but permanently contains the Author of grace Himself".[117]

So he exhorts the bishops not to tolerate those deviant liturgists who attribute dignity and efficacy only to the liturgical rtes. On the contrary, churches should stay open outside the times of Mass, lest adoration before the tabernacle be neglected.[118] Clearly he does not neglect the fact that in the course of the Church's history Eucharistic devotion has developed through different forms "ever growing in beauty and usefulness. . . for example devout and even daily visits to the Blessed Sacrament; Benediction of the Blessed Sacrament; solemn processions. . . adoration of the Blessed Sacrament exposed." Moreover he does not give normative value, in a narrow concept of Tradition, to only those forms known in Christian antiquity; he also gives high praise to all these developments.[119] In 1956 he emphasised once again that "separating the tabernacle and the altar is separating two things that by their nature and origin should stay united".[120] Eucharistic adoration in no way risks creating a "confusion" between the "historic" Christ and the triumphant Lord. On the contrary, the Church and the faithful find that they "are one".[121]

On the contrary, neglecting adoration before the tabernacle, as well as discouraging "devotional confessions", and despising the honour given to Mary - are "poisoned fruits, . . . most damaging to Christian piety; theymust be cut off, so that the life giving sap may nourish only the fruit that is sweet and good".[123]

"It is true that liturgical prayer, being the public prayer of the august Bride of Christ, is superior to private prayer"[124]; even so forms

125

of extra-liturgical devotion should not be despised: "It would therefore be damaging as well as erroneous to take it upon oneself to change all these practices of piety, and to try to fit them into the framework of the liturgy".[125] So he recommends the whole wealth of these forms of devotion - May devotions to Mary, prayers to the Sacred Heart, triduums, novenas, Stations of the Cross[126] and , in particular, the Rosary.[127]

Even so bishops should "be untiring in pointing out that the Christian life does not consist in a multiplicity of different prayers and devotional practices, but rather in the spiritual progress of the faithful. . . "[128]. The Pope thus foresees the dangers which are now appearing in certain quarters in reaction to the dominant rationalism and religious modernism.

He also recommends private devotional forms imbued with the spirit of the liturgy, such as the Divine Office and the canonical hours. It is the "prayer of the Mystical Body of Jesus Christ offered to God in the name of all Christians and for their benefit",[129] primarily by priests and religious, but it is also recommended to laypeople - particularly Sunday Vespers.[130]

A characteristic of the spiritual sterility of liturgical modernism, is that contrary to all recommendations, the recitation of the reformed canonical hours has in great part been abandoned both by clergy and laity.

Contrary to this loss of devotion, Pius XII, with St Thomas Aquinas defines devotion as "the chief act of the virtue of religion", [131] a "theocentric" life which affects all aspects of human life - individual, domestic, social and even economic and political.[132]

Pius XII also mentions "the whole family of mankind". But he sees only one possibility for restoring peace - through the Blessed Sacrament, people will "with one mind and heart sing that song of hope and charity".[133]

3.5   Ways and means

An important way recommended by the Encyclical for maintaining spiritual growth is liturgical formation both of clergy [134] and laity [135]. It is in this sense that the Pope calls the efforts made in his time "admirable initiatives" and speaks of "praiseworthy emulation" [136]. Nonetheless this recognition is accompanied by numerous restrictions. There is "an undue fondness for innovation and a tendency to stray from the path of truth and prudence" and "principles which either in fact or by implication jeopardise the sacred cause they are intended to promote and sometimes introduce errors touching Catholic faith and ascetical doctrine."[137]Various abuses in the past served to "the great advantage of heretics and the further

126

spread of their errors". It was for this reason that the Holy See created the Sacred Congregation of Rites.[138] Bishops too should watch over the liturgy [139]. To do this they will have recourse to decisions of diocesan application, or make use of a liturgical commission, which however will work within the norms applicable to the whole Church, and "no private individual, even though he be a priest, be allowed to use the Church for the purpose of arbitrary experiments".[140]It is a "sense of the universal" which "affirms the unity of the Church" and so the Encyclical enjoins obedience to the Pope and the Holy See on several occasions.[141]

This does not exclude an evolution of the liturgy, so the Church "always saving the integrity of her doctrine. . accomodates herself to the needs and conditions of the times".[142] Insofar as the liturgy includes both human and divine elements, the human elements can be modified to lead to an "admirable variety"[143]. The general growth of the liturgy brings to the foreground customs that were only vaguely present in former ages, and other "pious institutions" come back into use.[144]

For the Pope then, there is no question of considering a particular epoch as absolute - even the early Church. "The liturgy of the early ages is worthy of veneration; but an ancient custom is not to be considered better, either in itself or in relation to later times and circumstances, just because it has the flavour of antiquity".[145] Giving examples of such archeologism he affirms that "it would be wrong. . . to want the altar restored to its ancient form of a table; to want black eliminated from the liturgical colours, and pictures and statues excluded from our churches; to require crucifixes that do not represent the bitter sufferings of the divine Redeemer. . . "[146]. He also condemns the rejection of new liturgical rites established under the inspiration of the Holy Spirit, as well as the desire to revert to earlier conciliar formularies while rejecting more recent ones, or favouring ancient canons instead of more recent ones[147].

Does all this also apply to those who defend the classical Roman rite, that they wish to "revive obsolete rites".[148] Not at all, they rely in fact on a principle that Pius XII stresses: safeguarding "the integrity of her doctrine"[149], which is not spared by an arbitrary present. This principle justifies in particular the reasons they put forward for preferring Latin and which are identical to the Pope's. Latin is not only valued as an "imposing sign of unity" but also as an "effective safeguard against the corruption of true doctrine".[150]

Unlike the gross errors encountered today, Pius XII could still say of many of the errors of his time, that they were "subtle"[151]; he even considers it "indispensable"[152] that the bishops be vigilant against the enemy who sows cockle among the good grain. Apart from the above mentioned errors, he also mentions briefly again the dangerous "humanism: that leads souls astray", as well as a "false mysticism" and "quietism"[153]. Alluding to mystery theolgy he criticises writers, particularly Odo Casel with his theory of cultic mystery, who claim "that we ought to cultivate the "pneumatic or glorified Christ"and not the historical Christ".[154]

The Pope on the other hand presents the liturgical year as an opportunity to live through the mysteries of Christ as "constantly present and active".[155] To the temporal cycle of the mysteries of Christ are added the feasts of Mary and the saints. It is fitting to imitate the many saints, as they imitated Christ and as they loved God and neighbour, another reason for remembering them is to ask their help.[156] This is particularly the case with Mary, as "her life is most closely interwoven with the mysteries of Christ".[157]

Also, contrary to an iconoclastic archaism, images should always have their place in churches, and here the Pope includes contemporary art so long as it "takes into account the needs of the Christian community". It is a matter of finding a balance between an "excessive realism" and an "exaggerated symbolism".[158] On this point, contrary to the autonomy afforded in our days to the artist, the Pope attributes to the bishops the competence to "enlighten and direct" the artists.[159]

With regard to architecture, music and the other arts, the Pope's position is characterised both by accepting a multiplicity of forms and new creations and by a firm attachment to what is essential.[160]

Everyone then who influences or guides the position of the faithful should be examined. This is true in particular of those who direct spiritual exercises. They should encourage the faithful to share in worship and practise adoration. "If, on the contrary they hinder or prevent the observance of the rules governing divine worship, then it can be concluded with certainty that they are not directed by right thinking or prudent counsel".[161]

All this shows how much the Pope was concerned that the faithful should be guided to an *actuosa particpatio*[162]. But he gives this participation its deepest sense which is not always the case today. Certainly he considers it inappropriate that we have the "spectacle of a congregation either not joining in at all in the Latin or vernacular prayers of the community, or else contributing only a feeble murmur".[163] But for him the concept of participation appears in a different context. Pius XII recalls the will of Christ: "He has willed that all men should come and be brought to his Cross, especially by means of the Sacraments and the Mass, and so take possession of the fruits He has won for them. By this active and personal co-operation (*actuosa singulorum participatone*) the members become more and more like their Head. . ." [164]

4   The reception of the Encyclical after 1947

4. 1   What was done by Pius XII after 1947

In the year following the publication of the Encyclical a "Pontifical Commission for the reform of the liturgy" was created at Rome. This was to put into action the intentions of the Encyclical, which happened in subsequent years through a series of specific measures. Dogmatically – something the Pope watched over – the changes introduced were above all suspicion; liturgically and pastorally they were to a great extent sensible and useful. One should not however neglect the fact that propositions for change were presented to Rome by bishops won over to the reforms, and that in certain cases they were handled by persons who either sympathised with the reforms or who let themselves be impressed by the competence of certain experts.[165]

For many Sacraments, the use of the vernacular was extensively authorised in many countries, among which were France and Germany. After certain isolated authorisations issued in 1951, the reform of Holy Week began to be systematically prepared from 1953, being decreed in 1955. The Eucharistic fast was reduced in 1953. In 1955 the rubrics of the Missal were simplified, giving priority, for example, to the yearly cycle over the sanctoral. Faculties were also accorded for the celebration of Mass in the afternoon and evening.[166]

It is however noteworthy that in the 1950's papal declarations on liturgical questions are strongly marked by restrictions, calls to order and warnings. This is particularly the case with the desire for concelebration, which does not need to be discussed here as Mgr. Schmitz discussed it last year in detail[167]. This is also the case with the Encyclical *Musicae sacrae disciplina* of 1955, whose "retrograde influences" are deplored by Jungmann[168]; and it is particularly true of the allocutions addressed by the Pope to the bishops on the occasion of the canonisation of Pius X in 1954.

As *"magister"* the Pope enjoins the bishops to ensure that teaching in the Church is not carried out in an individual's own name, or as scientific theology, but in virtue of a mission conferred by the Magisterium[169]. For him appropriate vigilance is radically different from mistrust or ill-founded suspicion, but there are certain people who make themselves or the rules of non-theological disciplines absolute. There could be no autonomy for theology in relation to the Magisterium.[170]

As priest the Pope reminds the bishops that priesthood is founded on the New Covenant, *"cuius praecipua potestas et muneris functio est offerre unicum et celsissimum sacrificium"*, which Christ *"cruento modo in cruce obtulit et incruento in Novissima Cena anticipavit, continenter iterari voluit"* as he commanded [171]. Christ did not call every Christian to the priesthood, but only the Apostles, and he gave them its power: *"Itaque sacerdos celebrans, personam Christi gerens, sacrificat, isque solus; non populus, non clerici, ne sacerdotes. . . qui . . inserviunt"*[(172)]. He criticises those who wish to attribute the *"sacrificandi potestatem"* to everyone. Even though one may rejoice in the work of liturgical institutes and congresses, their conclusions remain nonetheless subject to the judgements of the Magisterium. According to *CIC* it is exclusively the preserve of the Holy See to regulate and approve liturgcal books [(173)].

Finally the Pope addresses the bishops as pastor. He is aware that in the modern age people wish to be treated as adults and are unwilling to accept any intermediary between God and themselves. However to lead people in an appropriate way is not treating them as children, but guiding adults according to the reality of the society to which they belong. God instituted the pastors of the Church not as a burden but for the good of souls. Keeping souls away from errors and vices, they lead them to true freedom; it would be against wisdom and charity to refuse this assistance.[(174)]

For a fruitful exercise of their ministry it is particularly necessary for bishops to maintain good relations with each other so that the faithful are not shocked by identical matters being regulated differently in neighbouring dioceses. Accordingly Pius XII recommends the bishops to meet in provincial and plenary synods. [(175)] For him there is no need to fear a conformism which gives way to the spirit of the age so long as a regular and vital contact is maintained with the Holy See in the areas of doctrine, morals and discipline.

The Popes do not speak in their own name but by virtue of the authority inherent in their function. They have no wish to impose uniformity or conformity in every matter, but they act according to divine law and according to the constitution of the Church of Christ. Insofar as they remain linked to the Apostolic See the bishops receive light and certainty on disputed questions, assistance in difficult matters and comfort in distress. Furthermore the Pope can recognise better and more quckly the ills that threaten the Church and so can apply the necessary remedies better and more rapidly.[(177)]

4. 2   The action of reformers after 1947

In his commentary on the *Constitution on the Liturgy* published in 1966 Jungmann declares that in *Mediator Dei* the Pope definitively declared himself to be in favour of liturgical renewal.[(178)]. However the text does not allow one to speak of "reform" in the way the term came to be applied later. In truth, as Abbé Martimort writes appositely, in my view, of Lambert Beauduin, "The cautions of the Encyclical did not deter him at all."[(179)]

130

Whatever the case may be, after 1947 the international structures and contacts of the supporters of reform strengthened. The Liturgical Institute at Trier was founded at the moment the Encyclical appeared, and in 1956 the Institut Supérieur de Liturgie of Paris was added to the CPL.

Liturgical congresses with participants representing several countries were organised, among others the "Semaines d'études liturgiques" in Luxembourg. Other countries also followed the movement, such as the United States and Italy, culminating in the Congress on pastoral liturgy at Assisi in 1956, "whose organisation was encouraged by the Sacred Congregation of Rites"[181] to which Pius XII addressed an allocution devoted among other things to the theme of concelebration[182]. Jungmann notes with satisfaction that bishops from various countries took part, indicating for him "how far the movement had spread through the world".[183] No less than four years later these contacts would be of decisive importance in the preparatory phase of the Council.[184]

With regard to Assisi, Jungmann stresses "the pastoral direction on which the efforts for renewal are based"[185]. So it can be seen how for many, liturgical reform was considered a pastoral tool. In this it is possible to see, as we have already noted, a step towards an anthropocentric shift.

On the matter of the reception of the Encyclical and the themes put forward by the "reformers", we will give as an example a study published in 1960 by Emil Joseph Lengeling.[186] It is found in *Unser Gottesdienst* with the subtitle "Reflections and suggestions: a working document" published under the direction of Alfons Kirchgaessner in the name of the Liturgical Commission for the German speaking countries.[187] In this sense this work can be considered a pendant to Nagel's book on the reform of the Mass.[188] This study appeared after Pius XII's death, when his sucessor had already announced the convocation of a council and indicated that he wanted to base his pontificate less on condemnations than on affections of the heart.

Lengeling's study is entitled *Uberwundenes in der Messerklarung* and is apparently a critique of the *Unitary Catechism* used in Germany between 1925 and 1955, replaced in 1955 by a *New Catechism*.[189] So Lengeling is criticising a work already replaced by the bishops, and so he can say things that in another context would have shocked or not gone without consequences.

In 1960 Lengeling could not criticise the Encyclical *Mediator Dei*, nonetheless many of his criticisms of the old catechism could equally in Lengeling's perspective be applied to *Mediator Dei*. He says for example, "Someone who strays from the Catholic (universal) Revelation is not just someone who denies a revealed truth but also someone who neglects aspects that are reliably attested in Scripture and developed in Tradition, and who restricts himself to solemn

131

definitions of the faith, which defending against heretical doctrines, put an accent on isolated elements without describing the whole".[190]

It is in this way that Lengeling criticises the old catechism for being almost solely centred on the Eucharistic presence of Christ and for hardly mentioning other "equally real modes of the presence of Christ". To justify his position Lengeling quotes *Mediator Dei* in a remarkable way: "There is not a word on the presence of Christ - nonetheless important for a full understanding of the divine worship in every liturgical action. . . in the holy Sacrifice of the altar. . . in the presence of His minister. . . , in the Sacraments. . . , in the praises and prayers addressed to God according to the word of Christ, 'Where two or three are gathered in My name, I am there among them' "(Mt. 18: 20).[191]

It is noteworthy here that Lengeling omits to mention the presence *"sub Eucharisticis speciebus"* that Pius XII nevertheless underlines with a *"tum maxime"*. This can possibly be understood from the context in which Lengeling is writing, but he further cuts out the reference to the Sacraments, *"praesens adest in Sacramentis"* without mentioning the specifically Catholic *"virtute sua"*, which follows immediately. With regard to presence, he quotes *"in Deo admotis laudibus"* omitting *"denique"* which provides the exact meaning.[192]

"One would look in vain," continues Lengeling, "for anything on the presence of Christ in the word of Scripture". On this Lengeling cannot quote *Mediator Dei* because this point is equally "absent". On the other hand it will be mentioned in the *Constitution on the Liturgy* and presented, as Jungmann observes, "in an ecumencal spirit".[193]

It would be doubtless not uninteresting to analyse other criticisms of Lengeling that appear under the titles "Isolated truths"[194] and "Expressions and phrases demanding reservations" [195], because they anticipate certain orientations of the "reform"; however bearing in mind the time available, I will content myself with noting what Lengeling also considers worth quoting from *Mediator Dei*, the truth according to which the Sacrifice of Christ is offered not only *for* the whole Church but also *by* her, and further, on "the participation of the faithful in the Sacrifice as sharers in the holy priesthood" or again "the right and duty to active participation, including Communion".[196]

4. 3 The Encyclical in the Council texts

In 1960 the *Commissio praeparatoria* charged with handling the liturgy still had no French and German members, but some were soon nominated along with the liturgists Martimort of Paris and Johannes Wagner of Trier[197]. In his foreword to Jungmann's commentary on the *Liturgy Constitution* Wagner confirms, "During the preparation and discussion of the *schema*. . . . there was a circle of experts at Rome

132

coming from the German speaking world, members of commissions and liturgical institutes in Germany, Austria and Switzerland, who through their close interrelationships were up to date with every phase of the development of this Constitution"[198]. Jungmann, the *doyen* of his circle, is the author of the commentary in *Lexikon für Theologie und Kirche*, which, apart from the more widely diffused commentary by Rahner and Vorgrimler in their *Kleines Konzilskompendium* has fixed the image of the *Liturgy Constitution* in the German speaking countries. Jungmann's text is however wider - and covers a vaster material - and in general is more objective than Rahner's and Vorgrimler's, which contains some virulently polemic elements.[200]

These commentaries also contain a number of references to *Mediator Dei*, to which the *Constitution on the Liturgy* refers a number of times. However, unlike other conciliar documents, the Encyclical is not mentioned in the official notes. It is accordingly impossible to make a complete list of quotations from and allusions to *Mediator Dei* in the *Liturgy Constitution*, because many formulations in the text make allusions in a broad sense which it is not always possible to find in *Mediator Dei*.

What is clearly taken from *Mediator Dei* are the modes of Christ's presence in the Mass, which I discussed in relation to Lengeling. As we saw, not only was there added "in an ecumenical spirit" a reference to the presence of Christ in Scripture, but also in the same spirit – or more exactly, to take account of Protestant positions – the phrase "instruments of salvation" added by Pius XII in apposition to "Sacrament", was not repeated. It was in vain that certain people in the *aula* of the Council right up to the final vote asked that "the Pope's text should be more closely adhered to". The resistance stemmed principally from "anxiety at seeing a lessening of faith in the Eucharistic presence".[201]

As this example demonstrates, and apart from certain unanimous references made by the Council, which certainly happened, the references to *Mediator Dei* and Pius XII can be grouped into two principal categories. They are either paradigms of the "reforming" majority presented in the words of Pius XII: such references are well founded and safe from criticism by the "conservative" minority. Or on the other hand, when just this minority voiced strong reservations with regard to new formulations, forms used by Pius XII were adopted, after sometimes lively discussion, which reassured and relativised the situation.

The passage in *Sacrosanctum Concilium* which recalls that "the Mass always retains its social and public nature"[202] comes from this latter category and was added by certain council Fathers who feared "that by insisting on the communitarian character of the Mass, the private Mass would be rejected".[203]

When the *Liturgy Constitution* expressly praises the Divine

133

Office, the least one can say is that it does not correspond with the ideas of Jungmann, the commentator. He is a supporter of the possibilities the text provides for reducing its recitation, and so speaks negatively of "panegyric tones drawn from *Mediator Dei*" to the glory of the Office.[205]

So it can be seen, as the example of the different modes of Christ's presence shows, that the quotations of *Mediator Dei* go with deletions and additions which change their sense. Thus the reference to vernacular languages, which was welcomed by the majority at the Council, says in the original of *Mediator Dei*, "*In non paucis tamen ritibus vulgati sermonis usurpatio valde utilis apud populum existere potest, nihilominus. . .*"[206] and this phrase is immediately followed by, among other things, a restrictive reminder of the competence of the Holy See. In the conciliar text the range of application is considerably broadened and it is presented in positive tones: "*Cum tamen, sive in Missa, sive in Sacramentorum administratione, sive in aliis Liturgiae partibus, haud raro linguae vernaculae usurpatio valde utilis apud populum existere possit, amplior locus ipsi tribui valeat, imprimis . . .*"[207]

Concerning the participation of the faithful in the Sacrifice, *Mediator Dei* is quoted with a characteristic omission. In *Mediator Dei* Pius XII says, "*Christifideles suo modo duplici ratione participant: quia nempe non tantum per sacerdotis manus, sed etiam cum ipso quodammodo Sacrificium offerunt*"[208]. In the *Liturgy Constitution* we read that the faithful should "*non tantum per sacerdotis manus sed etiam una cum ipso offerentes, seipsos offere discant. . .*" The restriction brought by "*quodammodo*" - "in their own way" - disappears from the quotation.[209]

Of course the reformers rejoice that with Benedict XIV, Pius XII praises "the devotion that prompts the desire of some, not only to communicate when present at Mass, but preferably to receive particles consecrated at that Mass".[210]

The *Liturgy Constitution* says this: "The more perfect form of participation in the Mass whereby the faithful, after the priest's communion, receive the Lord's Body from the same Sacrifice, is warmly recommended." But in Pius XII there is no question of a "more perfect participation". He in fact emphasises that by receiving hosts previously consecrated, there is also a full participation in the Sacrifice.

On this point, even Rahner and Vorgrimler mention the Encyclical, stressing that "it was a wish of the Encyclical *Mediator Dei* repeated with insistence, and the wish has great ecumenical significance".[212] They wrongly interpret these affirmations of the Encyclical as a link with the Protestant concept of a presence of Christ restricted to the time of the celebration[213].

In his commentary Jungmann is at pains to show that important pointers for the future had been made by Pius XII in the years that followed the publication of *Mediator Dei*. On the participation of the faithful he remarks for instance: "After centuries of a purely clerical liturgy, the people's participation was first expressly envisaged in a liturgical text in the *Ordo Sabbati Sancti* of 1951."[215] Concerning the rejection of any attempt at europeanisation he refers to certain passages of Pius XII's Encyclical *Summi Pontificatus*[216]. Concerning concelebration he can refer to the declaration of the Holy Office of May 1957[219], but he adds, "already before the Council, it was understood that it was not a matter - as at ordinations - of all saying the various prayers of the principal celebrant, on their knees, from the offertory onwards."[220]

When it appears opportune, Jungmann marks contradictions between PiusXII and his congregations. Concerning article 128 of *SC* he says that the evolution that led to the altar of reservation started with a decree of the Congregation of Rites of 1st June 1957, when even in 1956, Pius XII declared himself in favour of different solutions. So the instruction of 1964 reestablished the "former liberty".[221]

Naturally Jungmann does not omit to mention the praises addressed by the Pope to the Liturgical Congress at Assisi in 1956, which are quoted in *Sacrosanctum Concilium* 43. But what was unknown at the time was that many participants at this Congress already had a reform of the *Ordo Missae* in mind. Jungmann acknowledges it himself when he discusses article 50 of *Sacrosanctum Concilium*: "It can be said that among the dispositions of the reform, this is the most important article in the whole Constitution. The *Ordo Missae* is the entire fixed part of the Mass. It goes without saying that the Commission had very exact ideas about the reform to be strived for. In the ten years before the Council the majority of study meetings I earlier mentioned bore precisely on the reform of the *Ordo Missae*."[222]

Finally, contrary to what Jungmann hints at[223] there is no continuity between the diocesan liturgical commissions mentioned in article 45 of *Sacrosanctum Concilium* and those mentioned in *Mediator Dei*. The Council expressly gives these commissions the purpose of favouring the liturgical movement as a movement for reform, whereas for Pius XII such commisssions are to "promote the liturgical apostolate, so that under your watchful care the instructions of the Apostolic See may in all things be observed."[224] One may hold that their aims are opposite.

As we have said, in other Council documents the references to *Mediator Dei* are in the official notes to the Council texts. The criteria for quoting the Encyclical should be the same as in *Sacrosanctum Concilium*. *Lumen Gentium* frequently cites *Mediator Dei*: thus in *LG*10 "the common priesthood of the faithful" and the "ministry of service" are discussed,[225] or again in the following article on the presentation of offerings by the faithful[226] - two themes that play an important role in the *Liturgy Constitution*.[227]

On the other hand in other Council texts whose themes might make it appropriate, *Mediator Dei* is only quoted incidentally[228] or not even expressly mentioned.[228]

5 A final word on the role of the Encyclical in the post-conciliar Church

It is known that the liturgists are not of one mind in their appreciation of *Sacrosanctum Concilium*. So on its adoption Lengeling speaks of a great day because "a happily abundant harvest has been brought in, ripened over the last decades under the breath of the Holy Spirit"[230]; Vagaggini speaks of "a great step forward in the difficult reconquest of the essence of Christianity"[231]; Jungmann notes, "In numerous questions it was necessary to find a middle way between the ideal and the tradition, a way which showed the state of rival forces at each moment, a way which even in the text of the Constitution is not always straight, for example on the use of the vernacular or on the two linked concepts of Sacrifice and Sacrament".[232] Rahner and Vorgrimler note, "Now that the post-conciliar liturgical work has resolutely progressed, it is now [i.e. in 1966] easy to demonstrate that the requirement of a mysterious sacral language is absurd and that this language is a museum piece, contrary to the communicative nature of language. So the meritorious character of this passage [SC36] should not be forgotten. Doubtless the problems of language are not all resolved yet; the simple translation of the liturgical text, ossified for centuries, at the moment has only created new problems".[233]

It would not be difficult to continue the list of similar quotations. They demonstrate that for some even the words of the Council have no proper authority, but are in an expression of Rahner's "only the beginning of a beginning". How much more should for such people the Encyclical *Mediator Dei* and the dogmatic theology that underlies it be considered a thing of the past presenting only a historic interest?[234] Those who rely on them and approve them must expect to be treated at least as "preconciliar": which as Cardinal Ratzinger explained to to the Chilean bishops in his famous speech of 1988[235], must be considered a profound error.

It would be useful to study the presence of the Encyclical in post-conciliar documents of the pontifical magisterium, reviewing in particular Paul VI's Encyclical *Mysterium fidei* of 1965 [236], the declaration of the Congregation of the Faith *Sacerdotium ministeriale* of 1983 and the Holy Father's Maundy Thursday letters to priests.

Be that as it may, it is regrettable that references to the Encyclical are missing from the *Catechism of the Catholic Church*. Without doubt, this remarkable document is inspired by the spirit of the Encyclical. But it is only expressly quoted once on priesthood, "The priest then is the same Christ Jesus, whose sacred person is represented by His minister. The consecration which the minister received when he was ordained assimilates him to the High Priest and enables him to act by the power of Christ Himself and in His name (*virtute ac persona ipsius Christi*)".[238] On the other hand there is no direct reference to *Mediator Dei* with regard to the Sacrifice of the Mass or the liturgy, but it must be said that these are not particularly well developed parts of a work which otherwise we can only praise.

As for the presence of the Encyclical *Mediator Dei* in the declarations of the episcopal magisterium, unfortunately one can only be disappointed there. But fortunately, as this colloquium demonstrates, in recent times there have been glimmerings of a reversal in the trend. So I shall conclude by expressing a hope, the same hope expressed by Pius XII in the words of the liturgy in 1954:[239] "*nec pastori oboedientia gregis nec gregi desit cura pastoris*".

NOTES

1   Joseph Ratzinger, *La célébration de la foi*, Paris 1995, p. 77 et seq. (ET *The Feast of Faith*, San Francisco 1996).

2   ibid p. 81

3   ibid p. 82

4   Josef Andreas Jungmann, *Die Messe im Gottesvolk. Ein nachkonziliarer Durchblick durch Missarum Solemnia*. Freiburg 1970 pp. 7 et seq. In this work he refers to Charles Ruch, *La messe d'après les pères jusqu'à saint Cyprien*, in DThC X 1928, 963

5   Jungmann in *LThK* 12 p. 10. For Jungmann the decisive moment was a speech by Lambert Beauduin in 1909 at the Malines "Katholikentag".

6   Jungmann, *Messe*, p. 7

7   Jungmann, LThK 12, p.10

8   *Les origines du C. P. L. 1943-1949* R.P. Duployé, p. 338

9   *Le mouvement liturgique en Allemagne*, J. Wagner in *La Maison-Dieu*, 25/1951

10   Through such works as *Irrwege und umwege der Froemmigkeit* by Max Kassipe and *Sentire cum Ecclesia* by Doerner

11   Jungmann in *LThK* 12, p.11

12   J. Wagner in *La Maison Dieu* 25/1951. Wagner was to become director of the Institutum Liturgicum at Trier.

13   *Unser Gottesdienst* ed. A. Kirchgaessner, Freiburg 1960. A characteristic feature of the almost unlimited prestige enjoyed by Guardini in the German Church is that at the time of the breach which was appearing in 1960 his contribution was put at the front of this collective work which was to indicate the road to be followed.

14   ibid p. 3

15	ibid p. 3
16	ibid p. 4
17	ibid p. 5
18	ibid p. 5
19	ibid p. 5
20	ibid p. 5
21	ibid p. 5
21	ibid p. 5
22	ibid p. 5
23	ibid p. 6
24	ibid p. 6
25	ibid p. 6
26	ibid p. 7
27	ibid p. 7
28	ibid p. 8
29	ibid p. 8
30	ibid p. 8
31	ibid p. 9
32	ibid p. 9
33	ibid p. 10
34	ibid p. 10
35	Oswald von Nell-Breuning, "Quadragesimo Anno", in *Stimmen der Zeit*, 1971, p289 et seq.
36	cf. D. Albrecht, *Der Notenwechsel zwischen dem heiligen Stuhl und der deutschen Reichsregierung I*, Mainz 1965, esp. p. 402
37	Denzinger Huenermann (DH) 2600-2700
38	*MD* 68
39	For example his criticism of archeologism in 5 or the cofusion between the hierarchical priesthood and the priesthood of the baptised in 13
40	no. 14
41	no. 5
42	no. 17
43	F. Kolbe's commentary in *La Maison-Dieu* 74/1963
44	Ratzinger, *The Feast of Faith*
45	op. cit.
46	*Les origines du C. P. L. 1943-1949*, P. Duployé, p. 338
47	ibid.
48	The Latin text is in *AAS 1947* pp. 521-595, index pp. 596-600. The English text is quoted from the translation by G. D. Smith, C. T. S., London, 1960 with Smith's paragraph numbering.
49	*MD* 16
50	*MD* 15
51	*MD* 22
52	*MD* 2, 4
53	*MD* 17
55	*MD* 19

56   Cf. the brief critical study by Cardinals Ottaviani and Bacci, "Kurze kritische Untersuchung des neuen *Ordo Missae*", in *Schriftenreihe der Una Voce*, 4/1969, p. 9, or K. Lehmann and Wo. Pannenberg, *Lehrverurteilungen -kirchentrennend?*, Freiburg, 1987, p. 107, note 47a. On Mt. 18:20 see Ratzinger, *A Feast of Faith*

57   *SC* 7 and Jungmann's commentary, pp. 20-21

58   *MD* 174

59   *MD* 20. Furthermore for Pius XII, unlike certain widespread opinions today, the worship of God is a duty which is not limited to the individual but of "the whole community of mankind, linked together by social bonds"(*MD* 12)

60   *MD* 183

61   *MD* 23

62   *MD* 51,

63   *MD* 50

64   *MD* 52

65   *MD* 70

66   *MD* 3 cf. *MD* 218 "representing and renewing the Sacrifice of the Cross"

67   *MD* 72

68   *MD* 74

69   *MD* 81

70   *MD* 14

71   *MD* 21

72   *MD* 76: *ipsum altaris sacrificium per se gratiarum sit actio*

73   Taking the opposite position Lengeling stressed in 1960 that "the Canon (and thus the Eucharistic celebration of which it is the centre) is the Eucharist" ("Überwundenes in der Messerklarung" in *Unser Gottesdienst*)

74   *MD* 29

75   *MD* 29

76   *MD* 137

77   The famous para. 7 of the *Institutio Generalis* which prefaced the new *Ordo* and was modified on account of the protests it aroused. Cf. Ottaviani/Bacci op. cit. p. 7, also G. May, *Die alte und die neue Messe* (Una Voce Deutschland, 8/1975, pp. 61 et seq.)

78   "The 'community' is the new discovery of the postconciliar era. We have remembered again that in the ancient Church *synaxis* - assembly - was a name for the Eucharist." Ratzinger, *A Feast of Faith*

79   *MD* 122

80   *MD* 121

81   *MD* 127

82   *MD* 122

83   *MD* 124

84   *MD* 125

85   *MD* 126

86   *MD* 128
87   *MD* 85-86
88   *MD* 48
89   *MD* 48
90   *MD* 46
91   *MD* 45
92   *MD* 45
93   *MD* 44
94   *MD* 44 For Pius XII's doctrine of the priesthood see also the allocution *Solemnis Conventus* of 24 th June 1939, *AAS* 31/1939 pp. 245-251, Apostolic Exhortation *Menti Nostrae* of 23rd Sept. 1950, *AAS* 42/1950, pp. 657-702.
95   *MD* 88
96   ibid.
97   *MD* 217
98   *MD* 89. This is the only passage in the Encyclical that uses the term "concelebration". Doubtless PiusXII dealt with this problem in the 1950s but only in the form of allocutions. See Mgr. Schmitz' paper in *La Liturgie, trésor de l'église,* CIEL, 1996, pp. 119 et seq.
99   *MD* 88
100   It is typical that of this formulation the Liturgy Commisssion of the German speaking countries in *Studien und Entwuerfe* remarks that it is "not uncontested" and should be "suppressed without being replaced", Nagel, p. 38
101   *MD* 92
102   *MD* 94
103   *MD* 94
104   *MD* 96, 98
105   *MD* 101
106   *MD* 101
107   Ratzinger, *Ein neues Lied*, p. 146
108   ibid p. 147
109   *MD* 33
110   *MD* 112
111   *MD* 115
112   *MD* 130
113   *MD* 131
114   *MD* 135
115   *MD* 138
116   *MD* 138
117   *MD* 139
118   *MD* 144
119   *MD* 140
120   cf. Dieter Weiss, "La dévotion eucharistique dans l'église après le concile de Trente"in *La liturgie, trésor d'église,* pp. 155-156. In 1957 the Congregation of Rites published a decree on the tabernacle (ibid. 156).

121   *MD* 174

122   *MD* 188 "that devotional confession should be abandoned . . these are opinions . . . most damaging to Christian piety"

123   *MD* 188

124   *MD* 31

125   *MD* 196

126   *MD* 195

127   *MD* 186

128   *MD* 197

129   *MD* 150

130   *MD* 155

131   *MD* 35

132   *MD* 37-38

133   *MD* 145

134   *MD* 211

135   *MD* 215

136   *MD* 5

137   *MD* 7

138   *MD* 61

139   *MD* 198

140   *MD* 116

141   *MD* 69

142   *MD* 63

143   *MD* 66

144   *MD* 66

145   *MD* 65

146   *MD* 66

147   *MD* 67

148   *MD* 64

149   *MD* 63

150   *MD* 64

151   *MD* 216

152   ibid.

153   *MD* 216

154   *MD* 173 An explanatory letter published by the Holy Office in 1948 clarifies that it is a question of those who "teach that in liturgical adoration the mysteries are not historic but present in a mysterious and sacramental, but real, way."

155   *MD* 176

156   *MD* 180

157   *MD* 181

158   *MD* 181

159   *MD* 209

160   *MD* 207

161   *MD* 207

162   *MD* 212 He particularly mentions altar servers, chosen "from every

class in the community even of the higher and more cultured class. . .
properly instructed and encouraged. . . these boys may well prove a
source of candidates for the priesthood"(*MD* 213)

163   *MD* 204 quotes Pius XI in *Divini Cultus*
164   *MD* 82
165   Jungmann in *LThK* 12, p. 12
166   ibid.
167   *La Liturgie, trésor de l'église,* pp. 121 et seq.
168   LThK 12, p. 11: Jungmann notes that even before the Council there was strong oppositon to innovations from religious musicians, for instance at liturgical congresses.
169   *AAS* 1954, pp. 667
170   ibid, p. 316-317 refers the reader to *Humani Generis* and 2 Tim 4:3-4
171   ibid, p. 667
172   ibid,.p. 668
173   ibid.
174   ibid.
175   ibid., pp. 675-676
176   ibid.
177   ibid.
178   *LThK* 12, p. 11
179   Fr. Lambert Beauduin, A. G. Martimort, in *Les questions liturgiques et paroissiales,* September 1959
180   R. Falsini, *La Maison-Dieu,* 74/1963 for Italy; J. Daniélou, *La Maison-Dieu,* 25/1951 for the USA
181   Jungmann in *LThK* 12, p. 11
182   Schmitz, op. cit. p. 130
183   *LThK* 12 p. 11
184   ibid., p. 10
185   ibid.
186   For this author see W. Waldstein, "Le mouvement liturgique de Dom Gueranger à la veille du Concile Vatican II", in *La Liturgie, trésor de l'église,* p. 177
187   Freiburg 1960
188   The publisher of Guardini's letter to Bishop Stohr in 1940 (ibid p. 3)
189   This did not last long in spite of Lengeling's tactical praise. It was not used after the Council, although it still forms the basis of the catechesis of the community of the Fraternity of St. Peter in Strasbourg.
190   Lengeling op. cit. pp. 24-25
191   op. cit. 25; cites *MD* 15
192   ibid.
193   *SC*7 and *LThK* 12 p. 21. Lengeling adds "The presence of the saving actions of Christ in the liturgical year is, according to *Mediator Dei,* "Christ Himself who perseveres with his Church" (Lengeling ibid, *MD* 176). The quote "liturgical year . . . Christ Himself" does not conform to the text of *MD* or the Pope's thought. The Pope says that the liturgical

year is "no cold and lifeless representation of past events. . . . *Sed potius est Christus ipse, qui in sua Ecclesia perseverat*"It is erroneous to attempt to deduce a real presence of Christ in the liturgical year on the same level as the real presence of Christ in the Eucharist. The Pope here, as so often in his Encyclical, is speaking of the presence of the Head in His Mystical Body, the Church. There is in Lengeling no explicit reference to this essential biblical doctrine. Pius XII on the other hand in his Encyclical never ceases to recall that it is one and the same Christ who triumphs in heaven, who is present in the Eucharist and who is Head of his Mystical Body, the Church. (*MD* 174) To add anything to this is to fall under the condemnation of those who teach "in a vague and nebulous way"(*MD* 176)

194   In particular for the Mass, transubstantiation "almost the only matter considered", communion "with sentimental singing", "asceticism . . isolated acts the individual can scarcely perform", the names of individual parts of the Mass such as "preparation" for the liturgy of the Word etc. ibid p. 29.

195   In particular the concept of "renewing" the Sacrifice of the Cross, at Communion the former habit of speaking "personally about Christ, the Saviour, receiving God" instead of "gifts" or "offerings". For Lengeling the concepts of transsubstantiation, sacerdotal power, descent of Christ to the altar - and many others are questionable. He does mention formulartions rightly rejected as excessive. (ibid p. 32)He even criticises the *New Catechism* for its statements on the Mass(ibidp. 28) "Nonetheless this is a good starting point, while we await better - for a global concept of the Eucharist"(ibid) For Lengeling the Mass does not consist of among other things "a proclamation full of realities", "a communal meal for the faithful" but "is" these things (ibid p. 27)

196   ibid. p. 28

197   May *Die alte und die neue Messe* p. 5 note 8

198   Wagner in *LThK* 12 p. 10 May op. cit. p. 27 mentions "the determining influence in the work of the Council Fathers of the Jesuit Fr. Jungmann and the Swiss theologian Küng for the objectives of the reforming party at the Council. For Karl Rahner and his revealing correspondence from the time of the Council see:*Karl Rahner verstehen. Ein Einführung in Sein Leben und Denken* by H. Vorgrimler (Freiburg 1985)pp171 et seq. See also R. Wiltgren *The Rhine flows into the Tiber.*

199   K. Rahner, H. Vorgrimler *Kleines Konzilskompendium,* Freiburg 1966

200.   For instance they accuse those who prefer the ancient liturgy of an "inability to communicate" of "cultural arrogance" and "a sterile attitude to history". They are "tragi-comic secondary personalities in the Church, casualties of history" (ibid p. 40)

201   Jungmann in *LThK* 12 p. 212

202   SC 27 *MD* 85

203   Jungmann in *LThK* 12 p. 36

204   ibid p. 85

205   ibid
206   *MD* 64 .. the adoption of the vernacular in quite a number of functions may prove of great benefit to the faithful.
207   SC 36. 2 . . . the use of the mother tongue, whether in the Mass, the administration of the sacraments, or other parts of the liturgy, may frequently be of great advantage to the people, the limits of its employment may be extended.
208   *MD* 96-98
209   SC 48. Here again *"sed etiam"* was used to reduce to silence those Fathers who chose to speak only of a presentation of offerings "by" the priest. (Jungmann op. cit. p. 52 and note 8)
210   *MD* 126
211   *SC* 55
212   Rahner, Vorgrimler op. cit. p. 44
213   On the lines of the foregoing they show understanding for the fact that the Council " desirous of assuring a continuous transition (*to what? W. G.*) did not attempt to examine the questions, such as giving the celebration of the Eucharist the form of a meal, without completely abandoning stylised representation or overdoing the sacral and the artistic." ibid p. 44
214   *SC* 31
215   Jungmann op. cit. p. 38
216   ibid p. 43
217   ibid
218   ibid and note 31
219   ibid p. 60 and note 22
220   ibid p. 61
221   ibid p. 53
223   ibid p. 48, note 37
224   *SC* 45 *MD* 120
225   *LG* 10 *MD* 89
226   *LG* 11 *MD* 98
227   see also in the description of priestly ministry *LG*28, notes 103, 105 *MD* 88
228   *Christus Dominus* 9. 9 , Optatam totius 8. 15 *MD* 150
229   There is nothing in the decrees on Priests, on Ecumenism, on the Eastern Churches, or on The Church in the Modern World.
230   *LThk* 12 p. 13
231   ibid
232   ibid
233   Rahner /Vorgrimler op. cit. p. 42
234   Nagel uses the expression "liturgical archeologism"(op. cit. p. 41) cf ibid p. 41, note7 on "historicising"
        The same ways of thinking are found in *Dialog der Kirchen* by Karl Lehmann and various Protestant authors. *Lehrverurteilungen-kirchentrennend?* mentions *Mediator Dei* on those who wish to receive

Communion from hosts consecrated at the same Mass. Vol . III *Das Opfer Jesu Christi und seine Gegenwart in der Kirche* (Freiburg 1983) mentions in its conclusions "two important trailblazers for the present new thinking" - *Mystici Corporis* (and with it *Mediator Dei*) and strangely Odo Casel's "theology of mysteries" criticised by *MD* .

235   reproduced in *Der Fels* 12?1988 p. 343-344
236   DH 4410 et seq.
237   DH 4720
238   *Catechism of the Catholic Church* 1548
239   AAS 1954p. 677 see also postcommunion of the Mass *Si diligis.*

Theological and Pastoral Reflections on the History of Frequent Communion

Father Bertrand de Margerie SJ (France)

Father Bertrand de Margerie, a member of the Society of Jesus, was born in Paris in 1923, into a family of diplomats and writers. After his priestly ordination in 1956, he spent eight years in Brazil and taught theology in numerous countries, including the United States. He is the author of a number of books, notably on the Heart of Jesus (Mame, Editions Saint-Paul), on the exegesis of the Fathers (4 volumes, Cerf), remarried divorcees and the Eucharist (Téqui), the Eucharist (You will do this in memory of me, Beauchesne) and on the attitude of the great French authors towards the Sacrament of Penance (Of the confessional in literature, FAC, Saint-Paul).

I propose to present some brief reflections on a point of capital importance for the Christian life of each baptised person: what does God, the Fount of Revelation, teach us, through Holy Scripture, the Fathers, and the Magisterium of the Church, about frequent Communion and its temporal and eternal fruits? What pastoral conclusions has the Church drawn from these, and what might she glean from them in the future?

I   A brief historical review of the past teaching of the Church

It is not enough for us simply to consider the history of the practice of frequent Communion and the different ways of understanding it. We must also ask what Christ the Revealer wants to say to us about the nature, meaning and purpose of the practice.

1   Sacred Scripture

The decree *Sacra Tridentina Synodus*, published in 1905 by the Congregation of the Council with the approval of Saint Pius X, admirably summed up the revealed teaching in a systematic presentation that would be useful to quote here. Recalling the discourse of Jesus on the Bread of Life, the text comments: "by this comparison (Jn 6:59) between the Bread and the Manna, the disciples were able to understand *easily* that just as bread was the daily food of the Hebrews in the desert, so the Christian soul should nourish itself *daily* with Heavenly Bread. Moreover, when Jesus Christ tells us to ask in the Lord's Prayer for our "daily bread", we must understand by this, as nearly all the Fathers of the Church taught, not only material bread, the body's food, but the Eucharistic Bread which must

146

be received each day" (*Actes de Pie X*, Bonne Presse, Vol. 2, p.253).

In the light of John's Gospel, this text concisely recapitulates: firstly, the teaching of the God of the Old Testament through the figure of the daily Manna of the Jews in the desert, and then that of the God of the New Testament in the synoptic Gospels, introducing the petition for daily Bread, whose Eucharistic meaning is proclaimed clearly and virtually unanimously by the Fathers of the Church. Thus the text demonstrates in a most impressive manner how the Old and the New Testaments, and then the Fathers, come together to reveal God's will: that the Eucharistic Bread should be eaten each day by the members of Christ's Church.

The discourse on the Bread of Life, by presenting the Manna as a (rather negative) foreshadowing of the Living Bread come down from heaven, teaches us that the Living Bread must be eaten each day, as long as this earthly exile lasts, until we enter the Promised Land.

This document of the Holy See continues with the witness of the *Acts of the Apostles* (2:42,46) according to which the newly baptised "were persevering in the doctrine of the apostles, and in the communication of the *breaking of bread* ... And continuing daily with one accord in the temple, and breaking bread from house to house". The Eucharistic meaning of this repeated reference has been recognised by numerous exegetes, and has been illuminated by the discourse on the Bread of Life. [1]

On the other hand, exegetes are divided on the question whether or not the petition for daily bread in the *Pater Noster* bears a Eucharistic meaning. Some have thought that the literal sense concerns material bread, while the Eucharistic meaning would be secondary.

Nevertheless the exegetical criteria recognised by the Second Vatican Council enable us to retain a Eucharistic meaning with some degree of certainty. The *Catechism of the Catholic Church* (§§112ff) lists the three criteria mentioned by the Council: (1) Be especially attentive to the content and unity of the whole of Sacred Scripture, for Scripture is a unity by reason of the unity of God's plan, of which Christ is the centre. (2) Read the Scripture within the living Tradition of the whole Church, to which the Fathers are the privileged witnesses. (3) Be attentive to the analogy of faith, by which we mean the coherence of the truths of faith among themselves and within the whole plan of Revelation, for God never contradicts Himself.

By applying these three criteria the CCC (*Catechism of the Catholic Church*) (§§2835-2837) brings out what it terms the "specifically Christian sense" of the petition for daily bread: "[this petition concerns] "the Word of God accepted in faith, the Body of Christ received in the Eucharist".

The CCC goes on to analyse at length the twice stated temporal reference contained in the two formulations (in Matthew and Luke) of the fourth petition: "give us this *day* our *daily* bread" – *epiousios* – recalling the Eucharistic meaning of this word *epiousios* ("daily") which appears nowhere else in the New Testament. As the *Catechism* teaches:

- "Taken in a temporal sense, *epiousios* is a pedagogical repetition of "this day" (Ex 16:19-21), to confirm us in trust without reservation.
- Taken in the qualitative sense, *epiousios* signifies what is necessary for life, every good thing sufficient for subsistence.
- Taken literally, the word *epiousios* ("super-essential") refers directly to the Bread of Life, the "medicine of immortality" without which we have no life in us (Jn 6:35-56).
- Finally, in this connection, its heavenly meaning is evident: "this day" is the Day of the Lord, the day of the feast of the Kingdom, anticipated in the Eucharist that is already the foretaste of the Kingdom to come. For this reason it is fitting for the Eucharistic liturgy to be celebrated each day".

Hence the CCC is able to conclude that the Eucharist is our Daily Bread.

Bock and Carmignac have shown the profound sense of the petition, in the *Pater Noster*, for daily Bread seen as the continuation of the daily Manna; in this land of exile, we ask for our daily Manna, the new Manna of the new and eternal Covenant, the Manna which the Jews awaited in the inter-testamental period. Carmignac even states, in his *Recherches sur le Notre Père* (Paris, 1969, p.198): "Talmudic and Midrashic literature, the redaction of which certainly took place well before the time of Christ, contain sufficiently diverse ancient traditions to show that that the Manna continued to be regarded as the special food of messianic times". From this point of view, it would be appropriate to study the Eucharistic perspectives of the Fathers of the Church as they touch upon the daily Manna given to the Chosen People on their pilgrimage towards the Promised Land.

2 The Fathers

The commentaries of the Fathers on the usual understanding of the petition for Eucharistic Bread still enlighten the Church and our lives. Here we will quote from Cyprian, Basil, Ambrose and Augustine.

When quoting from the Fathers it is necessary to distinguish what they have to say about the practical effects of a given Eucharistic practice in their time and in their particular region, from how they interpret the will of Christ as shown in the New Testament.

If their historical descriptions illustrate a great variation in the

Eucharistic "rhythm", their testimony in favour of daily reception of the Eucharist is striking both in its depth and frequency. In the third century, Cyprian wrote, in his treatise *On The Lord's Prayer*, that it must "be feared that in abstaining from the Body of Christ, we separate ourselves from salvation: if you do not eat the Flesh of the Son of Man and drink His Blood, you will not have life in you" (Jn 6:54). And, consequently, we pray that we might be given each day our Bread, that is to say, Christ, in order that we who live and have our being in Him, might not separate ourselves from the sanctification of the Body of Christ." (§18). We should remember the statement *Christum dari nobis cotidie petimus.* Daily Communion is seen here as a means of persevering in the grace of Christ.

In about the year 372 Saint Basil, writing to a certain lady, told her: "to communicate every day, to participate continually in life, is to live to the fullest" (*Letter* 93, RJ 916). Then the Saint added: "We communicate four times each week (Sunday, Wednesday, Friday and Saturday)". Thus this Father was aware of a difference between the ideal and its concrete realisation. Pope John Paul II quoted this text of Basil of Caesarea in his letter about the Saint of 2 January 1980.

Not long after this, Saint Ambrose, bishop of Milan, in his treatise on the Sacraments, expressed himself in these terms: "What does the Apostle tell you? 'Each time we receive it, we proclaim the death of the Lord' (1 Cor 11:25-26). If we proclaim the death of the Lord, we proclaim the forgiveness of sins. His Blood was shed for the forgiveness of sins. I must always receive it so that it can always blot out my sins. I who sin continually, must continually have a remedy for sin. You mean to say that each time this Sacrifice is offered the death of the Lord is re-presented for the remission of sins, and you do not receive each day this Bread of Life! He who has a wound seeks medicine. That medicine is the venerable and heavenly sacrament" (*De Sacramentis*, IV 6:26 and V 4:25-26).

Let us try to understand Ambrose's thinking. The sacrifice of the death of the Risen Lord obtains for us the remission of sins: hence it is this sacrifice that we make our own when we offer and receive the Eucharist. Since we are well aware that we need to obtain each day the forgiveness of our daily sins, should we not communicate every day, as Our Lord invites us to when He makes us ask "each day for the Bread of eternal life which fortifies the substance of our souls", as Ambrose expressly puts it?

His spiritual son, Saint Augustine, followed the same line. Thus, in his *Sermon* 227.1, addressing on Easter Sunday those who had been baptised the night before, Augustine told them: "You must understand what you have received, what you are receiving, what you must receive each day: this Bread that you see upon the altar, sanctified by the word of God, is the Body of Christ". The text is very profound: "what you must receive each day: *quid quotidie accipere debeatis."* [2]

Of course, as Pius X would clarify later, this duty to receive the Sacrament daily is not a divine precept, but only the very earnest desire of Christ and His Church: a desire which the local community of Hippo had come to understand as early as the end of the fourth and the beginning of the fifth century, thanks to the preaching of Augustine.

With Saint Augustine (and this is true of the Fathers in general), the Eucharistic symbolism is not the only meaning of the Daily Bread: together the Body of Christ and His Word make up the Bread of Life eaten in faith – the Word proclaims the Eucharist, which inflames us with love for the Word. Together they are the soul's bread. This bread is eaten only by the children of God; whilst God gives material bread, the food of this mortal body, not only to those who sing His praises, but also – as Augustine reminds us - to blasphemers (*Sermon* 56). The same Church which recommends daily Communion with the Body of Christ, also advises the daily hearing or reading of the Word, which is offered to us as nourishment during the Eucharistic liturgy.

It would be possible to quote numerous sayings of the Fathers on the Eucharistic meaning of the Daily Bread; but that is not necessary. Let us rather turn to the history of the Church's teaching, that is, the teaching of the Popes and the general Councils. For these Fathers, who were themselves bishops for the most part, already expressed in their teaching the ordinary and universal Magisterium of the Church.

3 The history of the Church's teaching

It is a well known fact that, after the Patristic period, the fervour of charity, nourished by frequent Communion, diminished, and the practice became so rare that in 1215 the Fourth Ecumenical Council of the Lateran had to lay down the obligation of a minimum level of practice: all the members of the Church, in order to stay in a state of grace, had to communicate at least once a year.

The Council of Trent, without explicitly favouring daily communion, proposed it implicitly to all Catholics by expressing the "desire that the faithful communicate not only spiritually but also sacramentally at each Mass at which they are present, so that they might receive more abundantly the fruits of the most Holy Sacrifice of the Mass" (DS 1747, 1562 AD).

This text takes on its full importance in the context of an earlier declaration of the same Council, recapitulating the Patristic and mediaeval theology concerning the effects of sacramental Communion. In fact, in 1551, the Council had recalled (DS 1638) that Eucharistic Communion "frees us from venial faults, preserves us from mortal sin, binds us with the closest ties of faith, hope and charity to the Body of the Church, of which Christ is the Head, and constitutes the pledge of our future glory and of our everlasting beatitude". In other words, each sacramental Communion made in a state of grace, affects our sinful past, fortifies our present state of grace, preserves our earthly future, and merits our eternal one. Such are the intentions with which the Christian must communicate, according to the Council, so that his Communion, far from being that sacrilege and self-condemnation denounced by Saint Paul in his First Epistle to the Corinthians (2:27-32), would be, on the contrary, a Communion at once sacramental and spiritual.

From these Tridentine propositions, as from the whole of Catholic theology, it becomes evident that the communicant, through each new sacramental and spiritual Communion, receives a new increase of sanctifying grace, a new remission of venial sins, new and powerful assistance to avoid sin in the future, and new merit; and so prepares himself to receive new and wonderful degrees of glory in the eternal life to come: that is to say, knowledge and love of the One and Triune God, in the company of His elect.

In spite of the openings created by the Council of Trent, Jansenist rigorism continued to make access to frequent and daily Communion difficult, especially for those "living in the world", and for married people. There were debates about the necessary dispositions needed for Communion, and even theologians of note thought that Communion should be rare and submitted to numerous preliminary conditions.

This state of affairs was changed by the liberating interventions of two Popes: Blessed Innocent XI in 1679, and Saint Pius X in 1905 and 1910.

Saint Pius X settled the controversy: [3] basing his argument on the Fathers of the Church, he recalled "that no precept demands from daily communicants higher dispositions than those required for weekly Communion", and proclaimed a principle that is often forgotten nowadays: "the fruits of daily Communion are much more abundant than those of weekly Communion".

More precisely, to be able to communicate each day it suffices to be in a state of grace, and to have the right intention: that is, to approach the Eucharist, not out of routine, but in order to fight against one's faults, and to grow in charity and to respond to God's will.

Thus it is not necessary to be free from venial sin in order to communicate fruitfully – although that would be very desirable. Moreover, stated Pius X, it is not possible that daily communicants should not, little by little, be weaned off their affection for venial sin, and, by implication, grow daily in grace.

Hence at that time the commentators were right to stress that

151

while those who communicate once a week were able to do so more often, in fact they rarely availed themselves of the opportunity. This point seems to have been forgotten these days by a certain number of ecclesiastics who seem to think that Communion once a week is often enough. Thus it happens that the enemies of a certain kind of modern Eucharistic laxity (the victims of which are those who go to Confession too infrequently) fall into a sort of Neo-Jansenism by keeping quiet about the Church's invitation to daily Communion: even if certain people abuse that invitation, all have the right to know about it.

The Tridentine declarations and those of Pius X on the effects of Eucharistic Communion were magnificently taken up and deepened by Pope Pius XII in his encyclical *Mediator Dei et Hominum* of 1947. I say "deepened" because Pius XII, following Benedict XIV, introduced an idea that was not present in Trent concerning the very nature of Eucharistic Communion: it is *a participation in the sacrifice.* In other words, to communicate is to become one Victim with Christ crucified and risen for the salvation of the world. To eat and drink the Divine Victim is not only to take part in the heavenly banquet, but also to become part of the sacrificial oblation that this Victim makes of Himself for the eternal happiness of each human person. Hence it entails a readiness to offer up one's body and shed one's blood in union with and through the Divine Victim, and so merit for others the grace of sharing in the one and unique sacrifice.

In passing let us note that the encyclical of Pius XII on the liturgy remains the most beautiful and most profound of all the official documents of the Church on the Sacrifice of the Mass, the most useful for penetrating and understanding its inmost nature, and this is why its influence on the official documents of the Second Vatican Council has been so clear and profound, why it was quoted eight times in the Council documents, including five quotations in the Dogmatic Constitution on the Church, *Lumen Gentium* (10, 11, 28 and 50). In particular, Pius XII makes explicit mention of daily Communion when he says: "Would to God that Christians participate in the Divine Sacrifice by receiving in sacramental Communion daily, if they can, the Body of Jesus offered for all to the Eternal Father". By underlining the offering of Christ for us in the context of Communion, Pius XII was proposing to understand this as a participation in the offering of the Christ-Victim for the world. The Real Presence is not only that of God made Man, but that of the God-Victim making us participate in His state as a glorified Victim. To communicate each day is to become more and more a Victim in Christ, through Him, with Him and for Him. This is what the Second Vatican Council taught, in quoting from the encyclical of Pius XII in *Lumen Gentium* 11.

And so we come to the most recent Magisterium of the Church:

152

the teaching of Vatican II.

Whilst it is true that the *Constitution on the Liturgy* does not explicitly mention daily Communion, it is, nevertheless, strongly urged by the conciliar *Decree on the Catholic Eastern Churches* §15: "The faithful are strongly recommended to receive the Sacred Eucharist more frequently, even every day *(enixe quotidie)"*. *Enixe* means "strenuously". It is thus a text in perfect harmony with another conciliar recommendation made to priests – to celebrate the Eucharistic Sacrifice every day, as the supreme act of their priestly ministry.

Here we have the first explicit recommendation of daily Communion by an ecumenical council. How can we fail to notice the astonishing doctrinal progress concerning Eucharistic practice in the history of the general councils? Or note this "crescendo" in the exhortations of the Church, continually growing in her concern to have us participate in the Eucharist?

The First Council of Nicea, in 325, recommended that access to the Eucharist should be made easier for the dying. Lateran IV mandated, in 1215, the kindly, affectionate but grave obligation of yearly Communion. Trent recommended daily Communion implicitly but really in the context of a reminder of the Eucharistic interpretation of the Daily Bread given by the Fathers of the Church. [4] Vatican II crowned it all by explicitly recommending daily Communion for all the baptised. Without a doubt, it is one of the least cited, perhaps least discussed counsels of the last council! But it is nonetheless important: by definition it concerns the daily life of the Christian more than the undoubtedly useful declarations on religious liberty and episcopal collegiality!

Although the petition for Daily Bread also includes the idea of material bread and the Word of God, its Eucharistic sense, allied to the other two, maintained by the Fathers, by the Catechisms of the two Councils of Trent and Vatican II, and hence by the ordinary and universal Magisterium of the Church, is contained in the Revelation to which the Catholic Church adheres. [5]

Two later documents have completed, on a pastoral level, the stress laid by Vatican II on daily Communion:

- In 1967 the Holy See, in the Instruction *Eucharisticum Mysterium*, followed Saint Pius X in instructing parish priests, confessors and preachers to recommend frequently to the Christian people the practice of daily Communion. It recalled a point often misunderstood these days: it is appropriate to give Communion, even outside of Mass, when the faithful are really prevented from participating at Mass. It insisted that daily Communion should be available to the sick and to the elderly at any time, even when there is no danger of death.

•   In 1973 the Holy See published a ritual for the distribution of Communion outside Mass, providing a longer and a shorter rite, but with one point in common: the proclamation of the Word must shed light on and accompany the eating of the Eucharistic Bread. This is a particular example of the general principle of the liturgical reform carried out recently: the bread of the Word and the Bread of the Eucharist make up together the specifically Christian Bread of the New Covenant.

II   The Future: towards a fully Eucharistic Church.

If the declaration of Vatican II forcefully urging frequent Communion marks an important advance in the ecclesial awareness of Christ's desire to give Himself ever more fully to the Church, it above all invites us to a radical renewal of our pastoral approach to that end. I would like to set out here some fundamental aspects of the subject, which is nothing less than the elaboration of a pastoral praxis based entirely on that supreme evangelical counsel addressed to all, of daily Communion.

1)   Henceforth the preparation for the various Sacraments (especially those of adult Baptism, first Confession, Confirmation and Marriage) should be inseparable from preparation for daily Mass and Communion. It is pointless to object that many places are now without a priest, since the Code of Canon Law envisages the possibility of nominating laymen as Extraordinary Ministers of Communion (*CIC* 230). The Holy Eucharist is the *raison d'etre of* all the other Sacraments, and especially that of Holy Orders: our silence on the subject of daily assistance at Mass leaves numbers of young people without the superabundant sacramental power to answer God's call to a chaste marriage, to the priesthood or the religious life. The solution to the gravest problems facing the family and the Church depends upon the renewal of the urgent call to daily Mass. Without this, any true large-scale pastoral endeavour is impossible.

2)   The return to this call for daily Mass signals in the most concrete way the vocation (which was so clearly underlined by Vatican II) of each person to the perfection of charity: because the Eucharist is the Sacrament of fervent charity, the bond of perfection. How could anyone desire to become perfect even as our Father in Heaven is perfect, while scorning the principal means of achieving that perfection, daily Eucharistic union with Christ the Mediator?

3)   It is a paradoxical thought that, nearly a century after the liberating charter of Saint Pius X, there is not a single religious

Institute in existence that has as its main apostolate the propagation of daily Mass and Communion for the laity, while numerous Institutes have been founded to highlight other concerns which, while valid, are less fundamental.

Likewise, not one existing lay association seems to work for this end. It is permissible to imagine (and to pray) that the third millennium will be marked by the emergence of such Institutes and association.

4)   We must go further and recognise that the Church becomes most fully Church not only when her members come together around the Sacrament of the Cross continued in the Eucharist, but above all, when they do so every day. It is primarily through daily Mass and Communion that the Church grows unceasingly in essence and in love. Vatican II, quoting Saint John Chrysostom, tells us in its *Decree on Ecumenism* (§15) that it is by the celebration of the Eucharist that the Church is built up and grows.

Here we might perhaps explore an ecumenical digression. In 1783 an Athonite monk of the Greek Orthodox Church named Nicodemus the Hagiorite published a work on daily Communion presented to the French speaking public by the late Dominican theologian M.J. le Guillou. [6] According to this monk (who has been canonised by both the Greek and the Russian Orthodox Churches) anyone with a pure conscience must communicate each day, and thereby obey God's will. For Nicodemus, the Eucharistic Christ is that Daily Bread for which we pray to the Father. Moreover, for him the liturgy is, in essence, a Eucharistic assembly. The Church's *raison d'etre* is the union of each of her members with Christ, eaten and drunk after having been offered for the whole world. An ecclesiology is only fully Eucharistic when it recognises the necessity of each member of the Church to grow each day in love towards Christ and other Christians, through a more fervent participation in the Eucharist.

Our Father in Heaven wishes us to come together each day, and, together, to nourish ourselves with His only-begotten Son. By accepting our invitation to a worthily prepared daily Communion, we enable the Glorified Christ to continue to build His local and universal Church through us.

Let us not mince words: the simultaneous progress of Orthodox and Catholic believers towards daily Mass and Communion must constitute the foremost yet hidden means, obtained from Almighty God by the violence of a humble love, for our joint return to full and mutual hierarchical communion in the fullness of faith and in the shared Communion in the Immolated Lamb of God. To this end we hope that our

155

Orthodox brethren will lose no time in translating Nicodemus the Hagiorite's treatise on daily Communion into the various western languages.

5) Meanwhile time is short. Before the return of Christ in glory the Church must endure a final trial which will shake the faith of many believers. Perhaps already that mystery of iniquity, the Antichrist, is at work: that is to say, man who glorifies himself in place of the Eucharistic Christ (cf CCC §675, summing up several New Testament texts). The Church will only enter into the glory of the Kingdom by first passing through this final Easter, daily following her Lord closer in His Death and Resurrection (CCC §677). Indeed, time presses.

When will we see parish and presbyteral councils exchanging views on the best means of drawing members of the local community daily to Christ present on the altar and in the tabernacle? When will we see the bishops asking the Pope for an encyclical on Sunday Mass and daily Communion? When will we see a Pope convoking in Rome an episcopal Synod to examine the supreme evangelical counsel, urging daily participation for all in the Eucharistic victory of the Lamb of God? When will this supreme evangelical counsel of daily Communion (a counsel which, unlike the others, not only eliminates the obstacles to the obligatory perfection of charity, but actually positively nourishes it) be recognised as constituting a way of life which is to be found only in the One Church of Christ, and which is founded on faith in Christ? Such was the happy intuition of the great Spanish theologian Suarez: [7] the Christian way of life, which is the foundation of both the married state and the religious vocation, is itself founded on Baptism and Confirmation, and is a way of perfection. This way of life necessitates the perfection of charity, achieved by frequent, daily, reception of the Eucharist. The counsel of daily Communion is thus revealed as nothing less than Eucharistic perfection in charity. And thus it constitutes the highest point of the evangelisation of the living and sacramental economy of salvation. So in urging daily sacramental participation in the Eucharistic Sacrifice, the Second Vatican Council has thereby promoted a stable Christian way of life, leading to the eternal perfection of all the baptised and confirmed faithful.

NOTES

1   Cf. J. Daniélou, *Bible et Liturgie,* Lex orandi 11, Paris, 1951, ch. IX, pp. 194-219; P. Dumoulin, *Entre la Manne et L'Eucharistie,* Etude de Sg 16, 15-17, *Anal. Biblica* n. 132, Rome, 1994, chs. 7 to 11.

2   St Augustine, *Sermons pour la Pâques,* translation and notes by S. Poque, *Sources chrét.,* 116; especially *Sermon* 227, Paris, 1966.

3   Saint Pius X, *Actes,* B. Presse, Paris, t. 2, pp. 255ff.

4   Denzinger-Schönmetzer, *Enchiridion Symbolorum,* 35th ed., Rome 1963, nn. 1648 and 1649.

5   J.P. Bock, *Le Pain quotidien du Pater,* Paris, 1912, p. 485.

6   M.J. Le Guillou, O.P., *Essay on Athos and the Eucharistic life,* in the collection *Millénaire du Mont Athos,* t. 2, Paris, 1963, pp. 111 to 120; B. de Margerie, *Le mystère Eucharistique comme source d'unité,* a paper given during a symposum on P. Le Guillou held at Monmartre in December 1993, ed. Daint-Augustin, St Maurice, Switzerland, 1995, pp. 93-106, in the collection *Un homme pris par le mystère de l'Eglise.*

7   Suarez, *De Religione,* tract. 7, *Opera omnia,* ed. Vives, §§7-18; B. de Margerie, *Communion quotidienne et confession fréquente,* Resiac (Mayenne), 1988, pp. 36-36, §§42-43.

Supplementary Bibliography

Rouet de Journel, *Enchiridion Patristicum,* ed. 29, Fribourg en Brisgau, 1932.

B. de Margerie, *Vous ferez ceci en Mémorial de Moi,* Coll. Bibl. de Theologie Historique, Beauchesne, Montreal-Paris, 1989.

Homily delivered at High Mass on 10th October 1996

Dom Hervé Courau OSB (France)

Abbot of the Abbey of Notre-Dame de Triors

My most dear brethren,

Here, the Holy Mother of God has called us together, sinners each one of us. In this blessed place, Our Lady has recalled the importance of the nuptial robe. The sacrament of Penance restores the splendour of this robe, in order to give access to the Eucharistic banquet. It is not we ourselves who, by our generosity, made ready this wedding feast evoked by the Gospel. No, it is God Who takes the initiative in inviting us, in saving us, in loving us, and at what a price. He awaits sinners in order to save them; He does not await saviours who are full of themselves, but sinners who have renounced themselves, and seek conversion. He desires that we have a hunger and thirst for divine justice before we attempt to nourish the world, really and figuratively: *esurientes implevit bonis et divites dimisit inanes [Lk. I, 53].* In this place, the sacraments are approached with humility, because of the role accorded to the sacrament of Penance. By means of the very humiliation it involves, this sacrament makes a soul humble, and opens up a marvellously fruitful access to the greatest sacrament of all, the holy Eucharist. It makes the robe a nuptial one giving entry to the wedding feast, according to the last line in the Gospel of last Sunday.

I can say this particularly to you: one must admire the great and wise instruction included in the slow unfolding of the old lectionary. Certainly, it only gives us a selection of extracts from the Gospels, but they are very well chosen; they are often the very ones that the great Gregory commented on for his faithful; during many centuries they have educated Christian souls. In particular, St. Gregory explained this page of the Gospel in the Basilica of St. Clement, though we do not know at what date. *[cf. Bx. Schuster, Liber Sacramentorum, t.5, p.210].* The loss of Christian culture has caused the Church to rethink the liturgical presentation of the Word of God, but her traditional manner of liturgical reading has sufficiently proved itself, so as to yield its fruit in the few oases where such a tradition can continue to flourish.

It is not a question, however, of giving way to some sort of elitism, in contradiction to the humility and the feeling of contrition, which Laus so justly recommends. All the baptised belong to the royal race, participating in the sacred priesthood of the Unique Holy One, *regale sacerdotium, sacredotium sanctum [Peter 2, 5 & 9]*. Now, in royal families, it has been remarked, culture is transmitted at table: the history of a country is merged in the history of the family *[Dom Delatte]*. The table of the Scriptures is made for the baptised, who are prepared at the table of the Eucharistic feast. As is well known: what is learnt in this way in the family, is worth much more than what is acquired with difficulty on school benches. The latter culture always retains something artificial and strained; whilst in the former there is nothing forced, it flows from the source, it is in the nature of things. Liturgical culture flows from this source of sacramental life. Is there now no utterance, nothing transmitted from this table? For a very long time, too little confidence has been put in the catechetic efficacy of the rites in themselves, in the grace to be found in them, in the divine seed which they contain. The most active and fruitful participation is that of which the Holy Spirit is the chief master. Certainly, instructors are also needed to initiate movement, and God does not sanctify the idler who does not want to be interested in the one thing necessary. But a teacher will always be only an assistant; what is important comes from on high and from afar.

From this point of view, the Fathers of the Church are true models. Their immense genius willingly submitted to the sacramental life and to the primacy of grace; their catechesis was always liturgical, and sought only to reveal to their faithful the treasure placed in their heart by holy Baptism; they initiated the people into the liturgy with its double component parts, interior and exterior. At that time a spiritual life marked by self centred individualism was unknown. Such individualism was only to develop later, during the Middle Ages, after the discovery of the philosophical idea of "the person", an idea which was to become deformed in "the age of self-centeredness", to borrow the evocative expression used by Fr. Clerrisac to describe the Renaissance. The Renaissance was a time when people were inward looking rather than looking to the Creator to whom we all tend. It was an epoch which for this very reason had a grave tendancy to take itself seriously rather than looking seriously towards Him in whom all pure and simple solutions are to be found. Our ambiguous centuries have thus allowed the original egoism to attack anew the very rich notion of person and our human dignity. It is for us to find again the way of the Fathers, not in order to cultivate archaism in an affected manner, but in order to follow more profoundly the ways of recent saints, who have so marvellously emphasized the veneration due to the holy Eucharist.

The Eucharistic cult has, in effect, prolonged until our time this most wholesome spirituality that we admire in the Fathers. St. Thomas put into theological form this taking part in a cult, which each baptised soul carries within itself in an innate manner. In mingling

159

citations from the Fathers with those from St.Thomas, the council well indicated the depth of the exact view it maintained in order to understand profoundly the expression of active participation [cf. Liturgy No. 14 and Lumen Gentium No.11], to be associated with IIIa q,63, a 1 & 2]; it is partly bound up with the double notion inherited from the Fathers, namely the baptismal character and the common priesthood of the faithful [L.G. No. 10]. "The Sacraments of the New Law imprint a character, in so much as they appoint man to the worship of God, as it relates to the rite of the Christian religion", the angelic Doctor wrote; and he referred to Denys, the Syrian Mystic: "God, by the impression of a certain sign, gives to the baptised a participation in Himself.... He perfects the soul thus, in making it divine and a transmitter of the divine" [Hier. Eccles. c.2]. Divine worship consists in receiving divine things or in transmitting them to others, pursued St. Thomas; the character is a power, active or passive: in effect, the faithful receive, the ministers transmit the fruits of the redemption, providentially associated with the sacred signs which are the sacraments, and especially the greatest among them, the holy Eucharist. This passive power, inherent in the baptismal character is called, paradoxically in our day, active participation. But for a long time it had already been underlined that the highest action of the human spirit, the contemplation of divine things, is wholly imbued with docility, interior silence, and purity of heart. [cf. Vita Antonii, c.34; S. Pachomius, Greek Life No. 21; Cassian Conf. 1].

Of cult and culture, we can repeat: the link between the baptised person and the Eucharistic cult does not depend on an extrinsic, written culture, the soul has already within itself a disposition towards the divine through the sacraments; there is a connection between the nobility of its Christian being and the rites of the Church's prayer, even if this is not clearly seen, even if, only too often, it is not seen at all, because Christian initiation has not been bold enough to go to its ambitious conclusions.. The baptised person is not for all that less at home at the royal table, and his fundamental education takes place there, and he is brought up under the guidance of Divine Providence.. Nevertheless, in these times of uncertainty and disquiet, it is necessary to know how to account for the hope that is within us. In face of a culture of death, but also of a culture which, though good, is too dependent on the written word, we must know how to defend wisely what providence has entrusted to us. We are unprofitable servants. We must see to it that we are not also awkward servants, injudicious and imprudent, or worse, bad servants betraying the divine plan by making it too human, through the ends pursued or the means employed.

The object of your work is situated, I believe, at this high level. Also, as a monk, I accept willingly to leave the cloister for a moment, in order to encourage you in the battle of ideas, or better, in this spiritual endeavour, for what is at stake here goes beyond concepts. At this present time we are invited to live what we believe at a more profound level. *Imitare quod tractes.* St. Justin and St. Cyprian made answer for the thousands of less educated martyrs, who were less able to reply to the prefect. The strength of the Church lies, however, in the combined forces of great and small , *pusilli et magni, minores et majores.* [*Apoc.19, 5 and I-II q2, a 6*]. The world is at present suffering from not praying, from not finding its bearings in the - too often impoverished - liturgy which is presented to it. Guides are necessary to analyse this malaise, not in a spirit of meanness, but with the eyes of Faith. People are needed who know what they are talking about, and who live up to it. The formula of the Benedictine rule seems to me to be remarkably relevant: *mens nostra concordet voci nostrae,* our spirit should be in accord with the lips that pray, the exterior formulas must find an echo in the intelligence. Laus which evokes the moral purity necessary for union with God, is perfectly in line with your purpose: doctrinal purity, inseparable from purity of heart, moral purity, so necessary to anyone who speaks of divine things. May Our Lady help us to meet the needs of the present day, in fidelity and humility. Amen.

Eucharistic Rites
from Papal Ceremonial to the Roman Missal

Father Franck-M Quoëx (France)

Born in 1967 in Haute-Savoie, Father Franck Quoëx was ordained priest at Gricigliano (Florence - Italy) in 1992 by His Eminence Cardinal Pietro Palazzini. A member of the Institute of Christ the King Sovereign Priest, he is professor of liturgy and master of ceremonies at the seminary in Gricigliano. With a degree in theology from the Pontifical University, he lives in Rome where he is preparing a doctorate on the theology of acts of worship according to the teaching of Saint Thomas Aquinas, and where he carries out his priestly ministry. Interested in the liturgy since his youth, he has extensively studied the historical, theological and spiritual significance of the liturgical rites.

Introduction

It is important when one first enters into liturgical studies to form an idea of their dimension as ritual. The Sacred Liturgy, the comprehensive public worship of the Mystical Body of Christ, must be seen, over and above its social character and value, as a vast integrated complex of signs, actions and symbols transcending its time. The Liturgy, as seen and understood by a believer, is an assembly of signs; it is, in a word, the rites, symbolic rites - efficacious to a greater or lesser degree according to their nature - of sanctifying realities[1] . Furthermore, the liturgist would be well advised to increase his knowledge of the theological nature of each sign and thence its spiritual nature - what reality it signifies, why it requires this material agent or that, what value it has, whether it is men who give validity to signs or whether they derive their validity from the Incarnation which the Church consummates in the temporal order through the celebration of the Mystery[2]. The science of liturgy, provided it is based on sound theology, will include both a knowledge of rites - and not just for the sake of carrying them out with precision - and an understanding of their rationality and economy of grace achieved by studying the origins and the treasures of liturgical books. Such a study requires an acute feeling for the consistency and complete traditionality with which the forms of our liturgy have developed. If that evolution goes hand in hand with the development of doctrine, it is also linked with the formation of Christian civilisation at the heart of which the Church establishes itself as a perfect society. Her ritual functions, therefore, take on a social or political character, which makes the Eucharistic celebration of the Roman Pontiff and the Bishop a princely rite. This social or political aspect, which constitutes a fundamental key to understanding liturgical books, is particularly evident when one reads ceremonial books - from the Ordo Romanus I of the eighth century to the *Caerimoniale Episcoporum* of the post-Tridentine period - as well as the Roman Pontifical of which Mgr Andrieu wrote that it showed "the plan and foundation of the ideal construction."[3] ,which was "the edifice of medieval society". Now, as the inheritors of this Christianity, of "that time when, in the words of Leo XIII, States were ruled by the philosophy of the Gospel" [4], it is incumbent on us, whether we like it or not, regardless of the permutations of history, to accept its teaching and always remain faithful to its spirit.

Many things conspire to give to the post-Tridentine texts a character which nourishes the soul and the heart, inspires great zeal in young people and increases the number of vocations. This happens when young people discern the face of the Church as it appears in the sacred liturgy and especially in its purest Roman form. The many characteristics of post-Tridentine liturgical books include their perfect logic and congruence, the sobriety and magnificence of their rites when one takes the trouble to perform them as they should be, their feeling for order and sober elegance; in short, the atmosphere which seems to rise from these books in their very nature, as exemplified by the original editions of the Pontifical and Ceremonial of Clement VIII, so properly Tridentine in their style, midway between the over-ornate and an affected simplicity. Many of the rites which we do not understand and which will continue to puzzle even the most erudite liturgists, convey an atmosphere of antiquity which transports us to a former age and gives us a feeling of belonging in time and space to a Tradition which is not ossified but living.

As I had to undertake the task of studying these rites, I decided to conduct some research into their origins and discover the reason why they seemed to convey such a particular ecclesiological flavour. To do that, it was necessary to study pontifical rites, since a number of the rites of both Low Mass and High Mass can be understood only as they derive from a pontifical Mass or, better, Mass as celebrated by the Pope [5]. The family tree of Eucharistic rites has been plotted by a number of liturgists [6]. I propose, in this present discussion, to take an approach to reading Papal ceremonial which will lead us to study the transcriptions in the *Caeremoniale Episcoporum* of Clement VIII and the Roman Missal of Saint Pius V. It will be necessary in the first place to outline the apostolic Ceremonial, to describe its origins and later forms and to point out its influence on subsequent editions of the rubrics in Tridentine liturgical books. Then I

163

shall make this influence clearer by analysing certain Eucharistic rites from the papal *Ordo Missae* with specific reference to the ensemble of rites linked with Holy Communion. After examining these Eucharistic rites in their ceremonial context I shall try to determine, finally, what is the principle of interdependence between various Tridentine books and what, at the same time, is the difference.

I From the Papal Ceremonial of 1488 to the Roman Missal of St Pius V

1. The work of Agostino Patrizi Piccolomini

The Papal Ceremonial which was in use until recently, that is to say, up to the period after Vatican II [7] , was that of the first Renaissance, drawn up on the orders of Innocent VIII (1484-1492) by the master of ceremonies Agostino Patrizi Piccolomini, Bishop of Pienza and Montalcino. After publishing in 1485 his *Pontificalis ordinis liber* [8] he went on to consider matters related to the Pope and the Cardinals: the Conclave, Consistories, Councils, the Coronation and Consecration of kings, Canonizations, royal visits, the celebration of the Eucharist, the Divine Office, the liturgical year, the Sacraments, funeral rites, etc. The Ceremonial was first distributed in manuscript form but in 1516 a prelate of the Curia, Cristoforo Marcello, had it printed in Venice under the title: *Rituum ecclesiaticorum sive sacrarum caerimoniarum S.E.R. libri tres.* Marcello's edition contained modifications, variations, additions and omissions and it roused the ire of the then master of ceremonies, Paris de Grassi. [9] Among other things, the preface addressed by Agostino Patrizi to Innocent VIII, dated 1 March 1488, had been omitted. We are indebted to recent work by Father Marc Dykmans S.J. for the restoration of the preface in his critical edition of the work of the Bishop of Pienza. [10] In that preface the author laid bare the difficulties of the age, bound up as they were with the historical vicissitudes of the Papacy and the confusion they had caused to ritual, whence a great diversity of customs, disagreements between prelates and disputes between masters of ceremony which needed to be resolved by later legislation. And who would provide these rules? "Your Holiness", wrote Patrizi, "not wishing to see less order and beauty in divine matters than in worldly ones but a tranquility in all - a grave and dignified calm - has commanded me to use those old texts that you have extracted from the many archives of the Roman Church concerning the daily practices at the Papal Chapel. So I have applied myself assiduously for more than twenty years to arranging and editing the ceremonies as they were actually carried out by the Roman Pontiffs, omitting everything that is superfluous and outdated.[11]

This method of working must have been that of liturgists of the Tridentine period. It was characterised by a feeling for the purity and antiquity of the sacred rites and the unbroken, homogeneous development of the liturgy. Nevertheless, here and there, - as Dykmans comments, " Patrizi overlooked all the defects of a royal court with which the pontificate of his time was still afflicted. He wanted to find in liturgical tradition some elements which might save the Church of the Renaissance." [12]

Sources [13]

We do not have an exact list of the eight ancient volumes which Pope Innocent VIII consulted for his Episcopal Ceremonial, but we can observe their influence by studying Patrizi's text. If we need to establish the ancestry of the work, particularly as it concerns the rites for celebrating the Eucharist, then, given a knowledge of the *Ordines Romani* (the first descriptions of the solemn Eucharistic rites at Rome) of the 8th and 9th centuries, we must study the Roman books of the 12th to the 14th centuries which follow on from them. [14] *The Ordo Romanae Ecclesiae* [15] or the *Liber politicus* of Canon Benoit [16] (1140-1143), The *Ordo romanus* [17] of Cardinal Albino (1189) and The *Ordo romanus* [18] of Cencio Savelli, the future Honorius III, have all been edited by Monsignor Duschesne. The Papal *Ordo* Which Innocent III revised and which was followed in the papal liturgy before the move to Avignon, has been studied by Mgr Andrieu [19], and edited, thanks to Father van Dijk.[20]. Monsignor Andrieu has also edited the Pontifical of Durand de Mende, one of the sources cited by Patrizi, which provides only a few chapters on the liturgy of the pontifical Mass. [21] Mabillon attempted to collect the Roman ceremonial books from the *Ordo* of Gregory X, composed about 1273 (*Ordo* XIII of his collection) to the unpublished Ceremonial of Patrizi (1488). Father Marc Dykmans [22] has recently dedicated himself to this task.

Having studied the collected ceremonials of the Papal Liturgy from the end of the Middle Ages, Dykmans has been able to see at the same time what influence they had and what Patrizi contributed when he composed his Ceremonial. Patrizi's work is a work of synthesis, with the great merit of organizing, classifying and distinguishing its contents - his style remains always concise. "His sources are strictly traditional...the prayers are without change and often date back to before the year 1000. Rubrics are also taken from preceding centuries, especially the 12th to the 14th century...Patrizi quotes from the *Ordo* of Gregory X, the episcopal ceremonial of Cardinal Latino Malabranca Caetani, the Pontifical and other works of Durand le Speculateur, the ceremonial of Stefaneschi, the works of John of Sion, those written at Avignon up to Francois de Conzie, and those of Benedict XIII in Spain

165

and Pierre Ameil in Rome. He borrows also from his own works and those of Pope Pius II. His sources date from the 15th century and even if we can no longer retrieve the original in every case there is no doubt of their authenticity." [23] His book is the hinge between the Middle Ages and modern times.

Posterity

There is relatively little to say on the subject of Papal liturgy during the period from 1488 to post-Vatican II. We have the diary, or notebook, of Jean Burckard [24], at one time the efficient collaborator of Patrizi, which enables us to follow the evolution of Papal liturgy under Innocent VIII and Alexander VI and the work of the meticulous canon of Bologna, Paris de Grassi [25] under Julius II and Leo X. The edition of Cristoforo Marcello which dominated from 1516 to the reforms of Paul VI, though it was embellished, complicated and slightly distorted during the baroque period [26] - a peak period which must be distinguished, in Rome, from the strict Tridentine period which according to Mgr Jedin ends at about the time of the arrival of Urban VIII (1623). To that Pope we owe the edition of an *Ordo missae pontificalis in die Natalis Domini* for the use of the Pope. [27]

The secrecy which Paris de Grassi wished should surround the ceremonies of the Roman pontiff seems to have been well kept. Studies of the Papal liturgy, despite its being the model, were very few.

After the precious collections of documents and usages made by Dom Mabillon [28] and Dom Martene [29], the 18th century, thanks to the impetus which Benedict XIV gave to liturgical studies, produced the first and, we may say, the only great accounts of the rites of the Papal liturgy [30]. Dominique Giorgi, domestic prelate to Benedict XIV, made public the Papal liturgy and copied many hitherto unpublished documents [31]. Jean Baptiste Gattico, priest of the Lateran, undertook the publication of the *Acta caerimonialia selecta sanctae Romanae Ecclesiae* [32] which would have given the *Diaria* as well as descriptions of ceremonial if Gattico's work had not been suspended on the orders of Benedict XIV. Joseph Catalini, a prolific and hard-working liturgist, produced a commentary [33] on the ceremonial of Patrizi, in Marcello's edition which remains to this day the reference book for pontifical ceremonies [34].

Other commentaries, in greater or lesser depth, were published - those of Gaetan Moroni, in his monumental *Dizionario di eruditione storico-ecclesiastica* [35], should be mentioned. They were followed, at the end of the 19th century, by ceremonial protocols for the use of masters of ceremony [36] and indeed for the public at large [37]. We had to wait until this century before, thanks to Monsignor Michel Andrieu and, more recently, Father Marc Dykmans, there was published the complete set of ceremonial books for the use of the Roman pontiff [38], dating from the end of the 7th century up to the beginning of the Renaissance - a period when ceremonial, despite later additions, seemed to be fixed forever.

2. The Tridentine Liturgical Books.

After this very abbrievated account of sources and studies of Papal liturgy, it is important to recall the names of some who codified it: the original Roman Missal of Saint Pius V (1570), the Roman Pontifical (1595) and Ceremonial for Bishops (1600), both published by Clement VIII. These books, with the Roman Breviary of Saint Pius V (1568) and the Roman Ritual of Paul V (1614) were agreed to be compatible with the directives drawn up by the Fathers of the Council of Trent on 5 December 1563, in the twenty-fifth and final session [39]. One cannot over-emphasize that the principles of re-arrangement and revision for liturgical books which the Council of Trent formulated (as they appear for example in the Bull "Quo primum tempore" of Saint Pius V) are in substance contained in the two letters of Agostino Patrizi Piccolomini to Innocent VIII, one introducing the Pontifical of 1485, the other the Ceremonial of 1488. (The Roman Pontifical of 1595 derives from that of 1485.)

Furthermore, we know how effective was the contribution of Jean Burckard to the revision of the books of Innocent VIII, done on the advice of the Bishop of Pienza himself. The *Ritus servandus* of the Tridentine Missal is the same in substance, apart from a few details, as the *Ordo Missae* of 1502 in the Ceremonial for Alsace [40]. It is also known that Ceremonial of the bishops of 1600 was the product of those same sources which led to the drafting of the Ceremonial of Patrizi. Moreover, it is only proper to recognize, without exaggerating, the considerable influence of the Ceremonial which was written about 1508 by Canon Paris de Grassi [41], who succeeded Burckard as master of ceremonies at the Papal liturgy [42].

One arrives therefore at the following observations:

- Post-Tridentine liturgical books - and here I am referring to those which include or relate to the celebration of the Eucharist, that is to say the Missal, the Pontifical and the Ceremonial for Bishops - form a coherent body of texts on which, expert liturgists *(periti)* worked to develop ceremonies, especially Papal ones, using the sources mentioned.

- The coherence of these works presumes, beyond the categorisation and regulation of these rites, a doctrine or ecclesiological vision which imposes a discipline, an interior logic and a comprehensible form of ceremony. I therefore maintain the existence of fundamental charactertistics amounting to to a complete system throughout the post-Tridentine books, with evidence of their perfect compatibility and interdependence. This system can be appreciated only by reading the rubrics they contain.

Such a reading I am now about briefly to describe, by considering how certain Eucharistic rites from the Ceremonial of Pope Innocent VIII have been transmitted to the Roman Missal of Saint Pius V.

II Eucharistic Rites

The Papal Mass for Christmas Day, as Patrizi describes it in the second book of his Ceremonial, is, as far as the rules for its celebration, excepting minor details, the same as the medieval ceremony which preceded it. These rules apply also to the etiquette for princes and other nobles who are present and take part in the celebrations with the Roman pontiff. These rules, together with various testings and tastings, are the in novations which bear witness to the influence of the Renaissance. The preliminary rites of the Eucharistic celebration are rooted only in the Baroque age.

The text describes two different thrones for the Pontiff. The first is placed behind the High altar, in the apse, in the manner of a modest throne where the Pope, having come from his palace robed in cope and mitre, begins Terce and vests for Mass. Then, having blessed the incense, he goes to the foot of the altar for the penitential rite, receiving on his way the homage of three Cardinal-priests. Then he incenses the altar and is incensed by the Cardinal-deacon of the Gospel or one of the assisting cardinals, admitting him and the other two cardinal assistants to the double homage of the kissing of the papal cheek and breast , finally taking his place on the great throne, *ad sedem suam eminentem* [43]. Note that he does not take possession of this great throne at the far end of the apse, from where he can dominate the whole congregation, until the preparatory rites of the little throne and the confession and veneration of the altar are accomplished. From then on, until the beginning of the Eucharistic action, properly so-called - that is to say, up to the Offertory - all the ceremonies are directed towards the pontifical throne, all attention is directed towards it: it is from that vantage point that the Supreme Pastor presides over the liturgical celebration.

168

1. The Offertory and the offerings.

The singing of the Credo introduces the first steps in preparing the altar, which has so far remained unadorned except for the addition of the cross and seven candlesticks, which were at one time carried in procession. Patrizi states that the altar is the place where the *Regnum* (Papal tiara) is placed: statues of saints Peter and Paul are mentioned from the time of Clement V [44] onwards: later two reliquaries were allowed, but floral decoration was never allowed on the altar itself. The Cardinal-deacon minister and the Latin subdeacon laid a cloth of linen damask [45] on the altar and the deacon placed on it the corporal, the box of hosts and the purificators which had been carried by the subdeacon. The chalice, spoon and paten were brought by the sacristan after he had rinsed them at the papal credence-table: an acolyte followed him with the cruets and a silver cup for the pre-tasting, both rinsed by the sacristan. These last two rites were innovations. Previous ceremonials made no mention of anything which would suggest these ceremonies: as for the tasting of the matter of the sacrifice, the long ceremonial of Avignon, the draft of which dates between 1340 and 1362, refers to it as a possible usage [46]. Two assistant bishops placed the Missal on the altar, with its cushion and candlestick. The Pope, having taken off his gloves and washed his hands, left his throne and went to the altar where he began the Offertory rites.

Only slight vestiges remain in the Apostolic Ceremonial of the 15th century of the solemn presentation made to the Pope by oblates on behalf of the high nobility, and of the clerics of the court, and of the personal offering brought by the *subdiaconus oblationarius* - all rites described in precise terms by the *Ordo Romanus I* [47].

While unleavened bread gradually became the norm in the West from the 9th century onwards until its universal acceptance in about the middle of the 11th century [48], the oblation of the faithful, of great importance in France, comprised other objects among which, particularly, were oil, wax, candles and even gold and silver [49]. In the 13th century, the Ceremonial or *Ordo* of Gregory X no longer assumed a rite of oblation at a Papal Mass. Oblations took place only during extraordinary ceremonies. So it was that Patrizi described an Offertory rite for the Mass at a canonization: a Cardinal-Bishop was to offer the Pope two heavy wax candles, a Cardinal-Priest two large loaves and a Cardinal-Deacon two small casks of wine. Those Cardinals were escorted by gentlemen-in-waiting while an orator who accompanied each of the cardinals offered the Pope a candle and birds in a cage. The point here is that each personal offering was meant as a symbol to thank the Pope for a spiritual grace received. There must be no misunderstanding here: there was a clear distinction between the regular offerings and any additional elements introduced by the faithful [50]. This distinction, which is clear to any student of the Offertory rites, had been definitively formulated by St Thomas Aquinas. In his treatise on religion, he carefully distinguished between a simple gift made to God, freely and without prejudice, for the use of a religion or its ministers and the offering of some material things, in this instance bread and wine, which are to be used, in accordance with the prescribed offertory rite *sacrum facere*, to make a sacrifice [51]. We should therefore keep in mind the difference between a simple gift of offerings whose end is beyond the Holy Sacrifice and offerings which are part of that sacrifice. Only the bread and wine which the priests bring from the credence table -where they lie ready - to the altar, where the matter of the sacrifice is given to the Pope so that he can offer them in a distinctive rite as part of the sacrifice, can be the elements of the Offertory rite. A grasp of this basic distinction is therefore necessary for a true understanding of the nature of the Offertory [52]. What Joseph-Andre Jungmann calls "the completely hostile attitude in recent Roman liturgy towards the offertory procession" [53] seems to be explained by a desire to avoid all ambiguity about the significance of the act and the substance of the gifts being offered. The apostolic Ceremonial of Patrizi, as we have seen, kept the offertory for a canonization and the offering of gold for the emperor on the day of his coronation. The Roman Pontifical of 1595 provides, just before the Offertory rites, for the offering of a candle to the Pontiff by the candidates for the first clerical tonsure, to the major and minor orders and to those consecrated virgins. A newly consecrated bishop and a newly blessed abbot offer two large candles (*intortitia*), two loaves and two small casks of wine: a new abbess offers only the *intortitia* while kings and queens offer the Metropolitan Archbishop who crowns them as much gold as he is pleased to accept - "*quantum sibi placet*". The *Ritus servandus* of the Roman Missal of St Pius V says no more about the offertory than does the ordo for a Papal Mass according to Patrizi and that for an episcopal Mass in the *Caerimoniale Episcoporum* of Clement VIII. The *Ordo Missae* of Jean Burckard [54] in 1502 is much the same: it was left to Protestantism to put an end to it. One can, however, cite a multitude of examples of rites recalling practices derived from immemorial custom [55]. One knows also of recent attempts to restore something of these offering rites - alas, one cannot be unaware of the great extent by which they weaken the sacrificial aspect of the Offertory.

Let us continue our reading of the *Ordo* of the Bishop of Pienza.

When the Roman Pontiff reached the altar he received the paten with the Host and then the chalice, in which the deacon had poured enough wine for three people: the Pontiff, the deacon and the subdeacon. The latter mixed the wine with a little water, using a spoon. The Pontiff offered the bread, then the deacon, the ordinary

170

minister of the Precious Blood, together with the Pontiff said the form of prayer for offering the chalice. The celebrant put a silk cloth round the neck of the subdeacon so that he could cover the paten with it to protect it up to the Communion rites at the end of the *Pater Noster.* The paten is treated with reverence in this way in the *ordo romanus I.* However, at the end of the 7th century it was usually an acolyte who covered the large paten with a linen cloth and held it until the Canon, when a subdeacon *sequens* received the *super planetam,* and came in front of the altar until the subdeacon *regionarius* [56] took it from him at the end of the Canon [57]. There followed the incensing of the offerings, the altar, the Pontiff, the cardinals and the clergy etc, in order. The Pontiff continued with the Mass. For the Elevation and until after the Pontiff's Communion, eight apostolic acolytes held burning wax candles and another acolyte incensed the Blessed Sacrament.

2. Communion Rites

After the elevation the sacristan, his shoulders covered by a cloth, took in his right hand the golden tube which the Pope [58] would use to take Communion from the chalice: in his left hand he held the chalice. Preceded by an acolyte carrying the cruets and a golden cup and escorted by men at arms he went to the Papal credence table where, using wine and water, he washed the tube, the chalice and the golden cup and wiped them before placing them all on the altar. If it has so far clearly been the impression that the episcopal Mass described in the post-Tridentine *Caerimoniale Episcoporum,* apart from a few peculiarities and some recent rules of royal etiquette, is only an adaptation of a Papal Mass suitable for celebration in a cathedral, henceforth it will be seen as a unique rite which is being celebrated and which the Popes continue to preserve as a personal privilege, one which they did not grant even to the Patriarch of Lisbon [59] : namely *Communion ad sedem exaltatem,* that is at the throne[60] already mentioned in the *ordo romanus I.*

We know how complex are the Communion rites described in the *Ordo Romanus I.* I mention them here only in so far as they enable us to better understand the form of the rites about which we read in the Ceremonial of the Bishops of Pienza and the Tridentine books. First, the mixing in the chalice of a portion of the consecrated Host from a previous Mass with the wine, followed by the kiss of peace and then the placing on the great paten, held by the deacon, of the two consecrated Hosts that he had offered and from which he had broken a fragment to place on the altar. The celebrant then moved to the throne, followed by two subdeacons carrying the paten:the consecrated host was broken by the bishops and priests, the deacons doing the same with the host on the papal paten during the chanting

171

of the Agnus Dei. There followed Communion by the Pope, who retained a portion of the consecrated bread which he put in the chalice while saying the words for this second commingling: Communion of the Precious Blood in the chalice which the archdeacon presented to him: Communion by the clergy, under the species of bread, from the hand of the Pontiff on the throne and Communion under the species of wine received by the archdeacon at the altar and finally, general Communion of the Sacred Host and from a chalice *(scyphus)* in which wine had been mixed with the Precious Blood [61] .

The preparatory rites and the immixtion

Returning to the Apostolic Ceremonial of Patrizi, the formulae for the preparatory rites for Holy Communion which he describes are those found in the *Ordo Lateranensis* of 1145, the episcopal ceremonial of Prior Bernard [62]. The Eucharistic rites described by Bernard were those of the *Hadrianum*, amplified by Alcuin in the first years of the 9th century [63]. Non-Eucharistic worship closely followed the Romano-German Pontifical of the 10th century [64]. There followed thereafter only a single mixing of the bread and wine according to rites which are described in the Missal of the Roman Curia in the 13th century and the Roman Missal of Saint Pius V, that is to say: the replacing of the paten, the prayer *Libera nos*, breaking of the Host, *Pax Domini*, the first and only mingling of the bread and wine, the chanting of the *Agnus Dei*, the prayer *Domine Jesu Christe* and the kiss of peace.

It must be noticed however that the placing of the mingling of the bread and wine, kept by the Bishop of Pienza and before him in the long Ceremonial of Avignon (1340-1360) for a Papal Mass, is in no way like that described by Innocent III in *De Missarum Mysteriis* [65] and in the collection of ceremonies of the Papal chapel up to and including that of Stefaneschi, especially as commented on by Guillaume Durand [66].

These works place it at the very moment of the Pope's Communion. In this way the episcopal Mass of the Ordo lateranensis impinges on the papal liturgy and we are thus involved in one of those "interactions between liturgies", that is, between the Lateran basilica and the papal chapel, that Father Gy [67] has pointed out. In fact, up to the time of the long Ceremonial of Avignon, according to the writings of Innocent III, *Romanus pontifex alium in communicando morem observat* [68] . After the triple sign of the cross made with the fragment of the Host over the chalice while saying Pax Domini, he replaced the fragment on the paten: having given the kiss of peace, he remounted the throne and, in the sight of all, took the largest of the three fragments on the paten presented to him by the sub-deacon and divided it again, taking one part himself and putting the other in the chalice. Even though the mingling of blood and wine took place only once, it was still reminiscent of the *Ordo Romanus I* in recalling the solemn rite of the fraction at the throne and in retaining the second mingling *de ipsa Sancta quam mormorderat* [69] . The two other fragments provided Communion for the deacon and the subdeacon at the moment when these ministers received the sign of peace.

From here on, I return to the Ceremonial of Patrizi. The Pope had put down the fragment with which he made the sign of the Cross at the *Pax Domini;* he had given the sign of peace to the cardinal-bishop and finally he left the altar for the throne at the foot of the apse. At the altar the deacon-assistant raised to the level of his eyes the paten with the Host, made several circular movements and returned it to the subdeacon who carried it back to the left of the Pope. Having made the same movements with the chalice he took it to the right hand of the Pope. The Pontiff read the prescribed prayers from the book which one of the bishops held before him, then took and ate one of the fragments, sub-dividing the remaining fragment. Finally, the Pontiff drank some of the Precious Blood with the golden tube which the cardinal-bishop in attendance gave to him. So we see again the fraction at the throne and Holy Communion using part of the sacred species, the remainder being reserved for the sacred ministers.

We shall also see the close link which unites the sign of peace with the very act of communion.The celebrating cardinal-deacon who, along with the subdeacon had not received the kiss of peace at the altar with the attending cardinals and remained standing upright with the chalice and the tube, bowed, kissed the Pontiff's hand, received his Eucharistic fragment, kissed the Pope's cheek and then returned to the Epistle side of the altar where he received a little of the Precious Blood through the *fistula*. The subdeacon, on his knees with the paten, received Communion - in the form of the Sacred Host - from the hand of the Pope with the customary kisses of the papal hand and cheek and then returned to the altar to receive the Precious Blood after purifying the paten.

Catalani describes in his Commentary the old practice of giving a fragment of the main Host to some personage of importance, such as the Emperor. He gives the example of Pascal II and Henri V [70]. The *Ordo Lateranensis*, a Ceremonial for bishops, which therefore does not treat of the Communion of the Pope *ad sedem eminentem*, nevertheless prefigured it by treating of the Communion of the deacon and subdeacon with the Host of the celebrating bishop. During the Tridentine period this practice was reserved only to the Pope's Mass, at which the deacon and subdeacon were strictly required to receive Communion.

173

The kiss of peace and Communion.

We have seen that the reception of the kiss of peace by the sacred ministers was linked to the act of receiving Holy Communion The kiss of peace at the moment of Communion [71], a distinctive act in the liturgies of Rome and Africa from the time of St Augustine, was for a long time the customary practice. From the time of Gregory the Great it was retained at the *sicut et nos dimittimus* and in that became an essential preparation for receiving the Blessed Sacrament - the sign of unity between the members of the Mystical Body of Christ[72]. When the reception of Holy Communion became less widespread and took place less often, the kiss of peace which, beginning with the celebrant who kissed the altar and indeed the host and the chalice, was transmitted by the ministers and became a something of a substitute for the reception of the communion. In order to diminish this practice, which was coming to be seen as a mark of familiarity [73], the kiss of peace was ritualized in the Middle Ages and reserved for clerics during High Mass.

In the rites described by Patrizi the kiss of peace is restricted to the Communion, when the ministers kiss the hand of the Pope, receive Communion and then kiss his cheek. The same rite is to be found in Tridentine books, but at the altar. The *Caerimoniale Episcorum* has an echo of all this [74] on the assuming, Pontifical Mass at the Throne, in the Cathedral on Easter Day, for which it describes the general Communion of the ministers, the clergy and the people. Immediately after receiving Communion, the Bishop gives Communion to the deacon and the subdeacon with two Hosts taken from the ciborium and placed on the paten [75]. Each of them first kisses the Bishop's hand, receives the Host, stands up and kisses the left cheek of the Bishop (in a formal embrace) who pronounces *Pax tecum*, to which he responds *Et cum spiritu tuo*. The deacon then chants the *Confiteor*. The Bishop then says the *Misereatur* and *Indulgentiam*. During the distribution of Holy Communion, the deacon holds the ciborium on the right while the subdeacon holds the paten on the left [76] : the influence of the Papal Mass is obvious. The *Ceremoniale* specifies also that the canons who receive Holy Communion kiss the Bishop's hand before doing so and his cheek afterwards - the canons, let us recall, are dressed in their vestments. All the others, clergy and laity, kiss only the Bishop's hand. The Roman Pontifical of 1595 stipulates that those newly ordained shall kiss the hand of the Pope [77] . The kissing of the Bishop's hand or ring at the time of Communion, especially in connection with the rites prescribed for the ministers of Papal ceremonial and the Tridentine episcopal ceremonial can be seen as the vestiges of the kiss of peace signifying unity with the Bishop and through him, with the whole Church.

I would point out also another replacement for the kiss of peace: the kiss of the *osculatorium* or instrument of peace. This is the kiss that the Roman Missal of Saint Pius V [78] and the *Caerimoniale Episcoporum* [79] foresaw as possible, being given to the laity and even to clerics in non-solemn Masses. This same kiss was prescribed by Charles V of Spain in a formal document of 1548 in the *Formula reformationis* or *Interim* of Augsburg [80], as a way of answering the criticisms of the reformers.

We have seen recent attempts, with an archeological or pastoral flavour, to replace the kiss of peace by a simple form of a sign of peace not processing from the altar but being simply exchanged by those near together in the congregation: such attempts are not very convincing.

Communion from the chalice and the ablution

We have remarked on Communion under both species by the deacon and the subdeacon at a Papal Mass. Following the ancient practice, they had to take part in the completion of the sacrifice at the altar, of which they were ministers. They received Holy Communion in the form of the Precious Blood by means of the drinking-tube *(fistula)*. Patrizi, in his *Ceremoniale*, did not foresee that the Precious Blood could be given to anyone other than the ministers, not even the emperor. For that, he cited a precedent - the reception of His Imperial Majesty the Emperor of the Romans, Frederick III, who came to Rome on pilgrimages in 1468 [81] - a visit described by the first work of our author [82]. Notwithstanding that the Emperor read the lesson during the Matins for Christmas and that he processed on the left of the Pope during the Solemn Mass of the day, Paul II did not allow him to receive the chalice. Neither were the deacon and subdeacon allowed to receive from the chalice on that day, in order, as reported in the *Descriptio* of 1469, to answer the heresy of the Hussites in Bohemia, who maintained that Communion with the chalice was necessary for salvation [83]. The Roman Missal of Saint Pius V rejected the possibility of Communion with the chalice. Charles V of Spain hoped for a concession in respect of Germany: he had been dead (1558) for some years when, following the Council of Trent it was permitted, in 1564, under certain conditions. After experience of the practice, the concession was revoked, in Bavaria from 1571, in Austria from 1584 and, finally in 1621, in Bohemia and throughout Christendom [84].

Dom Martene has distinguished three ways of administering Holy Communion in the form of the Precious Blood [85]. The most ancient way consisted in drinking from the chalice itself. The *Ordo Romanus I* refers to a *pugillaris*, the first name for the *calamus* (pipe), which the people used to take the Precious Blood [86]. There is also the rite of intinction,

175

still practised in the majority of Eastern rites and recently restored in the West where, though accepted in the North before the 12th century, it had been rejected by the synods of Braga (675) and Clermont (1096).

One must however note that the chalice or cup *(scyphus)* from which, with the help of the *pugillaris,* the faithful of the *Ordo Romanus I* took Communion, contained wine with which the archdeacon had mingled a little of the Precious Blood [87].There used to be a practice of mixing a fragment of consecrated bread in the wine to bless it and make it holy - a rite which can be found in the Tridentine Mass of the Pre-sanctified for Good Friday, sadly abolished in 1955. In the same way there was in the 8th century, almost until the 12th, a rite for the blessing of the wine, by means of adding the Precious Blood, *ad confirmandum populum.*

At the period of the first great syntheses of dogma, the abandonment of Communion from the chalice put an end to the rite of sanctification described above. (Like Communion in the hand, which had been given up earlier, it had resulted in a number of accidents.) The rite itself one may think was already a restriction, whether it was seen as Communion of the Eucharist or a rite of purification. Whichever it was, in the 13th century the *ablutio oris,* the drinking of, or purifying the mouth with, wine[88], came into general use. The practice of taking a little water, or wine, or even nourishment, after the Eucharist, was a very ancient rite referred to by St Benedict in the West and St John Chrysostom in the East, among others. There was a fear that a fragment of consecrated bread - not yet unleavened bread - or some drops of the Precious Blood might fall out of the mouth in saliva. The practice remained after the introduction of unleavened bread and the ending of Communion from the chalice. A decree of Innocent III in 1204 required priests to rinse their mouths with wine [89]. The rinsing was oftern practised by all those taking Communion to whom a cup of wine was offered. No doubt this rinsing of the mouth was mistaken for Communion with wine mingled with the Precious Blood because it followed it. As Father Lebrun [90] wrote: "When Communion ceased to be given under both kinds it was thought necessary to offer wine to the faithful so that they would have enough drink to completely swallow the Host, which could adhere to the teeth or palate." The learned Oratorian was describing a practice which still prevailed in his day.

Therefore, one sees that in a Papal Mass the deacon and sub-deacon make their purification - the term used in liturgical books - from the chalice from which they have just received Holy Communion, while the Pope rinses his mouth with wine poured from a second chalice. The rinsing or purifying of the mouth by communicants is not at all unique to a Papal Mass. It is generally referred to in the chapter on rare practices in the *Ritus servandus* of the Roman Missal of

176

St Pius V as no longer in use. Jungmann however cites several recent examples of the practice. As the Missal described it [91] : away from the altar the server held a flask of wine in his right hand and a white towel in his left. Putting the purification to the lips of those who had taken Communion he gave them the towel to wipe their mouths. The Roman Pontifical of 1595 makes explicit reference to the practice during ordinations, not only for the newly ordained priests, with whom it was always used, but for all those involved in the ordination [92]. The *Caerimoniale Episcorum* prescribed it for the Communion of clergy and laity [93]. This was depicted in beautiful engravings of the time contained in two of the above-mentioned books. Only the requirements of convenience and hygiene can explain the almost total disappearance of so venerable a usage.

It was not only the mouth which was purified, but everything which came into contact with the consecrated species, including fingers and chalice. The Pope purified his fingers with wine from a golden cup, but did not drink this ablution. He sat, received the mitre, washed his hands [94] according to the requirements of princely etiquette and then returned to the altar for the Post-communion and Benediction. The Cardinal Bishops assisting then pronounced the absolution prayer and the ministering Cardinal Deacon put the *pallium* back on the Pontiff. Dressed in these sacred vestments the Pope returned to his palace.

Conclusion

Reading the *Ordo Missae* of Agostino Patrizi Piccolomini one is struck by the network of rites which surround the Sovereign Pontiff and amake manifest his status, as the words spoken at the putting on of the tiara express it, " father of Princes and Kings, lord of the world and vicar of Jesus Christ". We see him surrounded by many clergy: cardinals surround him, bishops assist him, princes are invited to wash his hands, each of the varied group of prelates of the Curia has his own function, often amounting to a liturgical ministry, as apostolic sub-deacons, acolytes, clerics of the Chamber. Around the Pontiff's throne is seen the highest point of the hierarchical structure of the Roman church. When, however, the Supreme Pastor leaves the throne from which he watches over the Church and the world to go to the altar in order to offer the Eucharistic sacrifice, the network of rites falls away: he becomes no more than a priest, magnificently surrounded indeed, offering the Holy Victim.

These comments on the nature of the pontifical celebration of the Pope apply also to a pontifical Mass celebrated by a bishop in his cathedral and indeed to a cardinal's Mass *extra Urbem* - though the

177

latter has less solemnity. The outline is the same, a sort of copy of the Papal liturgy: the chapter, priests and deacons, prepared, the prayer for terce and for resting at the little throne of the *Secretarium*, the rituals for washing hands, the presiding at the great throne etc up to the Sacrifice proper. As for the distinction between the pontifical ceremonial and the solemn priestly ceremonial, it is brought about by virtue of the distinction - strongly supported by the prescriptions of canon law - between the episcopal order and the priestly order. The presence, or the absence, of the papal insignia is the consequence of it.

In addition to some signs of honour and archaic practices of secondary importance, these are the rites prescribed for Communion *ad Sedem eminentem* which I have attempted to detail and which are notably specific, not being found in the episcopal Mass of the *Caerimoniale Episcorum*. Why did the Pope consume the Sacrifice not at the altar but at his throne? [95] There is no lack of explanations, some of them very allegorical [96]. I will simply remark that already in the *Ordo Romanus I* the Roman Pontiff had left the altar for the throne where he presided over the solemn fragmenting of the Eucharistic bread. Innocent III and, after him, Guillaume Durand, insisted on the public aspect of the fragmenting and Communion of te Sovereign Pontiff because, as the former said: *Christus in Emmaus coram duabus fregit, et in Jerusalem coram decem Apostolis manducavit* [97]. Whatever one makes of the allegorical aspect of this explanation, it is of importance insofar as it links closely the rite of infraction and consequently of immixtion to the Communion itself. Since the term *fractio panis* had been used in earliest Christian times to designate the Eucharistic sacrifice, the solemn fraction found in the *ordo I* which takes place at the throne, and the Communion which is linked with it, known to and described by Patrizi, tend to symbolize in the Eucharistic celebration of the Supreme Pastor, the unity of the Church through participation in the sacrament. [98] In a word, do these rites which are characterised by the greatest solemnity demonstrate, through and in the action of the hierarchy, that "the Eucharist makes the Church" ?

One cannot therefore say, as some of our "pastoral" liturgists have said ad nauseam, that the old liturgical books conceived of the Eucharistic celebration without participation in the Sacrifice by those present through the reception of Communion. From the 5th century there was a diminution in the frequency with which Communion was received by the Christian faithful. This phenomenon is accounted for by the obligation to receive Communion at Easter laid down by the Lateran Council (1215). Although it is outside the scope of this dissertation to analyse the causes of this phenomenon, I believe that the explanation as to why so few people received Communion during High Mass lies to some extent in the discipline of the Eucharistic fast. As these Masses were usually celebrated late· in the morning, people preferred to receive Communion during an early morning Mass, or even outside Mass. It was the actual rigours of the ancient Eucharistic fast that no doubt constituted a significant reason why people anticipated the functions of Holy Week by going to an earlier Mass.

As for the liturgical books, they merely sanctioned an established fact. I must, however, point out, with the help of the Roman Pontifical and the *Caerimoniale Episcorum*, that they present a liturgy of adminstration of Communion in common with that which is used in the *ordo romanus I*, even if they occasionally introduce certain peculiarities of Communion outside Mass. It would therefore be wrong to assume that the Tridentine liturgy makes an excessive distinction between the Holy Eucharist as Sacrifice and the Eucharist as Sacrament. On the contrary, the Communion of the Sovereign Pontiff *ad Sedem* highlights the function of Communion as a completion or consummation of the Sacrifice as a sacrament.

Pontifical Mass therefore is a Mass celebrated by a priest of the highest degree: the form of its ceremonial depends on the personal status of the celebrant - the Sovereign Pontiff, a bishop in his diocese, a cardinal in his titular church at Rome or anywhere *extra Urbem* - although with less solemnity for the latter. The details of the rites of the traditional pontifical scheme show how the role of master of liturgy is invested in the bishop: the unity of the Church is made manifest and fulfilled in the Eucharistic rite over which he presides. A priest of the second degree of the hierarchy is delegated by the Bishop to celebrate the Eucharist. He is not the originator of the ceremony but is delegated. He does not preside by virtue of being a priest of the second rank and his function is necessarily relative to his power to consecrate. That distinction enables one to understand the development of the pontifical rite, with its presiding at the throne, to the solemn rite where the priest-celebrant effects no presidential act beyond those at the altar for which he is empowered. In the Tridentine books on liturgy up to 1962 inclusive [99], a priest of the second order is given no liturgical status other than at the altar where he is empowered to carry out a sort of presidential function. It is on the basis of this fundamental distinction between priests of the first order and those of the second, rather than the absence of pontifical insignia, that the distinction between solemn pontifical ceremonial and solemn priestly ceremonial is made. The Tridentine works clearly express this distinction. Examination of the rites of a pontifical Mass, a scrutiny of a pontifical Mass with faldstool, the pure product of the Papal chapel, supports the proposition quite convincingly. The Pontiff who is celebrating does not have the personal status to preside over the occasion but is honoured for his episcopal function. He acts as if a pontiff, being given a special chair at the foot of the steps on the Epistle side. The chair is so placed in relation to the altar that he turns to the altar for each prayer and carries out at the foot of the steps the actions that a simple priest carries out at the corner of the altar on the

179

Epistle side. It is only the practice of turning the faldstool towards the altar that reminds one of the priest going from the centre of the altar to the epistle side.

It is a clear conclusion that the liturgical books, the pre-Tridentine Papal Ceremonial and the Roman Missal - not forgetting the Pontifical and Ceremonial for Bishops - see the celebration of the Eucharist as the act above all others in which the Church fulfills itself. They are all arranged around the central act of Sacrifice which is celebrated identically by Popes, bishops and simple priests. They are built on the foundation of two traditions of theology and liturgy, closely bound together and today, sadly, questioned. We should feel ourselves tightly bound to those traditions for all they have accomplished for civilization and culture as well as for Christians living in their own places and times. The last thirty years of struggle, sometimes bitter, always painful, on behalf of the traditional rites, have resulted, after a sort of journey across a desert, in this situation: that, despite some difficulties, those rites may be again officially practised. They can now be put within the grasp of young minds and the many souls that a sort of blackout of the Sacred has in a way disoriented. The overwhelming power of living Tradition has been shown in a way that many have judged, and still judge, impossible.

NOTES

1.Cfr. Saint Thomas Aquinas, *Summa Theologiae*, IIIa, q. 60, a. 2: Signa dantur hominibus, quorum est per se nota ad ignota pervenire. Et ideo proprie dicitur sacramentum quod est signum alicuius rei sacrae ad homines pertinentis: ut scilicet proprie dicatur sacramentum, secundum quod nunc de sacramentis loquimur, quod est signum rei sacrae inquantum est sanctificans homines.

2. Cfr. Fr. Joseph de SAINTE-MARIE, *L'Eucharistie Salut du monde*,Paris, 1981, pp. 295 et al.: "In themselves, Christ's Resurrection and Ascension accomplish everything. But subsequently we were given a sort of delay or time span for the accomplishment of the Mystery in and through the Church. If the Incarnation, the Passion and the Resurrection-Ascension are the three fundamental periods of the realisation of the Mystery through and in Christ during his life on earth, at a particular point in history, these three periods will in some way continue to live on in the life of the Church. They will be Pentecost, which is like the Incarnation prolonged in the Church, the Passion of this Church, established in her status as Body and Spouse of Christ, and his glorious Resurrection at the time of the Second Coming (Ap. 21, 2). Only then will the end of history, begun with the Ressurection of Christ, and even with his conception, be consummated. And that will be so because the Church, in the time allotted to her for that purpose, will have fulfilled her mission, which is precisely to consummate the Mystery of Christ. She does this by the power of the Spirit, in which she has been conceived and through whom she is born on the day of Pentecost. She does this through her witness and THROUGH HER LITURGY, that is to say, BY THE CELEBRATION OF THE SACRAMENTS OF THE MYSTERY, THE PERMANENT SOURCE OF THIS OUTPOURING OF THE SPIRIT OF THE RISEN CHRIST IN HIS MYSTICAL BODY. She does this through her whole life."
(pp. 298-299).

3. Mgr. M. ANDRIEU, *Le Pontifical Romain au Moyen Age*, T. III : *Le Pontifical de Guillaume Durand*, Citta del Vaticano, Coll. *Studi e Testi 88*, 1940, pp. VIII et seq. "If you have a sharp awareness of what Christianity was like in the days when its unanimity was not broken, if you want to know the ideal which she exemplified, the ideas on which she strove to model itself, you must spend time over these ancient texts, penetrate their meaning and come to realise how they were understood. At the end of the thirteenth century, they reflect all aspects of the constant relationship which the Christian people had with the supernatural world" (p. XIII).

4. Leo XIII, *Immortale Dei*. 1st November 1885.

5. Cf Mgr J. NABUCO, *la liturgie papale et les origines du Ceremonial des Eveques*, in *Miscellanea Liturgica* Mohlberg, Rome, 1948, vol I "...If one compares the pontifical functions in the Ceremonial for bishops with those in

the Roman Ceremonial, that is to say, the Papal Ceremonial, one sees immediately that one is the model for the other. I remember very well my first reading of the Ceremonial for bishops, at the time when I was beginning my theological and liturgical studies. I read and re-read the little book without understanding...I tried to put myself into the same state of mind as the authors or author of the book. Some chapters seemed to me well written, even beautiful...However, I still could not arrive at a satisfactory understanding of this mysterious book....At last, after long digressions, I came to understand that the Roman liturgy is the solemn Mass of a bishop in his cathedral. All the other functions described in the Ceremonial or Pontifical were derived from that principal one. The solemn Mass of a priest, following the Ritus servandus of the Missal was no more than the pontifical Mass without the throne, without pontifical insignia and with fewer clergy." (pp. 282-283)

6. Cf., among others, J.A. JUNGMANN, *Missarum Solemnia*, Paris, 1951, Vol I pp. 243-256: "The bishop, surrounded by his clergy, offering the sacrifice in the centre of the community, is the basic form of the celebration of Mass...The *Ordines romani* for a Papal Mass present the same picture...The *Ordines romani* for a Papal Mass having become, down the centuries, the rule for pontifical Mass in almost all of the West, the same arrangements are found elsewhere (p. 243)...Pontifical Mass in practice and in its highest form, the Papal Mass (where the presence of the faithful is a fact, not a necessary factor) are the direct continuation of the full Eucharistic ceremony presided over by a bishop. Even the High Mass with the deacon and sub-deacon, as said by a simple priest, a Mass, one might have thought, that could be explained as a Low Mass which is subsequently developed into a more solemn form, appears actually as a latin derivation from the pontifical Mass. That is why, even today, the difference between a pontifical Mass and a High Mass said by a priest is relatively slight in the Roman liturgy" (pp.248-249) (It is proper to add to this observation of J.A. JUNGMANN that the reduced rite of pontifical Mass with faldstool purely Roman in origin, is another level between a pontifical Mass and the High Mass of a simple priest. Closer to the latter than the former, the faldstool of a bishop outside his diocese, following the example of a priest's chair does not, unlike the Ordinary's throne, provide that bishop with a place to preside. All his ritual acts are related to the altar.) See also: C. VOGEL, in *Introduction aux sources de l'histoire du culte chretien au Moyen Age*, Spoleto, 1981, p. 128 and, for a bibliography, see pp 129-130 and 358-359: N.K. RASMUSSEN O.P. *Celebration episcopale et celebration presbyterale: un essai de typologie*, in *Segni e riti nella Chiesa altomedievale occidentale*, Spoleto 1987, Vol II pp 581-603, "the majority of these texts show that a priest's Mass has to be seen as a reduced version of a bishop's Mass and not as a Eucharist distinct from that of a bishop" (p. 602)

7. Cf the introduction to the new *Caerimoniale Episcoproum*, Citta del Vaticano, 1985, p. 8: *Qui liber, stilo mutato, a Christophoro Marcello, archiepiscopo electo Corfirensi...nostris quoque diebus, in caerimonius Romani Pontificis usui remansit.*

8. Concerning the revision of the Pontifical of Durand de Mende carried out by Agostino Patrizi Piccolomini, see M. DYKMANS S.I. *Le Pontifical Romain revise au XVeme siecle*, Citta del Vaticano, *Studi e Testi* 311, 1985, pp 108-123.

9. For the controversy of Paris de Grassi, cf: J. MABILLON-M. GERMAIN, Museum Italicum Paris. 1687-1689, II pp 587-592 = P.L. LXXVIII, 1401-1406: J. NABUCO- F. TAMBURINI, *Le Ceremonial apostolique avant Innocent VIII*, Rome 1966, pp. 33*-38*, 51*: M.DYKMANS S.I. *L'oeuvre de Patrizi Piccolomini*, Citta del Vaticano, Studi e Testi 293-294, 1980, Vol I pp 33*-42*.

10. M. DYKMANS: *L' oeuvre de Patrizi Piccolomini ou le ceremonial papal de la premiere Renaissance*, Citta del Vaticano, *Studi e Testi*, pp 293-294, 1980.

11. "Hec igitur, ut reor, provide considerans sanctitas tua, beatissime pater, cupiensque ut in rebus omnibus, tam divinis quam humanis, decus et ordo debite servetur, utque sine tumultu, quite, tranquille, cum gravitate et dignitate omnia peragantur, iniunxit mihi ut tam ex libris maiorum, quos ex archivis Romanae ecclesie complures deprompsit, quan ex quotidiano usu capelle apostolice, in quos annis supra viginti non sine labore assiduo versatus sum, cerimonias omnes, quibus nostro tempore uti consueverunt Romani pontifices, pretermissis superfluis et antiquatis, in ordinem redigerem." Cf M. DYKMANS S.I. *op. cit.* Vol I pp 5-8: trad. franc. pp 27*-29*.

12. M. DYKMANS, Op. cit, Vol I : "What was the spirit of the new book? Patrizi has left a memorable comment on the ceremonies of the liturgy. Ritual is essentially religious. 'Ceremonial is nothing other than the honour owed to God by men, because He is God.' The honour given to God can be found in those who have proclaimed it to men. It is in this sense that an author wishes to preserve everything of value handed down through the ages. He leaves out none of the old forms of prayer, but rather adds one when he finds one. He also keeps all the rubrics in the preceding books, trying always to make them more practical and precise...(pp. 31*-32*)

13. See A.G. MARTIMORT, Les *"Ordines"*, les Ordinaires et les Ceremoniaux. Brepols, Typologie des sources du Moyen Age occidental, Fasc. 56, Turnhout, 1991. For the papal Ceremonial, pp. 91-106.

14. For these books or "Ordinaries", cf. A.G. MARTIMORT, op. cit., pp. 71-73.

15. In M.P. FABRE-L.DUSCHENE, *Le "liber censum" de l'Eglise romaine*, Paris, 1905, Vol II, pp. 139-177.

16. "His 'Polyptyque' will remain a resource for his successors because all these authors will depend on one another. Their references, generally unacknowledged, can often be identified" in M.DYKMANS S.I. *Le ceremonial papal de la fin du Moyen Age a la Renaissance*, Bruxelles-Rome,

Bibliotheque de l'Institut Historique Belge de Rome, Fasc. XXIV. 1977, Vol I, pp. 7-8.

17. Ibid, vol II pp 85-137

18. Ibid, Vol I, pp 290-316

19. M. ANDRIEU, *Le missel de la Chapelle papale a la fin du XIIIeme siecle*, in *Miscellanea Francesco Ehrle*, Citta del Vaticano, *Studi e Testi* 38, 1924, Vol I, pp 348-376: The Missal of the Papal chapel "which had never left the soil of Italy...must be regarded as a very truthful witness of the Papal liturgy as it could be seen in the Lateran before the departure of the Curia." (p. 361): *Note sur un exemplaire de l'Ordinaire papal transcrit en 1365 pour le cardinal Albornoz*, in *Revue des sciences religieuses*, 5 (1925) p. 275. Msgr ANDRIEU published extracts from this *Ordo* in *Le Pontifical romain au Moyen Age*, T. II, *Le Pontifical de la Curie romaine au XIIIeme siecle*, Citta del Vaticano, *Studi e Testi* 87, pp 541-578: *Ordo qualitum agendum sit feria quinta, sexta et septima ante Pasch, ex Ordinario capellanorum Papae et e Missali romano s. XIII.*

20. S.J.P. van DIJK O.F.M. *The Ordinal of the papal court from Innocent III to Boniface VIII and related documents*, Fribourg-en-Suisse, 1975, Spiclegium Friburgense 22.

21. Cf M. ANDRIEU: *Le Pontifical romain au Moyen Age*, T. III, *Le Pontifical de Guillaume Durand*, Citta del Vaticano, *Studi e Testi* 88, 1940, pp 632 et seq.

22. M. DYKMANS S.I. has published six volumes, works of the highest erudition: *Le ceremonial papal de la fin du Moyen Age a la Renaissance*, Rome-Bruxelles, Bibliotheque de l'Institut Historique Belge de Rome: T. I, *Le ceremonial papal du XIIIeme siecle*, 1977, Fasc XXIV,L T. II, *De Rome en Avignon ou le Ceremonial de Jacques Stefaneschi*, 1987, Fasc XXV: T. III, *Les textes avignonnais jusqu'a la fin du Grand Schisme d'Occident*, 1983, Fasc XXVI: T. IV, *Le retour a Rome ou le Ceremonial du patriarche Pierre Ameil*, 1985, Fasc XXVII. To these four volumes should be added the two volumes of *L'oeuvre de Patrizi Piccolomini ou le ceremonial de la premiere Renaissance, loc. cit.* Father van DIJK had already published a critical edition of extracts from the *Ordinarium Gregorii X* in The Ordinal of the papal court from Innocent III to Boniface VIII and related documents, *op.cit.* including *De missa papali*, pp 583-589. One should note also, between studying the ceremonial books of the end of the Middle Ages and the Ceremonial of Patrizi, the edition of *Liber Caerimoniarum* of Nicolas V, published in the Ceremonial of Cardinal Stefaneschi (Ordo XIV of Mabillon) thanks to Pierre Gundisalvi de Burgos, clerk of ceremonies from 1445 to 1469. Cf. *Le Ceremonial apostolique avant Innocent VIII, loc. cit.* edited by F. TAMBURINI and J. NABUCO.

23. M. DYKMANS S.I.: *L'oeuvre de Patrizi Piccolomini, op.cit.*, Vol I pp 30*-31*.

24. Cf E. CELANI: *Johannis Burckardi Liber notarum*, in *Rev. ital. scr.* 32, I, 1-2,

Citta di Castello and Boulogne, 1906-1932.

25. Father M. DYKMANS advertised, in advance, an edition of the Diary of Paris de Grassi in three volumes, to bhe published in *Studi e Testi*, Bibliotheque Apostolic Vatican. It has not yet appeared. Was it completed before he died?

26. Cf J. NABUCO, *Le Ceremonial apostolique avant Innocent VIII, op. cit.* pp 22* *et seq.* : "Moreover, the Papal liturgy became so over-elaborate that it became necessary to prune it so that it did not become merely a brillant show. The Papal Mass, in itself, was not at fault: it was the preliminaries which were ornamented to excess." See also L. BOUYER, *La vie de la liturgie, Une critique constructive du mouvement liturgique, Lex Orandi* 20, Paris, 1956, pp 11-12.

27. I have not been able to refer to the first edition of the *ordo* of Urban VIII, but used that of D. GIORGI, *De liturgia Romani Pontificis in solemni celebratione missarum, ubi sacra mysteria ex antiquis codicibus, praesertim vaticanis, aliisque monumentis plurimum illustrantur,* Rome 1731-1734, Vol II 1. IV. Catalani often quotes from the *ordo.*

28. J. MABILLON-M.GERMAIN, *Museum italicum,* op. cit.

29. E. MARTENE, *De antiquis Ecclesiae ritibus libri tres,* Anvers, 4 vols 1736-1738 (Georg, Hildesheim, 1967)

30. Among the authors of the 18th century who devoted important works to the Papal liturgy, in addition to the better known ones that I have referred to, Monseigneur J. NABUCO has highlighted in *Le Ceremonial papal, op. cit.* p 39* the Protestant Christian Gottlieb HOFFMAN (1692-1735), adviser to the King of Prussia. His *Nova scriptorum ac monumentorum, partim rarissimaorum, partim ineditorum, collectio,* published in two volumes at Leipzig (1731-1732) contains the first edition of the Diary of Paris de Grassi preceded by a thesis on that author and on the Roman Ceremonials (Vol I): the *Liber Diurnus Romanorum Pontificum* and the Ceremonial of Patrizi in Marcello's edition. See also M. DYKMANS in L'oeuvre de Patrizi Piccolomini...op. cit. T. 1 p 39* n. 17 - where he corrects to HERMANN the name of the author whom NABUCO wrongly referred to as HOFFMAN.

31. D. GEORGI *op. cit., supra*

32. *op. cit.,* 2 Vols, Rome 1753

33. G. CATALANI, *Sacrarum caerimoniarum, sive Rituum ecclesiasticorum sanctae Romanae Ecclesiae libri tres a Patricio ordinati et a Marcello editi, nunc commentariis aucti,* 2 vols, Rome, 1750-1751.

34. :...It is no secret that at the Conclave of 1958 the question arose as to whether someone who was not a Cardinal could be elected. Catalini was consulted in preparing the response. The ancient Ceremonial had, in effect, foreseen the issue: the election of Saint Celestine V had not been forgotten. (J.

NABUCO, op. cit p 36*, n, 85)

35. G. MORONI: *Le capelle pontificie, cardinalizie e prelatizie,in Dizionario di erudizione storico-ecclesiastica*, Venice, 1841, Vols VIII and IX. See also F. CANCELLIERI; *Descrizione de tre pontificale che si celebrano nella Basilica Vaticana per le feste di Natale, Pasqua e di San Pietro*, Rome1788: *Descrizione delle Capelle pontificie e cardinalicie, Rome 1790: Storia de solenni possessi de sommi pontifici da Leone III a Pio VII*, Rome, 1802.

36. RINALDI-BUCCI; *Caerimoniale Missae quae a Summo Pontifice ritu solemni celebratur*, Ratisbon, 1889.

37. G.B. MENGHINI; *Le solenni cerimonie della Messa pontificale celebrata dal Sommo Pontifice*, Rome, 1904: See also J. BRINKTRINE; *Die feierliche Papstmesse und die Zeremonien bei Selig und Heiligsprechungen*, Freiburg, 1925.

38. I would commit an injustice if I did not refer here to the works of M.P. FABRI-I. DUSCHENE, *Le 'liber censuum' de l'Eglise romaine*, op. cit. See J. NABUCO- F. TAMBURINI, *Le ceremonial papal...op. cit.* See B. SCHIMMELPFENNIC : *Ein bisher unbekannter Text zur Wahl, Konsecration und Kronung des papstes im 12. Jahrundert, in Archivium historiae pontificae*, 6, 1968 pp 43-70: *Die Zeremonienbucher der romischen Kurie im Mittelalter,Tubingen, Bibliothek des deutschen historischen Instituts in Rom*, 40, 1973, etc. See also S.J.P. van DIJK-J. H. WALKER, *The ordinal of the papal court...op. cit.* etc. Cf F. WASNER, *De consecratione, inthronisatione, coronatione summi pontificis, in Apollinaris*, 8, 11935, pp. 86-125, 249-281,428-439: *Texte des 15 Jdhs. zu Zeremoniell*, in *Traditio*, XVI, 1958, etc.

39. Cf H. JEDIN, *Concilio tridentino e riforma dei libri liturgici,in Chiesa della fede, Chiesa della storia*, Brescia, 1972, pp 391-425: see also, by the same author: *Il Concilio de Trento*, 1981, T. IV, Vol II, pp 344-347.

40. The *Ordo Missae* of Jean Burckard was published by W. LEGG, *Tracts of the Mass*, H. Bradshaw Society, London 1904 pp 126 *et seq.* : cf also the Appendix to *Ephemerides liturgicae*, Rome, 1924.

41. Paridis GRASSI, *De caeremoniis cardinalium et episcoporum in eorum diocesibus libri duo*, Rome 1564. This posthumous edition - Paris de Grassi died in 1528 - was the work of Francesco Mucanzio, one of Grassi's successors. On Paris de Grassi, see J. NABUCO ; *La liturgie papale et le Ceremonial des Eveques, op. cit.* pp 287-292, and, by the same author, *Le Ceremonial papal avant Innocent VIII, op cit.* pp 33*-34*. See also L. GROMIER : *Commentaire du caerimoniale Episcoporum*, Paris 1958, in which the author reveals the influence of the canon from Bologna in the text of the *Caerimoniale Episcoporum* of Clement VIII.

42. For the precise influence of the Ceremonial of Paris de Grassi on the editors of the Ceremonial of 1600, see M. DYKMANS, Le pontifical romain revise

au XVeme siecle, op. cit. p 122.: "The book by Patrizi begins now with a long liturgy which Durand left out and which the Roman Pontifical (of 1595) made the mistake of ignoring in order to reserve it for the Ceremonial of Bishops. In fact, it is the most solemn pontifical ass. This Mass takes up 17 pages, of which I will say only that they come half way between Latino Malabranca (about 1280) and the *caerimoniale episcoporum* of 1600. The latter is closer to the 15th and 16th century editions of the Pontifical than to Paris de Grassi: *De caeremoniis cardinalium et episcoporum in eorum diocesibus* (1564). It is Patrizi's text which would have shown the place where it was printed, rather than the other."

43. Cf. n. 867 in DYKMAN'S edition, *op. cit.* T. II p 302.

44. Cf. M. DYKMANS, *Le ceremonial papal*, T. II p 342.

45. "Among the ceremonies of the Papal Mass whose origin and meaning are unknown, one must mention the cloth for the *Incarnatus est*, called the '*strogolo*'. It is a cloth of damask linen, divided in three parts and decorated with golden lace, and of the same size as the altar table. It is put on the altar before the Mass and folded towards the candlesticks. After the *Incarnatus est* and before carrying the purse with the corporal, the Cardinal deacon, aided by the sub-deacon of the Mass, unfolds the cloth." (J. NABUCO, *Le ceremonial papal...op. cit.* p 48.) See also L. GROMIER, *Commentaire du Caerimonial de Episcoporum, op. cit.*, pp 249-250. J.A. JUNGMANN (*op. cit.*, T. II p 328) regards it as a vestige of the old corporal which stretched the whole width of the altar.

46. "Et in fine (incenset) episcopum non cardinalem, si serviat pape, ut vidi fieri, tam in parando altare quam in eligendo hostiam per papam consecrandam , ac ponendo vinum et aquam in calice, et probam de illis fieri faciendo", ed. DYKMANS, in *Le ceremonial papal, op. cit.*, T. IV p 155 n 32.

47. Cf M. ANDRIEU, *Les ordines romani du haut Moyen Age*, Louvain, ed. 1971 Vol II pp 91-94.

48. Cf J.A. JUNGMANN, op. cit. pp 287-291.

49. Id, T. II pp 279-298.

50. J.A. JUNGMANN, op. cit. pp 287-291.

51. Saint THOMAS AQUINAS, *Summa Theologiae*, IIa. IIae, Q 85, A. 3. ad 3 um: " 'sacrificia' Proprie dicuntur quando circa resDeo oblatas aliquid fit: sicut quod animalia occidebantur, quod panis frangitur et comeditur et benedicitur.Et hoc ipsum nomen sonat: nam sacrificium dicitur ex hoc quod homo facit aliquid sacrum. ....

'Oblatio' autem directe dicitur cum Deo aliquid offertur, etiam si nihil circa ipsum fiat: sicut dicuntur offerri denarii vel panes in altari, circa quos nihil fit. Unde omne sacrificium est oblatio, sed non convertitur". See also Q 86 A. 1: "...Nomen oblationis commune est ad omnes res quae in cultum Dei exhibentur. Ita quod si aliquid exhibeatur in cultum divinum quasi in aliquod sacrum quod inde fieri debeat consumendum, et oblatio est et sacrificium...Si vero sic exhibeatur ut integrum maneat, divino cultui deputandum vel in usus ministrorum expendendum , erit oblatio et non sacrificium".

52. Cf Dom B. CAPELLE O.S. B. *Nos sacrifices et le sacrifice du Christ a la messe,*in *La messe et sa catechese,*Paris, 1947 coll. Lex orandi: 7, pp 154-179: "At the offertory execute in their minds the act which at one time the whole congregation carried out in advancing towards the altar: each one giving his offering to the priest for him to consecrate. The offering, as in former times, is no more than the bread and wine. The faithful know very well that the significance, the efficacy and the importance for our good and that of the Church of the act, derive from the fact that the bread and wine will become the body and blood of Christ. The scope of the offertory is no less vast than that of the whole Mass: our spiritual participation cannot be narrower or more restricted... To entrust the matter of the sacrifice to the priest so that he then can take action to bring us close to God, is to join ourselves in advance and in the depths of our being, to the offering which he will make a few moments later. So one can see that the offertory is in no way a potential, unrealized part of the actual oblation. It is wholly of the oblation in being its preparation: *'tuo nomine preparatum'*. The offertory is not a partial act which will become absolute: it is, on the contrary, a complete but relative act - that is to say that the Christian anticipates, as a spiritual reality, his participation in the consecration, his attention already fixed on the imminent ascrificial offering in an essential union with it...What one gives to God, with total respect for the priest, is indeed the bread and wine, already in effect the body and blood of Christ"...(pp171-172). See also the *Debat sur l'Offertoire* which follows the intervention of Dom CAPELLE and the discussion of the question put by Dom L. BEAUDOIN: Does not the way in which these things are offerede excessively reduce the participation of the faithful in the Mass, contrary to the whole intention of the liturgy? We touch here on the crux of the contemporary liturgical problem.

53. J.A. JUNGMANN, *op. cit.* T. II p 291.

54. Cf W. LEGG, *Tracts on the Mass, op. cit.* p 149 : dicto offertorio, si sint volentes offerre, celebrans accedit ad cornu epistolae, ubi stans detecto capite, latere suo sinistro altari verso, deponit manipulum de brachio sinistro, et accipiens illud in manum dextram porrigit summitatem ejus singulis offerentibus osculandum dicens singulis: Acceptabile sit sacrificium tuum omnipotenti Deo, vel: Centuplum accipias et vitam aeternam possideas. (Quoted by J.A. JUNGMANN, op. cit. T. II p 289 n 89)

55. Cf. E. MARTENE, *De antiquis Ecclesiae ritibus, op. cit.* 1 pp 386 et seq.: P. LEBRUN, *Explication litterale, historique et dogmatique des prieres et des ceremonies de la Messe,* Paris 1716 pp 226 *et seq.* See also J.A. JUNGMANN, *op. cit.* T. II pp 281-298.

56. For the different categories of sub-deacons and their various functions in the Papal liturgy in the course of history, see A. CUVA: *Pagine di storia del ministero suddiaconate alla messa papale, in Fons vivus - Miscellanea Vismara,* Rome 1971 pp 287-314. After describing the function of the sub-deacons in the Ceremonial de Patrizi, the author concludes: "As far as one can discover it, even in the Ceremonial of Patrizi the role of the sub-deacon at a Papal Mass is varied and divided among several sub-deacons. One remembers that the sub-deacons truly constitute the college of apostolic sub-deacons. It must be allowed, however, that the responsibilities given to the apostolic sub-deacons in Patrizi's Papal Mass are very reduced in comparison with the earlier ones in the *ordo romanus I* and the *ordo* of Canon Benoit. This shows that even in the times which followed Benoit's *ordo* the inexorable simplification of Papal functions continued, as it had in the 10th and 11th centuries." (p 308, author's translation).

57. Nam quod intermisimus de patena, quando inchoat canonem (understand this as the Preface which, for the editor of the *ordo,* begins the Canon), venit acolytus sub humero habens sindonem in coll ligatum, tenens patenam ante pectus suum in parte dextera usque medium canonem (read, the Te igitur). Tunc subdiaconus sequens suscipit eam super planetam et venit ante altare, expectans quando eam suscipiat subdiaconus regionarius. Finito vero canone, subdiaconus regionarius stat cum patena post archidiaconem". Cf OR 1. ed. M. ANDRIEU, *op, cit.* Vol II pp 96-97.

58. On the origin and usage of the Calamus, besides J.A. JUNGMANN (*op. cit.* T. III pp 316-318) see J. BRAUN, *Das christliche Altargarat in seinem Sein und seiner Entwicklung,* Munich 1932. (Georg, Hildesheim, New York, 1973) pp 248-265, with a representation of the Papal *fistula* (p 264).

59. In the liturgical privileges granted to the Patriarch of Lisbon by Clement XI (1716), Benedict XIII (1724), Clement XII (1737) and confirmed by Pius VI (1778) and the Mass which he celebrated *more papali,* etc, see the authoritative work of Msgr J. NABUCO: *Jus Pontificalium - Introductione in Caerimoniale Episcoporum,* Paris 1956 pp 51-57 and p 361 (bibliography).

60. On the Papal Communion at the throne, see A. ROCCA, *De sacra summi pontificis communione,* Rome, 1610: G. CATALANI: *Sacrarum caerimoniarum sive rituum ecclesiasticarum, op. cit.,* T II pp 78-86 (It is Catalani I have mostly consulted.)

61. On the practice of mingling the Precious Blood with non-consecrated wine, see M. ANDRIEU, *Immixtio et consecratio,* Paris 1924.

62. L. FISCHER, *Ordo Officiarum Ecclesia Lateranensis,* Munich 1916. For a comparison of the *Ordo romanus I* with the *Ordo Lateranensis,* see Dom B. CAPELLE, *Fraction et commixtion,* in *Travaux liturgiques,* Louvain, 1962, T II ?? pp 319 *et seq.*

63. On the Gregorian Sacramentary: *Hadrianum* (named after Pope Hadrian who

sent it to the court at Aix-la-Chapelle about 785) and on the *Hadrianum* with Alcuin's additions, see C. VOGEL *op. cit.* pp 72-82 with the bibliography.

64. For the Romano-Germanic Pontifical cf. M. ANDRIEU, *Les Ordines romani, op. cit.*, Vol I, pp. 494-548; C.VOGEL- R. ELZE, *Le Pontifical germano-germanique du Xeme siecle*, Citta del Vaticano, 1963, coll. *Studi e Testi*, 226-227; see also C. VOGEL, *Introduction aux sources, op. cit.*, pp. 187-203, with the bibliography.

65. This work, written by Pope Innocent III, (1198-1203) before his elevation to the pontificate, is better known under the title given by Migne *De sacro altaris mysterio*, PL 217, 763-916. The passage to which I have referred is at L. VI. 9.

66. GUILLAUME DURAND, *Rational ou Manuel des divins Offices, trad. franc*, Paris, 1854 T. II pp 394-398. On the work of Guillaume Durand, Bishop of Mende, see M. ANDRIEU, *Le Pontifical romain au Moyen Age, op. cit.* T. III, *le Pontifical de Durand de Mende*, pp 3-22. See also P.M. GY, O.P., *Guillaume Durand, Eveque de Mende (vers 1230-1296), canoniste, liturgiste et homme politique; Actes de la table ronde du CNRS*, Paris 1992.

67. P.M. GY, O.P., *Interactions entre liturgies. Influence des chanoines de Lucques sur la liturgie du Latran*, in *Revue des Sciences religieuses*, 58. 1984, pp 537-552 and, by the same author, *L'unification liturgique de l'Occident et la liturgie de la curie romaine*, in *Revue des Sciences theologiques et philosophiques*, 59, 1975 pp 601-612. See also M. MARCHETTI, *Liturgia e storia della chiesa di Siena nel XII secolo*, Siena, 1991, pp 45-48.

68. *De Missarum mysteriis (De sacro altaris mysterio) op. cit.* L VI. 9: Summus pontifex non statim particulam hostiae dimittit in calicem, sed eam, post trinum crucis signaculum, in patenam reponit, et post osculum pacis ad sedem adscendens, ibi consistens, universis cernentibus, partem majorem suscipit oblatae de patena quam ei diaconus repraesentat, ipsamque videntibus dividens, unamque particulam sumens, aliam mittit in calicem quem tenet coram ipso subdiaconus, de quo sanguinem hautit cum calamo. Deinde particulam unam tradit cum osculo diacono, aliamque subdiacono sine osculo, quem ad altare ministrantem ei calicem diaconus osculatur. Et tunc subdiaconus particulam dimissam in calice sumit cum sanguine.

69. *Ordo romanus I*, ed. ANDRIEU, *op. cit.* T II p 101.

70. J. CATALANI, *op. cit.* T II, L II, Tit I, C XIV, para XIII, XI.

71. See J.A. JUNGMANN, *op. cit.*T III pp 249 *et seq*. See also Mgr M. RIGHETTI, *Manuale di storia liturgica*, Milan 1966 Vol III pp 486-489.

72. St THOMAS AQUINAS, *Summa Theologiae*, Q LXXIII, A 3, Res sacramenti est unitas corporis mystici, sine qua non potest esse salus: see also l'ad l um of the same article: Q LXXIXm, A 1.
THEODORE OF MOPSUESTIA (quoted by J. DANIELOU, *Bible et Liturgie*, Paris 1951 p 182): " They give the sign of peace one to another, and by this

190

kiss make a sort of declaration of their unity and charity. In effect, baptism gives us a rebirth, through which we are united in nature and it is the same nourishment that we all take when we take the same Body and Blood : we all, however numerous, form a single body because we share the same bread. Before we approach these mysteries, we should follow the rule of giving the sign of peace by which we signify our union and mutual charity. It is not right that those who form the single body wich is the Church should have any feeling of hate for a brother in the faith". (XV, 40).

73. See J.A. JUNGMANN, *op. cit.* T III : "....Nowadays we cannot help feeling that the use of a kiss in this way - a sign of the closest familiarity - is bold and risky. A sign, after all, no longer given in the closed circle of a young community, filled with high idealism, but a regular use in public meetings. We must take account of certain features from earlier cultures. Whatever is the case, throughout the ages a formalized use of the kiss has prevailed in all the Christian liturgies, attenuated in form.

74. *Caerimoniale Episcoporum*, L.II, C. XXIX. See Mgr P. MARTINUCCI, *Manuale Sacrarum Caerimonialum*. Rome, 1870-1873, L.Vt.III, pp 118-124: L. STERCKY C.S.Sp. *Les fonctions pontificales selon le rite romain*, Paris 1932, pp 128-131 : Mgr L. GROMIER, *Commentaire du Caerimoniale Episcoporum, op. cit.* pp 439-442.

75. One finds, in the Ceremonial of Patrizi, two hosts carried on a paten by the sub-deacon to the Pope's throne after has has taken Communion: These are for the Emperor and Empress. (Cf M. DYKMANS, *L'oeuvre de Patrizi Piccolomini, op. cit*, T. I, p 104.)

76. Mgr GROMIER (*op. cit.* p 440) makes clear that this way of giving Communion, which derives from the Papal Mass, is reserved to the bishop (the Ordinary of the diocese) chanting the Mass from the throne.

77. If the bishop who is ordaining is not the local Ordinary, he himself holds the ciborium: the newly ordained priests however kiss his hand at Communion (cf Mgr J. NABUCO, *Pontificalis Romani - Expositio juridico-practica*, Paris 1962 p 135). In the case of ordinations and other extra-ordinary pontifical functions, a bishop not the Ordinary replaces the Ordinary: he receives the offerings and makes the sign of the Cross etc. but in accordance with the appropriate restrictions (Mass at the faldstool).

78 Cf *Ritus servandus in celebratione Missae*, X, 3: Tunc manibus junctis super Altare positis, oculisque ad Sacramentum intentis, inclinatus dicit secreto: Domine Jesu Christe, etc. Qua Oratione finita, si est daturus pacem, osculatur Altare in medio et instrumentum pacis ei porrectum a Ministro juxta ipsum ad dexteram, hoc est, in cornu Epistolae genuflexo, et dicit: Pax tecum. Minister respondet: Et cum spiritu tuo.

79. *Caerimoniale Episcoporum*, L, 1, C. XXIV nn. 6-7.

80. Cf H. JEDIN, *Il Concilio di Trento, op. cit.* T. III, pp 277 et seq.

81. Cf M. DYKMANS, *L'oeuvre de Patrizi Piccolomini, op. cit.* T. I pp 190-195.

82. *La descriptio adventus Friderici III Imperatoris ad Paulum papam II* - published by MABILLON, Museum Italicum, op. cit. T. 1, pp 256-272.

83. Cf *la Descriptio adventus Friderici III*...Communicavit Summus Pontifex Altaris Sacramentum cum Imparatore, Diacono, et Subdiacono de pane tantum; de Calice autem, etsi consuetudo sit, communicantes cum Pontifice participare; propter insurgentem tamen Hussitarum, acf Bohemorum damnatum haeresim, quae Calicis potationem ad salutem necessariam putat, praeter Pontificem, nemo bibit (quoted by CATALANI). Communion from the chalice was refused at first by the Council of Constance but conceded later in Bohemia from 1433.

84. Cf J.A. JUNGMANN: *op. cit.* T. III, p 319.

85. Dom E. MARTENE, *De antiquis Ecclesiae ritibus, op. cit.* 1, pp 438-439.

86. For the different names and usages of the calamus see J. BRAUN. *Das christliche Altargerat, op. cit.* pp 249 *et seq.*

87. *Ordo Romanus I*, ed ANDRIEU, II, nn. 108, 111, 115.

88. Cf J.A. JUNGMANN, *op. cit.* III pp 347-356.

89. *Corp. Jur. Can., Decretales Greg.* L. III, 41, 5 (quoted by JUNGMANN, *loc. cit.* p 349).

90. P. LEBRUN, *Explication...op. cit.*, pp 506-508.

91. *Ritus servandus*, X, 6 : Minister autem dextera manu tenens vas cum vino et aqua, sinistra vero mappulam, aliquanto post Sacerdotem eis porrigit purificationem, et mappulam ad os abstergendum.

92. Unus ministrorum Pontificis stat juxta cornu Epistolae altaris Calicem habens, non illum cum quo Pontifex celebravit, sed alium cum vino, et mappulam mundam in manibus, ad quem singuli communicati accedunt, et se purificant, os extergunt, et ad partem se locant.

93. *Caerimoniale Episcoporum*, L. II C. XXIV, nn. 3-4.

94. Cf Mgr L. GROMIER, *Op. cit.*: " In former times, after taking Communion under both species, the celebrant drank pure wine for the purification, then washed his hands with water which had been put in the piscina. Later, he rinsed his fingers with wine, before drinking the purification and washing his hands. Washing the fingers and mouth with wine and water, a later development which did away with the washing of the hands (except for a bishop), met more opposition than is generally believed. Now, at a Papal Mass, the Pope does not drink the water with which he has washed his

fingers". (p 311)

95. I must point out that prior to the Ceremonial of Patrizi, when the Pope was celebrating the pontifical Mass more frequently, the practice of Communion ad Sedem was used only on formal occasions, never during penitential rites or at requiems.

96. Cf J. CATALANI : *Op. cit.* T. II, L II, Tit. I, C. XIV para XIII, XVII-XXII.

97. Quoted by CATALANI, *loc. cit.*

98. Cf. St Thomas Aquinas, *Summa Theologiae*, IIIa q. 73: aa. 1,2,3,4, etc.

99. St.Thomas Aquinas,ibid.IIIa,q.83,a.5: in celebratione hujus mysterii quaedam aguntur ad repraesentandum passionem Christi; vel etiam dispositionem corporis mystici; et quaedam aguntur pertinentia ad devotionem et reverentiam usus hujus sacramenti.

Gregorian chant
as a sign and witness of faith and its relation to the Most Blessed Sacrament of the Altar

Professor Jan Boogarts (Netherlands)

Professor Boogaarts, doctor in musicology, teaches at the University of Utrecht. For over forty years he was a professor at the seminary and the conservatoire of Haak. He is renowned for his competence in musicology, but also as an organist and composer. Responsible for more than 30 records of Gregorian chant and sacred music, he is vice-president of the International Centre of Sacred Music (C.I.M.S.) whose chair is in Rome.

Introduction

When one greets a person one gives that person one's hand. This gesture has no material objective, it is a material sign with an immaterial significance. Since man consists of body and soul, matter and spirit, there are always two forms that determine his communal life: the one serves the preservation of his bodily existence, the other is nothing other than a symbol of immaterial concepts and values that give form to his awareness and enable communication on the spiritual level. Just as man's soul may be recognised in his bodiliness, so too may spiritual and intellectual values be transmitted only by means of concrete, palpable, material signs.

The first category that serves the preservation of bodily life may be termed FUNCTIONAL, the second category, as the symbol for immaterial values, the *signa şensibilia*, may be termed MONUMENTAL. [1]

Since man constitutes a unity of body and soul, the functional forms may be recognised as human forms, as opposed to the world of purely natural forms, by their power to express the intellect: everything that belongs to the elementary requirements of life: eating, drinking, clothing and habitation. The monumental forms by contrast can only serve as symbols for immaterial values when their original functionality has been removed. By dispensing with normal practices, an expressive functional form can be raised to the level of a monumental form. There is a difference between a genuflection of reverence and kneeling to pick up a handkerchief. And one does not button up one's jacket with a medal.

There are yet further characteristics which must be presupposed in the case of monumental forms. These forms have arisen in the course of centuries - ancient traditions; they cannot be

194

ordered into a coherent whole from one day to the next.

A highly developed society knows many - and often complex - monumental forms. If one wishes to preserve a certain standard of civilisation, one must proceed extremely carefully in the education of children, so that they learn to operate with these forms and above all to understand their spiritual content. Where it is attempted to use monumental forms and to explain them at the same time the spiritual communication is lost . A third feature is that the quality of the visible forms is proportionate to the clarity of the immaterial objective. Monumental forms possess another remarkable quality: if they are observed well they not only effect a spiritual communication on other persons, but also lead to a deeper awareness of the spiritual objective for the person who observes them. Finally the mere trace of an original functional form may be sufficient to serve as a symbol: not the complete embrace but only a handshake, not a complete house but only an obelisk. The proviso however remains that the original functional form has disappeared. When one makes a toast one raises the glass, one sips, and one does not quench ones thirst.

Liturgy

In the liturgy only monumental forms are used. They are not the monumental forms of society which serve communication between persons, but (as a type of super monumentality) material forms as symbols of communication between the human spirit and the absolutely immaterial Being, the omnipresent and timelessly existent spirit, God, to whom we render homage in the liturgy.[2]

Liturgical forms differ from social forms in the sense that they embrace the entire complex of social forms: the functional conjoined with the monumental as the total expression of the human intellect. A church is a real house; one can feel safe in it, yet one seeks safety there not on account of bodily necessities but as a sign that one is taken up into the heavenly hierarchy. In the same way, liturgical nourishment is real food and real drink, liturgical vestments are real clothing. Gregorian chant is real music.

Moreover liturgical forms must correspond to all the characteristics of social monumental forms, although they can only serve the liturgy when they are deprived of their normal social usage: if a church building is also used for social gatherings, reverence for the house of God disappears.

Additionally, liturgical forms are bound up with tradition. The liturgy is there: it can be celebrated. One cannot simply think up the liturgy in a discussion on a Saturday night. St Benedict says: *Sic stemus ad psallendum ut mens nostra concordet voci nostrae* (Let us sing psalms in choir in such a way that our heart is in accord with our voice).[3] The complexities of our society and the long tradition of our

195

Christian culture built upon Jewish, Greek and Roman foundations occasions by definition a complex world of liturgical forms. If we wish to preserve the richness of our liturgy, a thoroughgoing education of all these who perform functions in the Church and of the entire community is indispensable. This must not remain a solely formal explanation of the signs, as it usually has in the past, but must be above all an introduction to the spiritual content that is expressed and realised by the sign and the form. It is constantly coming to light that many priests are insufficiently trained and that they are not acquainted with tradition. What is much worse is that they lack any understanding of the principles of liturgy. Again and again in the liturgy one is confronted with remarks such as: "Now we stand for the Gospel", "We open our book at page ..." and at the sign of peace: "Give each other your hand as a sign of peace and reconciliation". The last is apart from anything else a social form and does not belong in the liturgy. Instructions and directions must never be given during the liturgy.

The training of choir leaders and organists with respect to the liturgy leaves much to be desired. The average standard of melodies and texts and their performance is so deplorable that one actually can no longer speak of a standard at all. In a concert hall they would be booed off the stage. In the Mass, where the quality of the material forms should be the highest, it seems that everything is acceptable. Through a mistaken and limited interpretation of the concept of *participatio actuosa*, Gregorian chant and polyphony[4] have been banned from many parish churches. The monument of the *Thesaurus Musicae Sacrae* is not only a marvellous art form but above all a witness of our faith. Here too it is true that the performance of really good *musica sacra* gives rise to reflective dispositions both for the musicians and for the listeners, to a deepening of faith, and also the realisation that it is not only necessary but also that it is our primary duty to give all honour to God.

Gregorian Chant

Liturgical texts must have certain characteristic features which distinguish them from the speech patterns of social intercourse. A simple way that this can occur is through the use of Latin or - and this is not so simple - through a particular liturgical form of the vernacular.[5] In the Roman Catholic tradition one further distinguishing feature which constitutes a particular element of expressive monumentality is the use of music. The liturgy of Christendom has always been a sung liturgy. Even the readings were always sung up to quite recently (*Cantus Ecclesia Orans*). Gregorian Chant is, then, a musical form which has arisen out of the expressive structure of the texts.

196

Much more might be said concerning the power of expression in general. One feature should be mentioned at all costs: free natural rhythm. It is based on mathematical, often metrical values it is true, yet it is always analogous to the rhythm of living nature. This is one of the essential features of Gregorian Chant.[6] It has a long tradition originating in times prior to Western European civilisation. Because of its dissociation from normal social usage this musical form is pre-eminently suited to liturgical chant.

This chant was not established in writing during its process of formation until the ninth century. It attained its fullness in the course of an oral tradition, for which reason minor variations were continually occuring and being incorporated. These were finally smoothed out and crystallised into a monumental form unique in western civilisation. By reason of this perfection, Gregorian chant is capable of expressing great and ineffable mysteries. Music gives expression to that which words cannot say. St Augustine says in his *Enarrationes*: Songs of joy are a particular type of song that expresses the fact that the heart utters something which cannot be put into words. To whom is this song of joy more appropriate than to the inexpressible God: He is inexpressible because He cannot be grasped in words. *Si eum fari non potes et tacere non debes, quid restat nisi ut jubiles?* If you cannot *speak Him* and you are not permitted to be silent, what else can you do but rejoice? What else but exult in your heart with a joy beyond words, with a superhuman joy unlimited by syllables? Rejoice before God in your singing![7]

In Gregorian chant there is not only the exultation of the Allelujah melodies; many pieces are oligotonic or possess rich melismas. Apart from this, however, the simple songs, the antiphons, and the psalms give one the impression of being directly connected with the centuries old songs of praise of the Catholic Church; one feels taken up in the communion of believers and saints that have preceded us in the celebration of the Eucharist, the mystery of our faith. In every Protestant church there are many different hymns to be heard, whereas Gregorian chant is proper to the Catholic Church alone: *Cantus proprius sanctae Romanae ecclesiae.*

Gregrian Chant and the Blessed Eucharist

There are many chants which celebrate the Real Presence of Christ in the form of bread and wine. The best known are of course the chants on the Feast of Corpus Christi, although these do not belong to the original repertoire, but are predominantly adaptations of old melodies, or parts of melodies, to new texts. Most of these texts stem from the hand of St Thomas Aquinas (ca 1225-1274).

The Feast of the Eucharist was celebrated first in the diocese of Luettich in 1246. It was introduced by Bishop Robert von Torote

197

on the basis of a vision of the holy Augustinian Juliana von Cornillon (1193-1258). The motivation for the feast was a reaction to erroneous teaching, an atonement for neglect of Eucharistic adoration, and a memorial of the institution of the Sacrament of the Eucharist at the Last Supper. As early as 1264 it was established for the whole Latin Church by Pope Urban IV and in 1317 it was confirmed by Pope John XXII. [8]

The Feast is celebrated on a Thursday in memory of Maundy Thursday. It is a feast of thanksgiving that directly adjoins the period which forms the climax of the church year: the Easter period. Many of the melodies and texts of Corpus Christi became very popular, since they were continually sung in the course of the centuries and secured a firm position in Eucharistic devotions and Holy Hours-in divine services of a paraliturgical nature centred on the Blessed Sacrament exposed in the monstrance. Many of you will be able to recall to mind in a lively fashion the texts and melodies that were used: the Magnificat antiphon of first Vespers, *O quam suavis est*, the Benedictus antiphon of Lauds, *Ego sum panis vivus*, the Magnificat antiphon of second Vespers, *O Sacrum Convivium*, and in addition various parts of the hymns, and the sequence *O Salutaris Hostia* from the hymn of Lauds *Verbum supernum*, *Ecce panis angelorum* from the sequence of the Mass *Lauda Sion*, and *Tantum ergo* from the processional hymn *Pange lingua* which is also the hymn of second Vespers. The latter is a text of St Thomas which alludes to an older hymn of Venantius Fortunatus (d.606), *Pange lingua gloriosi lauream certaminis*. In addition to this we have *Panis angelicus*, the last two strophes of the processional hymn *Sacris Sollemniis* (which is also the hymn of Matins). Innumerable composers have used these texts for polyphonic compositions and in so doing have contributed to a deepened awareness of the most Holy Sacrament of the Altar. Some examples are *Ego sum panis vivus* by Giovanni Pierluigi da Palestrina (1525-1594), the grandiose, measured tones of *Tantum Ergo* in A flat major by Anton Bruckner (1824-1896) and the almost heavenly motet *O sacrum convivium* by Olivier Messiaen (1908-1992).

In the period prior to 1965 there were in many parish churches practically daily devotions before the Blessed Sacrament exposed. It was a continual reminder of the Feast of Corpus Christi and therefore also of the Real Presence of Christ in the Holy gifts of the altar.

In The Netherlands the devotion has now disappeared; the day of the Blessed Sacrament has for a long time been an ordinary working day.

One musical peculiarity of the office of Maundy Thursday is that the antiphon and responses, as they follow on each other, progress through the Church modes. The first antiphon is in the first Church mode: doric (authentic); the second in the second mode (plagal), the third in phrygian (authentic) etc. [9] In the old *Ordo* before

198

1960 there were a few changes so that the key of the responses followed a divergent pattern. [10] In the *Novus Ordo* after the Second Vatican Council the original scheme can no longer be recognised.

The chants of the proper of the Mass are also to some extent adaptations. Just as the gradual of the Requiem Mass refers to the Resurrection by introducing the melody of Easter Sunday, so the Alleluia *Caro mea vere est cibus* reminds us of the psalm text *Laetabitur iustus in Domino et sperabit in eo*. It was assumed into the *Novus Ordo* as the Alleluia verse for the common Mass of martyrs. The earlier communion antiphon *Quotiescumque manducabitis panem* summons ones thoughts to the Holy Spirit, to the great feast of Pentecost with its Communion chant *Factus est repente*. The Communion antiphon *Quotiescumque* is no longer a part of the *Novus Ordo*. In its place is the chant *Qui manducat carnem meam* for the ninth Sunday after Pentecost in the Old *Ordo*.

The melody of the sequence *Lauda Sion* comes from another sequence dating from the 11th century that was sung at the Feast of the Exaltation of the Cross: *Laudes crucis attolamus*. It is a melody that has developed out of the Alleluia *Dulce lignum* which at the same time fits the Alleluia *Caro mea*. The text of *Lauda Sion* treats the dogma of the Blessed Eucharist, *Dogma datur Christianis*: the central point of Christian faith where bread and wine are transformed into the Body and Blood of the Lord. Under two forms that are only signs, and not substances (*non rebus* - not material functional forms) is concealed the sublime reality, the Real Presence of Christ. Perhaps this lecture will encourage you to open up the text again. Ancient and original compositions were taken for the Introit, the Gradual, and the Offertory - compositions which had a position in other places through the Church year. The *Missa Votiva de Sanctissimo Sacramento* had the same proper with the exception of the sequence.

Although the entire liturgy concerns the Blessed Eucharist – how could it be otherwise since the Holy Sacrifice occupies the position of central importance? – the Feast of Corpus Christi is completely centred on the Blessed Eucharist – a feast that wanted to make an emphatic statement against the erroneous doctrines being promulgated at that time, in which the dogma of Transubstantiation was denied, namely by Berengar of Tours (ca. 1000-1088), a pupil of Fulbert of Chartres, who in 1050 denied the Real Presence of Christ in the form of bread and wine. A few centuries after the introduction of the feast of Corpus Christi, the denial of the Real Presence contributed to the rise of Protestantism. In one of his sermons held on this feast day Luther stated: *In no Feast is God and His Christ so blasphemed as on this day and above all by the procession.*

Even in our day this dogma is in for attack of a more or less open kind. The following example throws a harsh light on the situation. Some time ago the regional schola of Arnhem was asked to sing a Gregorian Requiem in a city church. In the sacristy there were two bare uncovered dishes of hosts. A priest from outside asked whether the hosts were consecrated, upon which the Sacristan replied: Yes, one of the two dishes is – but I don't remember which. In this church they cobbled together their own type of liturgy that in many respects can no longer be recognised as Roman Catholic. Has all of this come about through the introduction of the vernacular? Let us recall the discussion about the definition of the Eucharist in the *Instructio Generalis* for the new missal of 1970 (a year later a correction followed). The texts of the Cantus Gregorianus derive mostly from the Bible. As for the postconciliar vernacular texts, a particularly critical examination would be necessary, which would perhaps evolve from the outlines of this lecture. Let one citation suffice at this point, which is taken from the German language: one of the earlier hymns of union by Friedrich von Spee (1591-1635): *O Christ hie merk*. In the second and third strophe there is a clear and easily understandable expression of the Real Presence of Christ together with a brief indication of the erroneous interpretations:

2.   In the monstrance is Christ entire, no substance of bread; of bread thine eye beholds merely the form and appearance.

3.   No bread is there neither in nor by the Host. That which is there, Lord Jesus Christ, art Thou Thyself. [11]

Remarkably enough this hymn is no longer included in the so called E.G.B. (united hymn book of the German speaking dioceses). One asks oneself why. Does this serve the truth, or a misconceived Ecumenism?
Let us return to the substantive theme of our lecture: Gregorian chant. To the Gregorian repertoire belong not only the greater chants of the proper and ordinary but also those texts in the liturgy of the Roman rite which are sung in a very simple, practically recitative, style, for example the psalms and the orations. Almost the entire liturgy as such belongs to the Gregorian style of chant: in this connection there are scarcely any texts that have to be excluded. Albert Blaise offers an excellent treatment of the various different subjects in his book *Le Vocabulaire Latin des principaux thèmes liturgiques*. Apart from the Vocabulary, the book is divided into three sections: *première partie: Lex Orandi; deuxième partie: Lex credendi; troisième partie; Lex Vivendi*. In the middle of the second part of *Lex Credendi* the theme of the Blessed Eucharist is treated, the central position which it merits by reason of its importance. [12]   Blaise subdivides the chapter on the Eucharist into eight paragraphs:

1.   The sacrifice of the Old Law

200

2.	The memorial, the re-presentation of the Last Supper
3.	Nouns and verbs that relate to the Holy Sacrifice and its celebration
4.	The offering of the sacrifice
5.	The prayers for acceptance and propitiation
6.	The gifts received and the effect of the Holy Sacrifice
7.	The participation in the holy sacrifice
8.	Body and blood of Christ: the Real Presence. [13]

Viewed in this way, there are several hundred chants which refer to the Holy Eucharist; they are too numerous to be enumerated in the present outline: but let us simply mention a few examples.

Alleluia, cognoverunt discipuli Dominum Jesum in fractione panis. This is the first Alleluia of the 3rd Sunday in Eastertime. The text is taken from St Luke (24,35) from the account of the disciples at Emmaus. The melody is not original but derives, probably in the 7th or 8th century, from another Alleluia: *Domine Deus salutis meae.* For this reason the singing of the text *Cognoverunt* gives rise in the back of the mind to the thought: The Lord is the God of my Salvation. The same applies to the text: *Alleluia, Si testimonium hominum accipimus testimonium Dei maius est.* It is related to the same melody as are the two texts mentioned above. The *Alleluia, Si testimonium* appeared in the Old *Ordo* on the 1st July in the *Festum pretiosissimi Sanguinis Domini Nostri Jesu Christi,* the Feast of the Precious Blood. Not until 1849 was the Feast established by Pius IX for the entire Western Church. In the new Gradual (1974) it has no place.

The offertory *Portas Caeli* from the Wednesday after Easter: this well known text derives from Psalm 78 (23-25) and prefigures the gift of the Blessed Eucharist - 'He opened the gates of Heaven. He made Manna rain down upon them for food and gave them Heavenly bread. Men ate the bread of angels. He sent them nourishment in its fullness.' In the original form of the offertory, which contained different verses that had already become obsolete almost 1000 years ago, the last sentence *Panem angelorum* bore a particular significance since it was sung after each verse as a refrain.

The communion song *Hoc Corpus* used to be the Communion song of Passion Sunday. In the *Novus Ordo* it is sung on Maundy Thursday. The text from 1 Corinthians 11 (24-25) is a direct allusion to the words of consecration in the Mass.

The communion song 'Manducaverunt': Previously this was the communion song of the Sunday Quinquagesima, now it appears on the sixth Sunday in ordinary time. The text, like the offertory, *Portas Caeli,* is taken from Psalm 78 (29-30). 'They ate and were well filled; he provided for them that for which they hungered. In their wishes they were not disappointed.' Here again the Blessed Eucharist is prefigured in the Old Testament. In our liturgy it appears as a

201

confirmation.

The Communion song *Gustate et Videte* of the eighth Sunday after Pentecost: This text is taken from Psalm 33. It also appears as the last sentence of the Offertory *Immittet Angelus*: 'Taste and see how good the Lord is.' Orlando di Lasso (1532-1594) wrote a magnificent motet to these words as a procession chant for Corpus Christi. It is recounted that in Munich on the Feast of Corpus Christi in 1580 it rained so terribly after Mass that it was impossible for the procession to leave the church, but 'as soon as they left the church and he (Orlando) with his schola, just as he was approaching the princely company, and was about to begin singing the motet *Gustate et Videte*, then upon all those present by the grace of God the sun rose up to shine.[14] The Communion song *Gustate et Videte* is sung on the 14th Sunday in ordinary time in the *Novus Ordo*. In the liturgy of the following six Sundays, all of the Communion texts bear witness to the Blessed Sacrament of the Altar: *Qui manducat carnem meam; Acceptabis sacrificium iustitiae; Honora Dominum de tua substantia; Panem de caelo; Panis quem ego dedero; De fructu operum tuorum.* These chants all belong to the original repertoire. They are to be found in the most ancient manuscripts of the pregothic era. Ancient Latin liturgy is – as it were self-evidently _ permeated with texts that refer to the mystery of our faith. The false doctrines of Berengar and others were followed by a wave of reaction, but by this time the finest flowering of Gregorian chant was centuries past. The new hymns for Corpus Christi are at best only adaptations that have turned out well.

During that period the custom arose of elevation at the Consecration. Various prayers were composed for this purpose, which the faithful were able to say while looking at the Sacred Host. Most of these were poems in metrical form. This was how the well known 14th century hymn *Adoro te devote* came into being. The popular melody can no longer be described as Gregorian. It first appeared in the 18th century. In addition there is a yet older melody to this text. It is the same as the melody of the hymn already mentioned by Friedrich von Spee, *O Christ hie merk,* included in the Cologne hymnal of 1623.

The well known poem *Ave verum corpus natum* is also a prayer for the elevation from the 14th century. On account of Mozart's composition the text is almost universally known. Johann Baptist Hilber (1891-?) wrote of it: '... and finally the *Ave Verum* composed in 1791, the year of his death, and close in time to the Requiem, which is so often kept as a 'beautiful piece' rather than a Eucharistic dirge written by a man already marked by death, who certainly in the resonances of his church music, if not perhaps always in his life remained faithful to the innermost mystery of his faith! For that is just how it is: the works speak of Mozart's faith, in them is sung his exultation in God, his church prayer, his Marian devotion, and his

202

Catholic spirituality in all its convincing, heartfelt beauty.' [15]

Although we cannot count all of Mozart's church music as genuine liturgical music, one must agree with Hilber concerning the improper use of much liturgical music. The masses of Josquin des Prez, for instance, were composed in order to lend the Mass a particular lustre. Today they are heard in concert halls. It is a similar situation when hordes of tourists shuffle through a cathedral chattering noisily without the slightest reflection that they are in the house of God.

Even Gregorian chant threatens to become a consumer article. Only when we proceed with the most extreme caution and preserve Gregorian chant, reserve it, and by not permitting it to be used outside the church, give it pride of place, namely in the liturgy. Only then can it retain its proper symbolic value; only then will it be able to lend expression to the Catholic faith, above all to the greatest mystery, the highest good: God's Real Presence in the Blessed Eucharist.

1. Dom Hans van de Laan O.S.B., *Het vormenspel der liturgie*, Leiden, 1985.

2. J Boogaarts, *Inleiding tot het Gregoriaans en de Liturgie*, Bussum, 1985/1994, 2; Sec. 66ff.

3. St. Benedict of Nursia, *Regula Benedicti, Caput XIX: de Disciplina Psallendi*.

4. *Musicae sacrae ministerium*, Journal of the *Consociatio Internationalis Musicae Sacrae*, Anno XXIX-XXX, no. 1 & 2, Rome, 1995. See: Boogaarts, *Les formes de pièces polyphoniques des propres au début de la polyphonie et d'aujourd'hui*, Sec. 58.

5. Chr. Moorman, *Liturgical Latin*, Washington, 1957.

6. H.P.M. Litjens and G.M. Steinschulte, *Divini Cultus Splendori. Liber Festivus in Honorem Joseph Lennards*. See: J Boogaarts, *Saecularisatie in Europa. Van ritme naar metrum*, Rome, 1980. Sec. 10 ff.

7. St. Augustine, *Enarrationes in Psalmos* 32, 11, Sec. 1, 8.

8. L. Brinkhof O.F.M. u.a. *Liturgisch Woordenboek*, Roermond, 1965-1968. Sec. 1195 and 2494.

9. F. Wagner, *Einfuehrung in die gregorianischen Melodien*, Leipzig,

1921. Teil III, S. 351.

Dom Joseph Pothier O.S.B., *Revue du Chant Gregorien*, XVIII, S. 173.

Die Jesuitenkirche Sankt Mariae Himmelfahrt in Koeln: Dokumentation und Beitraege zum Abschluß ihrer Wiederherstellung 1980, Dusseldorf, 1982.

Albert Blaise, *Le Vocabulaire Latin des Principaux Thèmes Liturgigues*, Turnhout, 1966.

Ibid., Sec. 379 ff.

1. *Les sacrifices de l'ancienne Loi*
2. *Le Memorial, la "re-presentation"de la Cène*
3. *Noms et verbes désignant le saint sacrifice et sa célébration*
4. *Sacrifice d'offrande*
5. *Demande d'acceptation, d'agrement, de propitiation*
6. *Les Dons reçus, les effets du saint sacrifice*
7. *La participation au saint sacrifice, la reception du saint sacrifice*
8. *Le Corps et le Sang du Christ, la présence réelle*

14. Fr. X. Haberl, *Orlando di Lasso's Werke - Magnum Opus Musicum*, Bd. V.S.V.

15. Johannes Overath, *Musica Sacra als Lebensinhalt, Eine Auswahl aus Aufsaetzen und Vortraegen von Johann Baptist Hilber*, Sinzig/Rhein, 1971.

Homily delivered at the closing Mass of the Colloquium 11th October, 1996.

Bishop Bernard Jacqueline (France)

Former Apostolic Nuncio.

Today we celebrate the feast of the Divine Maternity. It was Pope Pius XI who instituted this feast in 1931, to celebrate the fifteenth centenary of the Council of Ephesus, the council which on the 24th June 431 proclaimed the BlessedVirgin to be truly *Theotokos*, that is the Mother of God.

Already St. Luke tells us that one day while Jesus was speaking to the crowd a woman cries out, "Blessed be the Mother that bore You, the Mother that fed You with her milk." But Jesus answered, "Blessed rather whoever hears the Word of God and puts it into practice," thus praising His Divine Mother.

At Rome just after the Council of Ephesus, Pope Sixtus III dedicated a basilica to the Virgin Mary on the Esquiline Hill, St. Mary Major's. Since the new Missal came out the Universal Church celebrates the feast of Mary, Mother of God on the 1st January, while continuing to commemorate on the 5th August the dedication of St. Mary Major's, the oldest church in the West to be dedicated to the Mother of God.

In her Magnificat, which we take up each day at Vespers, our Lady praises the Lord, her heart full of joy on account of God her Saviour.

The night of Christmas the angel of the Lord announced to the shepherds of Bethlehem the glad tidings of great joy: the birth of the Saviour. And there was with the angel a great multitude of the Heavenly host, praising God and saying, "Glory to God in the highest and on earth peace to the men He loves." And we each Sunday and feast-day unite our voices to those of the angels as we sing, *Gloria in excelsis Deo.*

The shepherds, having heard the message of the angels, hurried to Bethlehem. They found Mary and Joseph and the Child Jesus laying in a manger and they went home glorifying and praising God for all they had seen and heard.

As for the Wise Men led by the star, they were filled with great joy, and entering the house they saw the Child and His Mother and, falling down worshipped Him. Opening their gifts they offered Him gold, frankincense and myrrh.

If we in turn fall down and worship the Holy Eucharist it is because we see there the Divinity of our Lord Jesus Christ. In the

205

liturgy of the Mass we express our faith in the real presence of Christ, under the appearances of bread and wine by genuflecting as a sign of adoration. But also, as *Mysterium Fidei* recalls, "The Catholic Church has always and still does worship the Blessed Eucharist not just during Mass but outside Mass as well, by conserving with the greatest care the hosts which have been consecrated, by presenting them to the faithful for their veneration, by carrying them around in procession"; those processions where we sing with St. Thomas Aquinas, "Godhead hidden I Thee adore, truly present under the appearances of bread and wine."

Besides the joyful adoration of the Lord, the feast of the Divine Maternity is also an occasion for us to admire Mary's fidelity to the observance of the rites of Israel.

When the eighth day came when they should circumcise the Child, they gave Him the Name Jesus, this Name which had been given him by the angel before His conception.

When the day came on which, according to Law, she ought to be purified, they took the Child to Jerusalem to present Him to the Lord and to offer as sacrifice a pair of pigeons or two turtle-doves, according as the Law prescribed.

If the Mother of our Lord, the Mother of God, submitted herself to the Law of Moses. how much more ought we to observe the norms of the Liturgy - for only the Pope and the bishops in communion with him can modify the Liturgy. No priest can.

Just as Jesus at Nazareth was subject to His Most Holy Mother so we too ought to obey the liturgical norms laid down by the Church, our Holy Mother.

Lastly, it was at Calvary that the Lord as he offered His supreme sacrifice, gave the Blessed Virgin Mary to be our Mother. That is why in our trials and temptations we invoke Mary and end the *Ave Maria* by saying, "Pray for us sinners now and at the hour of our death."

206

Communion under Both Kinds:
Theological and Pastoral Considerations

Father Wladimir-Marie de Saint Jean OM (France)

Born in 1939, Father Wladimir founded the community of Opus Mariae in 1969 ; this semi-contemplative community lives according to the rule of the regular canons of Saint Augustine. Ordained priest in 1977, he has a degree in philosophy from the Pontifical Gregorian University, a degree in theology and is preparing a theology doctorate. The community of Opus Mariae, settled in the Gap diocese, is recognised canonically of diocesan right and includes a female and a male community.

As long as we maintain the dogmatic principles established by the Council of Trent, Communion under both kinds may be extended to both clergy and laity at the bishops' discretion, in cases to be determined by the Holy See: for instance to the newly ordained at their Ordination Mass, to newly professed Religious at the Mass of their profession, and to the newly baptized at the Mass which follows their baptism.[1]

Thus speaks the second Vatican Council, in the Constitution on the Sacred Liturgy.

- I -

It is common knowledge that Communion under both kinds is far from being a recent innovation. The first eucharistic Communion was received by the Apostles themselves at Our Saviour's own hands, and was effected under two kinds, both consecrated bread and wine, for it was thus that Christ instituted the Sacrament of the Eucharist. (Lk. 22:19-20)

From the apostolic period until the twelfth or thirteenth centuries, this manner of communicating was virtually universal, although not exclusive, in both East and West, as the Council of Trent itself declares: "From the beginning of the Christian faith the use of both kinds was not unusual" (Sess. XXI, c. 2). This is certainly not the only witness, for beginning with St Paul (I Cor. 11:28) we can cite among others the Didachè, St Ignatius of Antioch, St Justin, Tertullian, St Cyprian of Carthage and St Cyril of Jerusalem.[2] This evidence is not confined to the first five or six centuries, witness Nicephorus of

Constantinople (d. 829) in his *Antirrheticus adversus Constantinum Copronymum*.[3]

The Fathers, contemplating the Eucharistic mystery in the light of this rite of Communion received under the two species of bread and wine, were fond of elaborating the symbolism of the Chalice, notably in regard to the theology of salvation, and the links between Communion and the study of the Last Things, or the theology of the Holy Spirit. Fr Lebeau, S.J., from Leuven, has dealt with these themes in several works in which he quotes among others these fine extracts from the Fathers:

"The cluster of grapes which hangs on the tree in the last days, whose blood becomes the draught of salvation for those who believe," writes St Gregory of Nyssa (Life of Moses, II, 268). "As we communicate in His blood, poured out for us, we receive the Holy Spirit," adds Pseudo-Chrysostom.[4] St Ambrose invites us: "Come to the banquet of Christ, the banquet of the Body of the Saviour, the sacramental banquet; come to this cup which gladdens the heart of the faithful, to be thrilled with the joy of the remission of sins, to forget the cares of this world, the fear of death, and all anxiety. Elevated by this draught, the body feels itself renewed in strength, without weakness; dissolved, the soul is not herself but made one with God."[5]

St Irenæus writes against the Ebionites, who failed to recognize Jesus Christ as the Messiah of the Ages, and in their ceremonial followed the "aquarian" heresy, refusing to *consecrate* anything but pure water in their eucharist; he says "They repudiate the mingling of the wine of heaven, and wish to be no more than water springing from the earth; they refuse to accept God in union with them."[6]

For the Fathers, as for St Paul, (I Cor. 10:3-4) the Eucharistic Bread is also a "spiritual food", which Fr Lebeau defines as "the vehicle of the Holy Spirit, a spiritual food, a spiritual drink."[7] The Fathers *also* emphasize the symbolic aspect of *koinonia*, of which the Chalice is the vehicle, consistently demonstrating its oneness with the Bread, the sacred Body of the Saviour. St Ignatius of Antioch writes to the Philadelphians: "Be sure not to celebrate more than one Eucharist, for there is only one Body of our Saviour Jesus Christ, only one Chalice to unite us in His Blood, and one Altar, just as there is only one Bishop, with his college of priests and deacons."[8] The Anaphora of St Basil, immediately after the invocation of the Holy Spirit, says "may all of us who share in the One Bread and the One Cup be one with each other in the Communion of the one Holy Spirit."[9]

This clearly refers to the ordinary manner of receiving Communion, as was still practised until about the twelfth century, even in the West. Nevertheless Communion under both kinds does cause difficulties in the practical and pastoral sphere, which arise from communicating through the Precious Blood. These difficulties are not unconnected with a genuinely theological concern over the respect due to the Real Presence of Christ under each of the two species, a respect which Communion from the Chalice cannot always guarantee, through fear of spillage.[10]

This may be seen in the development of how Communion in the form of wine was distributed. Originally people drank from the chalice. By the eighth century communicants used a tube, (*pugillaris*, since as the *Ordo Romanus Primus* indicates: "It was difficult to communicate the whole congregation, at least with the chalice."[11] Because of this very difficulty the usage grew up of the "eucharistic spoon", as early as the seventh century, as it seems, in Syria.[12] J.B. Pitra has recorded its use in the West, where it appears in a ninth-century regional conciliar text.[13] Most of the East adopted this custom, as we are informed by Cardinal Humbert (d. 1061).

It is in the seventh century that we first find evidence for intinction, when it was condemned by the third Council of Braga.[14] If the Latins have several times condemned this practice, it is because they feel it to contradict the way in which the sacrament was instituted at the Last Supper (as well on as the less serious objection that it looked too like the communion of Judas). The East, however, adopted it in some rites, particularly the Byzantine. If a spoon is used, the command "drink this, all of you" is not fulfulled, and the significance of the chalice is obscured, to say the least.

We can be sure that it would be wrong to say that the Orientals, who have retained Communion under both kinds, have never had problems with it. But they, as M. Jugie remarks, have "never considered the manner of Communion observed at the Last Supper as being ordained by the Saviour for everyone, indefinitely, and without any possible development."[15] This development has led in some regions giving Communion in one kind only (i.e. the Armenians and Maronites[16]), and, according to J. Jungmann, among the separated Byzantines "the Hosts destined for the communion of the faithful are not usually consecrated - so they only receive the Precious Blood, with a symbolic morsel of bread."[17]

To proceed, all historians agree that the useage of Communion ynder one kind only is found in earliest antiquity, especially when outside a church building. From the third century it is documented by, for instance, Tertullian and St Cyprian.[18] The faithful could be licenced to keep the Reserved Sacrament in their homes : St Basil records this practice in Egypt and Africa, and St Jerome gives evidence for the custom of home Communion at Rome in his own time. It was a common practice in the periods of persecution, and even later, so that the fourth century councils (Saragossa and Toledo) had to make regulations to avoid or suppress abuses.[19]

Besides this, the sick, the ordinary healthy faithful in time of persecution (or even otherwise), and hermits, all communicated under the form of bread alone, witnessing to their desire of union with Christ

209

in the Communion of His Body. We must emphasise the link that the mystique of martyrdom had with eucharistic spirituality, as well as the latter's connection with the origins of the monastic life, the desire to be incorporated into the mystery of Christ. So it was that Communion, even under the species of bread alone, expressed "union with Christ in his triumphant passage into death, or rather, through death to life."[20] Can we not see here the beginnings of belief, at least implicitly, in "concomitance", by which we mean that Christ is present whole and undivided? Fr P.M. Gy has observed that the expression *Christus totus* is already found in St Augustine, even though we cannot claim that it carries an exclusively eucharistic meaning with him.[21]

Moreover, although since the researches by Cardinal Bona (d. 1674) historians like to distinguish between "Communion outside the church" from "Communion in church" (i.e. in the context of the liturgical assembly), and restrict communion under the form of bread alone (or wine alone) to the former case, other historians have shown that our knowledge of the facts has been obscured by oversimplification. We have evidence for the practice of the church of Constantinople under St John Chrysostom (see Sozomen and Nicephorus Callistus[22]), of the church in Jerusalem from Cardinal Humbert,[23] of the fifth-century church in Rome from Pope St Leo:[24] the Manichees, who refused to communicate in the Precious Blood, hid themselves among the faithful for the reception of the Body of Christ, which would have been impossible had not communion under one kind been customary. Later texts from Gaul in the sixth to ninth centuries seem to refer to the rite *sub specie panis* being used in the context of the liturgical assembly;[25] again in the seventh century at Rome under St Gregory the Great communion under one kind was normal, as we learn from Mabillon, quoting Paul the Deacon.[26]

We should also mention the custom of making up for a shortage of consecrated wine by adding a few drops of the Precious Blood to ordinary wine. This mingling did not effect the consecration of this wine, since it was only an aspect of the "symbolism", and the usage demonstrates that communion under one kind was familiarly practiced.

We may also cite the Communion under one kind in the Mass of the Presanctified, known in the East in the fourth century, and its mention among the Latins in the Sacramentary attributed to St Gelasius. The communicating of children also was most often done under the form of wine alone.

We cannot maintain that the faithful of these centuries would have considered these customs to be "mutilated rites", and that they did not believe in a true Sacrament. But neither in the theological sphere nor in that of pastoral practicality were the difficulties and particular controversies resolved (saving the abuses alrady mentioned of communicating the healthy at home, and the Latin diffidence about intinction).

- II -

It is generally agreed that since the thirteenth century the custom of non-celebrants receiving the Precious Blood virtually disappeared. The Church did not oppose this development, and eventually made Communion under the form of bread alone obligatory in the Latin rite. A. Dublanchy comments pertinently to this question, "The new custom established itself gradually, without the aid of any formal legislation for the Universal Church."[27] In his *Treatise on Communion under Two Kinds*, Bossuet explains how the transition from one method to the other had happened "without objections", and he adds "the most certain way of telling whether a custom is freely held is when it changes without dissension."[28] He cites in particular the peaceful practice in the church of Jerusalem, as reported by Cardinal Humbert, Legate to the East from Leo IX.

Nevertheless, the teaching of Berenger of Tours might have led some to imagine that communion under both kinds was necessary, and as Megivern notes, Rome would not have reacted so passively to this development, "if the truth of the Real Presence of Christ under either kind had not been denied."[29] That is why it is vital to give the authentic motives for this change of rite, which certainly did not happen without good reason.

Some historians, like Gregory Dix,[30] have maintained that the chalice was abandoned at this period due to doctrinal reasons, of which the most important was the theology of Concomitance. This position is not convincing, and many other authorities stress practical motives, or those resulting from pastoral liturgy: a large number of communicants on a few occasions in the year (partly due to the decline of frequent Communion, which brought the Church at Lateran IV to impose the discipline of yearly Communion), or for reasons of hygiene.[31] That does not of course exclude theological or spiritual reasons. Fr Gy in turn makes more of the motive of danger of spillage, the fear of losing the Precious Blood, "but this motive could not have played a decisive role except in a new theological and spiritual climate" as he says.[32] That is what matters.

This new "theological and spiritual climate" was that of the devotion given to the sacred humanity of Christ especially in His Passion. At the same time devotion to *Corpus Christi*, the Blessed Sacrament, was increasing, leading to important developments in mystical spirituality. The sacred Host was reserved - not the Precious Blood - and the popularity of adoration of the Real Presence developed without ever excluding (quite the contrary) awareness of the Passion and the Blood, with a reference to the Chalice. However we can at the same observe that the eschatological aspect of the Chalice was to some extent obscured.

At the beginning of the thirteenth century, the revelations which St Julian of Mont-Cornillon received regarding eucharistic devotion had a definite influence on the decision to establish the Feast of Corpus Christ at Liège. Following the miracle of Bolsena, Pope Urban IV confirmed this in 1264. Fr Browe has collected eucharistic miracles and demonstrated how this phenomenon is concentrated in the twelfth to fifteenth centuries.[33] Do not these bleeding Hosts prove to the faithful, in their own manner, that the whole Christ is present in the consecrated bread? These miraculous occurences also contributed to an understanding of the sacrificial nature of the Eucharist, and a growing devotion to the Precious Blood.

We must also note how the faithful wanted to gaze on it: this "need to contemplate the Body of the Saviour was so strong that from the early twelfth century it suceeded in establishing a notable innovation in the middle of the Canon, which had so long been considered to be sacrosanct and unchangeable : the elevation."[34] The Chalice, usually now covered by the rear portion of the corporal folded forward, was not elevated until somewhat later - after all one could not see the Precious Blood itself.

According to J.J. Megivern, there was a progressive loss of the symbolic understanding since a period difficult to specify - he says it was the Carolingian age. But if this is true with regard to the Chalice, it is because the stress laid on the Real Presence of Christ under each of the two consecrated species led to particular care lest the Chalice be spilt - can we call that an impoverishment? G. Daneels writes "The theology of the Real Presence, typical of the epoch, inspired a sense of realism which reinforced the desire to surround the Sacred Species with the greatest possible reverence."[35]

The teaching of Berengarius, and his challenge to Lanfranc, stirred up a theological process which led to the doctrine of concomitance, showing that Christ is fully present under each of the two kinds. Developed while the practice of Communion under both kinds was already dwindling, this process was not the cause but the accompaniment of a liturgical movement, giving it a theological justification. We can therefore speak of a double influence, the fear of the danger of spillage, and the doctrine of concomitance.

The term "concomitance" seems to derive from the Arab philosopher Avicenna,[36] and what it means is to establish a link between a given reality and something which is not part of its essence but cannot be separated from it. In the sphere of the sacraments, the development of this doctrine is the flowering of a general belief in the Whole Christ, explicitly and specifically defined in the wake of the Berengarian crisis. All the great theologians embrace this doctrine, especially William of Champeaux, Hugh of St Victor, and Peter

Lombard. The influence of Lombard meant it was commonly taught in the Schools, until St Thomas Aquinas brought it to its perfection (J. Megivern[37]). The Councils of Constance (Denzinger-Schönmetzer 1198), of Florence (D.-S. 1320) and Trent would make it their own, and the term was canonized in the 13th Session of the latter, in 1551: "In virtue of the connection and natural concomitance by which the members of Christ the Saviour, who himself was raised from the dead in order to die no more, are bound together." (Chap. 3, D.-S. 1640; cf 1729).

In these texts the Council adopts the theology of St Thomas (IIIa, q.76, art. 1,2,3) on the total presence of Christ in either form. Aquinas cites this doctrine again in qu. 80, precisely to justify Communion under one kind only: "The Body can be consumed by the people without their consuming the Blood, and they suffer no disadvantage theough this, because the priest who represents them all offers and consumes the blood, and because Christ is present whole and entire under each of the two species." (art.12, ad 3).

You will have noticed that in the thought of the Common Doctor the argument from concomitance takes second place. St Thomas thinks first of the role of the priest, the celebrant "who represents them all, offers and consumes the blood" in the person of all.

To speak in this way does not diminish the importance and strength of the doctrine of concomitance, which the Church has made her own. As Fr Roguet writes, "The reasoning which forms the doctrine of concomitance has the virtue of depending on a fact, guaranteed to our faith by the word of God : Christ himself is alive and glorified in heaven, he will die no more, his flesh and blood cannot be separated again."[38] It is worth emphasizing this again.

In any case, before appealing to concomitance in his discussion, the Angelic Doctor invokes the argument of the celebrating priest who "takes the place of all". "This does not mean that he personally occupies a higher rank than that of the layman in the ontology of Communion" writes Fr Roguet (p. 362), but it is because he celebrates the Holy Sacrifice that the priest represents the entire assembly.

This point made by St Thomas is affirmed by Roguet to be "much better than the argument from concomitance, because it places itself on the sacramental plane, that of symbolism."[39] St Thomas' argument is entirely theological, in both sacramental and ecclesiological aspects. Certainly its effects in the latter area have been of historic importance, but we must take on board Fr Bouyer's apposite comment in order to avoid the typical opposition between priest and layman: "There was no question of withdrawing the cup from the laity, contrary to what the Protestants claim, it was

213

withdrawn simply from all communicants other than the celebrant"[40], in other words also from communicating clergy.

Fr Roguet's opinion as to the superiority of the first argument invoked by St Thomas can be accepted, since it does not involve abandoning or even disparaging the doctrine of concomitance which, as the same author says "is far from being a mere scholastic speculation, since it applies to the practice of the Church, which is the normal rule for sacramental theology."[41]

We must not forget that the Resurrection and the Hypostatic Union of Christ are the truths on which the doctrine of concomitance is grounded, although of a higher order. Christ is now risen. In that state his body and blood are inseperable: that is the reality. It is this reality which is brought under the sacrament in virtue of concomitance, even though this must not be confused with the sacramental reality in itself, that is to say that which is "defined and effected by the words, *vi verborum*." (ibid., p. 313.

The Eucharist, sacrament inseparable from sacrifice, makes present for us the entire Paschal Mystery (Passion, Death and Resurrection) which is the work of the Incarnate Word, the Redeemer. Through Communion (de usu as St Thomas says, IIIa q.80) we are associated with it and enjoy its fruits.

The Eucharist is therefore perfectly and validly effected through the fact that the celebrating priest consecrates the matter[42] and communicates in the Body and Blood under the two kinds of bread and wine, performing all this in persona Christi and, inseparably, in persona omnium (q. 80 a 12, ad 3) because he takes the place of the assembly which, in some manner, is "personified" in him.

Thus the faithful who receive the entire Christ, communicating sub specie panis are deprived neither of the reality of the Sacrament nor of the graces which flow from it. They suffer in fact "no deprivation" (aliquod detrimentum, ibid).

Because of these two motives, the transition to Communion under the form of bread alone happened in a peaceful manner without provoking any dissension, as we have already noted.

- III -

Despite this, there arose in the fifteenth century the Utraquist rebellion of the Hussites and Calixtines. The latter, the moderate partizans of Jan Hus, made Communion from the Chalice their most prominent demand. It has been said that it was the Chalice which made Hussitism, and Jakubek who was the "author of the Chalice".[43] It is not our intention here to recount the history of this debate. It is well described in articles by G.Bareille and E.Dublanchy in the *Dictionnaire du Théologie Catholique* under "Calixtines" and

214

"Communion under both Kinds", as well as in the work by D.R. Holeton dealing with these questions. He demonstrates especially how the Utraquists tried to use texts of St Cyprian, William of Laon and even St Albert the Great to support their revolt. Thus speaks Jakubek, citing St Albert: "In the Sacrament, the Church does not only understand that we receive Christ as one might receive Him through growth in grace and merit, but she understands that we receive Christ as nourishment, perfect nourishment. And perfect nourishment is not found in the sacrament of bread alone, but in the sacrament of bread and wine."[44] This is not convincing, since communion sub utraque is effected at every Mass by the Celebrant, and the reality of the sacrament is therefore assured.

The Council of Constance condemned them on 15 June 1415, in its 13th Session, declaring that the Utraquist revolt "concealed a doctrinal error on the Real Presence"[45] and casting doubt on the entire presence of Christ under either kind.

We should note that the Council of Basle, operating in the absence of the Supreme Pontiff, did concede to the Bohemian Calixtines the "privilege" of communicating sub utraque, but safeguarding the conditions laid down in the treaty of Prague in 1433 known as the Compactata.[46] This concession was revoked by order of Pius II on 13 August 1462.

We have finally arrived at the Council of Trent (1545-1563). This did not make communion under one kind a definite rule, which was unnecessary, since the obligation for non celebrants of communicating in this manner was already well established. Before Constance, which formally stated "it is to be held as a law" (D.-S. 1199) the local Council of Lambeth in 1281 had forbidden the faithful to communicate in the consecrated wine, without incurring any criticism or censure from Rome.

Trent however did apply itself to correct the error of the so-called "reformers" (i.e. Protestants) who had revived the Calixtine claim. The latter, be it noted, held to the real Presence, but we cannot make the same assertion with regard to the Protestants who differed among themselves on this article of faith. There is another difference to take into account: the Hussite movement was strongly motivated by a desire for frequent, even daily, Communion, linked to a genuine devotion to Christ in the Eucharist.[47]

In the case of the Protestants, can we consider the reappearance of communion from the cup as bearing on sacramental theology or eucharistic piety, or does it belong to the realm of ecclesiology, being rooted in the rejection of Church order and its hierarchical structure, in particular the distinction between priest and layman, as well in that systematic opposition to the Magisterium, which is institutionalised as "protestantism"? J. Megivern quotes

Luther on this perverse attitude: "If a council granted the chalice he would oppose it, and vice-versa".[48]

Trent, reacting to these protestations, was concerned to defend the doctrine and practice of communion sub specie panis. It does so in affirming that communion under both kinds can not be called a divine command: "The Sacred Council, instructed by the Holy Spirit, the Spirit of Wisdom and Intelligence, of Council and Piety, and following the judgment and custom of the Church, declares and teaches that no divine command obliges the laity and non-celebrating clergy to communicate under both kinds, and that one cannot do so without casting doubts on the faith, whether communion under either one or other kind be sufficient for salvation." (Session XXI, c.1)

To prove the truth of this definition, the Council turns to scriptural arguments, taken especially from chapter 6 of St John's Gospel. In the discussion they compared the texts "He who eats my flesh and drinks my blood will have eternal life" (v.24) with "How can this man give us his flesh to eat?" (v. 52), and "He who eats this bread will live for ever" (v. 58), and showed that "flesh and blood" (v. 54) did not imply any divine command for the faithful.

As for Matthew 26:27, "drink this all of you" and Luke 22:17 "and taking the cup he gave thanks and said 'Take this and share it among you'", these verses express Christ's specific commmand in context, addressed to the Apostles. In the same way Luke 22:19 "Do this in memory of me" expresses the power conferred on the Apostles, in view of the mission which would be continued by their successors. That is to say the power of offering the Eucharistic Sacrifice, a power which implies the consecration of both kinds, and Communion under both kinds, since, as E. Dublanchy says "this communion completes the Sacrifice".[49]

The Council Fathers also put forth arguments from tradition, going back to the Church's practice for centuries, and showing that in parallel with communion under both kinds, communion sub una was practised since the earliest days of the Church in certain circumstances, as we have already seen (cf. note 25).

In the second place, Trent goes on to defend Communion under one kind by invoking the disciplinary authority of the Church with regard to the dispensation of the sacraments:[50] "The Council moreover declares that the Church has always had the authority to establish (statuerunt) or modify the distribution of the sacraments, as long as their substance is preserved (salva illorum substantia), as she judges most useful for the faithful and appropriate for the sacraments.... Hence, although in the early days of the Christian Faith the practice of communicating in two kinds was common, nevertheless custom has changed everywhere in the passage of time, and the Church, recognising this disciplinary authority in the administration of the Sacraments, and moved by good and serious reasons, has approved

216

this custom of communion under one kind only, and has decreed that it will in future be kept as a law, a law which no one can modify on his own initiative without the authority of the Church. (Session XXI, cap. 2; D.-S. 1728).

We have already examined the reasons, rooted in the history of the Church's pastoral practice, which brought the Council to define and promulgate the decision which we have just read. The Council Fathers rejected the erroneous opinion of some of their number who suggested that it was possible for the Church to change a law of Divine right.[51] The question was addressed in Session XIV, on Extreme Unction, and the phrases *statuerunt* and *salva illorum substantia* show clearly how the Church intended to state a principle. (This principle was several times invoked, especially by Pius XII in *Sacramentorum Ordinis* with regards to the matter and form of a sacrament, and in *Mediator Dei*.)

Finally, Trent cited theological reason, based on the presence of Christ "whole and entire" under each separate species, and the real communication of the grace of the Eucharistic sacrament through Communion in one kind: "The Council declares as well that, although the Redeemer did as we have said institute this Sacrament at the Last Supper under two kinds, and distributed it thus to his Apostles, we must nevertheless recognize that even under one kind we receive Christ whole and entire, and the full reality of the Sacrament, so that as a result when we consider the fruits of the Sacrament, those who receive only under one kind are not deprived of any grace necessary for salvation." (cap. 3, D.-S. 1729)

"Grace necessary for salvation". We must understand, in reading this Conciliar text, that the last phrase refers only to the effect of the Sacrament in itself, affirmed by the words *verum sacramentum*, and not to its integrity. The question remains open to theological discussion, for the Fathers had no intention of closing the debate.[52]

It appears that we can classify theological opinion in this area under two headings: 1) a single sacramental effect, 2) a two-fold sacramental effect.

1) According to the first opinion, the sacramental species signify the unity of the spiritual repast. In the spiritual realm, food and drink have no separate meaning. Sacramental effect is proportionate not to the form of the sign, but to that which it signifies, and remains the same when only one kind is present. An analogy can be drawn in the sacrament of baptism between immersion or simple infusion. It is enough in fact to remember that the Eucharistic species are efficacious virtute *corporis et sanguinis*. This principle of sanctification remains even under one kind, *vi concomitantiæ* and not *vi consecrationis*. In fact, the distinction of species is due simply to the integrity of the eucharistic sacrifice, not to its sacramental effect.

217

St Thomas made this position his own (according to most commentators) in IIIa q. 80 a. 12 ad 3, as did St Bonaventure, even though the latter maintained a distinction between the perfection of the effect and that of the sign.

2) In the second opinion, there is a double sacramental effect corresponding to the twofold spiritual repast which the species signify. One grace has an effect on the soul parallel in the spiritual sphere to physical nourishment, and the other likewise parallel to physical drink. These graces are distinct, although very similar, and are beneficial to the communicant, but deprivation of one is easily compensated by the very similar graces received frequently in communion under the other kind. There is therefore no significant spiritual loss.

All ths depends on the hypothesis of a twofold manner of spiritual repast, which is in no wise proved. One can on the contrary appeal to the "specific unity of the Eucharistic sacrament, which presupposes a unity of nourishment for the soul despite the distinction of species."[53]

Some Fathers maintained that in communicating under both kinds grace is better received because of a better disposition, *ex opere operantis.* But this subjective element, while not negligable, is outweighed by the more general consideration of *periculum effusionis* (which is common to the whole congregation), as well as the arguments from the discipline of the Latin Church (which are of a much greater order, taking into account the varied motives which are well expressed in the Catechism which emerged from the Council, as A. Michel says).[54] There was as well a concern for Church unity prominent in the mind of the Council. We must remember also that the doctrinal question was immersed in an atmosphere charged with politics. That is why the eventual permission granted for the Chalice caused such debate, in the anxiety to safeguard unity if possible. St Charles Borromeo, indeed, and other cardinals, as well as the bishops of Hungary, were in favour of the concession (generally confined to Bohemia), as Pallavicini reports in detail.[55] Later on even Bossuet considered the possibility of restoring communion in both kinds to "facilitate the return of England and Germany". He thought that in this manner "we shall see the total eclipse of heresy."[56]

The Fathers opposed to the concession spoke of expediency, which required that no exceptions to a universal law should be made at a time of doctrinal heresy (J.B. Castano), lest such heresy grow as a result of a practice which might seem to justify it,[57] and because it would be likely that further exceptions be wanted. The Fathers could not agree, and they referred the matter to Pope Pius IV, who appeared to be much in favour of the concession. He granted it to certain metropolitans of the Empire in 1564. However the chalice, which had

218

become the symbol of the reformation, was rejected by the Catholics themselves.[58] The concessions were therefore finally annulled.

- IV -

As we come to our own time, in quite a different climate, we have seen a resurgence of Communion under both kinds, and that at the highest level, since the second Vatican Council itself treats of it in the Constitution Sacrosanctum Concilium §25 : "As long as we maintain the dogmatic principles established by the Council of Trent, Communion under both kinds may be extended to both clergy and laity at the bishops' discretion, in cases to be determined by the Holy See (*concedi potest, in casibus ab Ap. Sede definiendis, de judicio Episcoporum*).

The *Missale Romanum*, promulgated by the Apostolic Constitution of that name dated 3 April 1969, uses a similar wording in §241 of the General Instruction, urging the pastors to remind their people as clearly as possible of the Catholic Doctrine on Holy Communion according to the definitions of Trent, and in particular on the presence of Christ whole and entire under each species, so that the Sacrament is received in its fulness and no grace necessary for salvation is wanting to those who communicate under one kind.

The instruction *Eucharisticum Mysterium* of the Sacred Congregation of Rites, dated 25 May 1967, uses the same terminology on the necessity of holding to the principles established by Trent (§32).

The *Catechism of the Catholic Church* says "Since Christ is sacramentally present under each of the species, Communion under the species of bread alone makes it possible to receive *all the fruit of Eucharistic grace.*[59] For *pastoral reasons* this manner of receiving Communion has been *legitimately* established as the most common form in the Latin rite. But 'the sign of communion is more complete when given under both kinds, sinc in that form the sign of the Eucharistic meal appears more clearly' (GIRM, 240) This is the usual form of receiving Communion in the Eastern rites." (Cat., 1390).[60]

The Code of Canon Law prescribes as follows: "Holy Communion is to be given under the species of bread alone, or, in accordance with the liturgical laws, under both species or, in case of necessity, even under the species of wine alone." (CIC 925). In this canon Communion *sub una specie* is mentioned twice, *sub specie panis* and *sub specie vini*.

None of these references, even if you take into account the degree of authority with which they are indued, can be treated lightly. All of these texts, explicitly or implicitly, refer to the teaching and canons of Trent. They could hardly have done otherwise, but it is still important to emphasise this fact.

219

From the pastoral point of view as well, the principles of Trent must be maintained, and the faithful need to be taught and reminded of them. This means that these truths must not be merely alluded to, in passing or once only. A real catechesis and faithful preaching must really happen; this is a command and an obligation, not a mere recommendation.[61]

Now we can see that while Communion under both kinds is practised in obedience to the Church (the doctrinal justification for a pastoral practice), it can on occasion of give rise to the serious and weighty problems for which communion in one kind only had "legitimately" become the "most common form" of Communion in the Church of the Latin rite, without in so doing obscuring its proper value. Thus, Communion under both kinds can not legitimately bring about a devaluation of Communion under the form of bread alone.

The second Vatican Council and the other Magisterial documents did not intend to break with the age-old practice of communicating *sub specie panis* in legislating for the possibility of Communion under both kinds in certain circumstances. We can cite in evidence the Roman decree of 7 March 1965 which authorised concelebration of Mass and Communion under both kinds in the so-called Tridentine rite itself. It is worth while emphasising this while we watch the reappearance of a custom which had fallen into disuse in the Latin church from the 12th or 13th century until it was finally forbidden.

From the pastoral point of view again, may we not express surprise at the fact that despite conciliar and magisterial requirements for the necessary instruction needed for a proper understanding and right use of Communion under both kinds, we have actually seen very few examples of such preaching, and many major catechetical resources give it little or no space?

For example the *Catéchisme pour adultes* of the French bishops (1991) does not specifically mention it as a rite, although it quotes John 6:51-55, and I Cor. 11:27-29. (§410-411, 421-423). The same applies to the *Le Livre de la Foi* of the Belgian bishops (Tournai 1987) which quotes I Cor. 11:27 without precision. In contrast *Katolischer Erwachsenen Katechismus : Das Glaubensbekenntnis der Kirche* (Bonn, 1985), the adult catechism published by the German bishops, gives it a paragraph, saying it is "authorised in certain occasions" and briefly reviewing the principles of Trent as well as the positive aspects of the chalice which are mentioned in GIRM 240.62   On the other hand, *Le Nouveau Livre de la Foi - La foi commun des Chrétiens*, which has a particularly ecumenical perspective, does not invoke it as a factor for reconciliation (rather, it prefers to repudiate the "reification" which according to the authors derives from notions of substance and accident![63]) *La Foi des Catholiques* (Paris 1984) by B. Chenu and

220

F.Coudreau, does not even mention Communion under both kinds (according to the index under the word "Communion").

Without claiming to have exhausted the subject, it does seem that the catechism of the German bishops and the *Catechism of the Catholic Church* are almost the exceptions in dealing with a subject on which, in contrast, the Catechism of the Council of Trent devotes a long passage. The reason for this scanty treatment, or even omission, can hardly be lack of interest, still less discretion on the part of the authors of these texts with regard to Communion under both kinds : what, then, can it be?[64]

It is even more remarkable that the *Dictionnaire Encyclopédique de la Liturgie* (1992) under the heading "Eucharist" does not say a word on the subject,[65] while L'Eglise en prière, (vol II) an older reference book edited by A.G. Martimort, gives it several pages.[66]

Let us now turn to the question of ritual. According to what ritual should Communion under both kinds be administered where it has been re-established?

1) Communion by drinking from the Chalice. The ritual is minutely described in §244 of the GIRM of 1969.[67] But despite these precautions, we cannot see how the danger of spillage has been avoided or even really minimised.[68] The detailed rubrics which comprise §245 also demonstrate that in the case of a large congregation this manner of communicating cannot fail to lengthen the ceremony considerably.

2) The use of a tube. In this manner the danger of spillage is actually mentioned in the rubric itself (§249b, *attendens ne quid defluat*), so the risk is possible or even probable. Moreover, if we observe what the rubrics of §249b suggest, the ritual becomes complicated, and even (as Fr Roguet notes) slightly comic, since this "modern style of drinking" is more likely to remind us of the familiar "drinking straw"![69]

3) The use of a spoon. This seems more straightforward as far as action goes, but the rubric (*attendens ne eorum labia aut linguam cochleari tangat*) makes the practice more complicated and really impracticable. Here too remains the danger of spillage (§251) and the precautions recommended confirm this.

4) The rite of giving both kinds by intinction. Here the celebrant must hold both the chalice and the sacred vessel contining the Hosts in the same hand, which presupposes small vessels and therefore small congregations. The rubric does make provision for larger numbers, when a small table must be provided, covered with a cloth and a corporal, for the chalice to stand on. These necessary instructions do not lead to a simplification of ceremonial, a point worth mentioning for both practical and pastoral reasons. But we will return later to the question of intinction.

It is not slightly surprising to observe that the risk of spillage is more or less taken for granted, while at the same time the formal obligation of a gesture of reverence towards the Real Presence is clearly prescribed (§244 et seq, *singuli communicantes accedunt, debitam reverentiam faciunt...*) Simply presenting oneself for communion does not of itself constitute the gesture of reverence required.

Moreover, it is clear that liturgical preparation is necessary in view of the practicalities of these different complicated procedures, and that if such preparation fails to be repeatedly made, communicants are uncertain what to do, which hardly contributes to the dignity of worship.[70] This uncertainty, almost too obvious to reiterate, is a matter of common observance in these situations. The point is relevant to actual pastoral concern, not just theoretical.

It seems that we must now return to the question of Communion under both kinds by "intinction". The simple re-establishment of this rite on the same basis as the three others raises legitimate questions, since this manner of communicating was the subject of much criticism and even a number of condemnations, especially between the 7th and 13th centuries.[71]

The use of intinction is not recorded before the Council of Braga in 675 which condemned the practice in its second canon.[72] The alleged motives are that the Gospel narrative asserts the separation of the two species, and also that the dipped bread was given only to Judas. The latter point is obviously of limited value. The practice reappears in the 11th century, according to the *Micrologus de ecclesiasticis observationibus*, which treats it as a blameworthy innovation.[73] In 1095 the Council of Clermont, presided over by Pope Urban II, condemned the usage in its 28th canon.[74]

In 1175 the Council known either as of London or of Westminster also prohibited intinction.[75] But what is more significant is the intervention of Pope Innocent III in the 13th century in his *De sacro altaris mysterio*. The Pope declared that it was the Church which had fixed and decreed as a norm "*eucharistia non detur intincta*." In joining in this prohibition of intinction, the Pope gives as a reason the necessity of eliminating the heresy (*pro hæresi extirpanda*) which fails to recognise the whole presence of Christ under either species.[76] This is of quite a different order of importance.

"Receiving bread treated with a few drops of wine cannot be called taking a drink, which communion under the species of wine would require".[77] Paradoxicaly, intinction actually demonstrates that communion from the Precious Blood is neither of necessity nor of obligation or rule.

Now we cannot deny the theological and pastoral value attached to communion under both kinds from the point of view of symbolism (*ratione signi*, see GIRM §240 and most of the subsequent documents). We have already referred, you will remember, to the

222

teaching of several of the Fathers of the Church on the particularly rich symbolism of the Chalice. We may specify the sign of the Covenant sealed in the Blood of the Lamb, which is certainly recalled by communion in the form of wine (cf Heb. 9:15-22). Moreover, the "sign of the eucharistic banquet" and the "connection between the eucharistic banquet and the eschatological banquet of the Kingdom" (GIRM, 240) are certainly brought out by communion under both kinds and in particular in the form of drink,[78] even though we must stress that all this remains in the realm of sign, "*quo signum eucharistici convivii plenius elucet*" as the GIRM repeats at the end of §241. (Note also that this Instruction repeats the terms of the 1965 decree.)

These texts take on themselves a theological, spiritual and pastoral dimension which is not without interest. They make no claim to express the entire doctrinal content of the Eucharist, but coming from a point of view that stresses the symbolic aspect of sacramental theology, they lay much more emphasis on the sacrament as sign, than they lay, for example on the sacrament as means of grace.[79]

The limitations of a short article constrain us to make these general comments and to oversimplify, without making any pretence at discussing the question technically and fully. But we should add that the community dimension of the Eucharist - *koinonia* - which we have already pointed out in the Fathers, has become the central aspect of the sacrament in a theological climate which affects even some Magisterial documents. As the liturgist A. Ganoczy says, "all other aspects, even those of the real presence and the sacrifice, are subsumed and viewed in the light of this over-riding consideration.... Real presence and sacrifice can be subordinated, so to speak, to the encounter between God and man, and among men, to the extent that neither can be taken as an end in itself."[80]

It follows that for this school of theology the sign of the convivial feast - *signum convivii* - which is stressed by communion under both kinds, again considered from the point of view of symbolism, gives this practice a privileged status.[81]

Can we conclude that the circumstances which (apart from formal legislation) had gradually led to communion under both kinds becoming rare for non-celebrants have now completely disappeared? Have the motives which justified this development simply vanished, like empty delusions?

Is it that we are now at last, with communion under both kinds, emerging from a long theological, liturgical and pastoral eclipse, or at least a shadow? Will the Eucharist now rediscover the pre-eminent place in the life of the Church which it ought to have, will it be the object of a more enlightened faith, a better understood truth and authenticity?

Will respect and devotion to the Real Presence be strengthened in the secrecy of our hearts, or in liturgical expression? Then what is the meaning of those alarming opinion polls about belief in the Real Presence among the faithful?[82]   What is the significance of some assertions which we would rather not hear about?[83]

Will communion under both kinds finally establish itself as a return to normal conditions after so many centuries of exceptional circumstances?

This string of questions was not meant to be ironic. They reflect and express positions which are common knowledge. Here is what the Italian pastoral encyclopaedia says: "Communion in bread alone nullifies our catechesis on the eucharistic sign ... Without the chalice, all discussion on the symbolism of eucharist and the Last Supper would be a pious fraud ... [by communion under both kinds] the Church is rediscovering the necessity of faithfulness to the word of the Lord ... moving beyond ritual inadequacy and symbolism reduced by half. Communion including the chalice is the rule - that which is limited to bread alone or wine alone is the exception due to particular circumstances (we are not talking about an utopia, nor theorising in isolation from reality, but dealing with a state of affairs which is part of the sacramental reality, which must be accepted without mental reserve). The expressions "communion under both kinds" or "under one kind" are derived from the limited imaginations of the scholastics, whose vocabulary has become virtually incomprehensible.   These expressions should be forgotten, and the simple term "communion" used, no more. There is still an enormous amount of psychological ground to be made up to make the liturgical reform a reality."[84]

Once again, we are not here talking about ideas circulating in secret, and I would not have quoted this unless it reflected a theological climate and pastoral practice widespread enough to be significant.

These ideas are put forward in the context of an encyclopædia, and their author is but one of many involved in the project. We should take note of the polemical tone which becomes strident, "the Church is rediscovering the necessity of faithfulness to the word of the Lord"!   How would they react if the defenders of communion under one kind used such language?   This phrase contains enough material for a theological debate, for which we have no room here. We should not delay on this consideration, although it betrays a mentality not unlike that of the sixteenth-century reformers. Let us proceed to the most important consideration:

The theology of sign and symbol, let us take careful note (although we are far from denying that it can help to illuminate matters), is here privileged, not to say exalted almost to an exclusive position.

"Communion including the chalice is the rule." This is what should catch our attention, as is the intention of the encyclopaedia itself, which urges us to avoid any "mental reserve" on this question, with some panache, and remarkable doctrinaire arrogance. Beware of the closed mind! How do we reconcile their assertions with the scriptural sources (thinking of John 6) where it is impossible to find a divine command on communion under both kinds, as Fr Roguet among others admits (see note 49)? How do we reconcile it with the theological and pastoral "rule" so clearly and strongly repeated in the General Instruction of the *Novus Ordo* itself? How do we fail to detect the spearhead or at least a new incarnation of the disruptions raised by the "utraquists", who bear such responsibility for the prohibition of the chalice for non-celebrants?[85]

How can one call a liturgical practice of the Church "the exception" when it had been given strong doctrinal support and practiced for eight centuries? Was that really the result of theological reflection? Isn't it more a question of confusing wishful thinking with the truth? And that to the extent of imposing the idea with an assertion of infallibility : "which must be accepted without mental reserve"?

We are not exaggerating - the Encyclopaedia makes the claim of "sacramental reality" in case anyone should oppose its teaching.

Doesn't this imply that in the theology and practice of the Church "sacramental reality" has been missing? Is this what we have been looking at in detail, communion under one kind practiced from the beginnings of the Church (in circumstances which we can call "particular" but not "exceptional")? These questions are raised, if not answered, in such phrases as "the simple term 'communion' [should be] used, no more", since the only genuine "real" communion is that under both kinds?

Does no other manner of communicating merit the name? Surely we see here an exaggeration, an excess which the Church cannot fail to correct (after a period of careful examination of its dogmatic, liturgical and spiritual consequences)?

So who are the opponents of communion under both kinds?

They are not to be found among the priests and faithful who, in virtue of their "justified aspirations" (Motu Proprio *Ecclesia Dei*) make use of the 1962 liturgical books, for they are not opposed in principle to communion under both kinds, and concede that the practice may be justified by important particular circumstances, according to both letter and spirit of the conciliar document re-establishing the possibility of this practice (Constitution *De Sacra Liturgia*, and C.I.C. canon 925). All are agreed that the Church "in the disposition of the sacraments, not touching on their substance, has always possessed the authority to institute or to modify what she considers most useful for the good of the faithful, and the dignity of the sacraments" (Trent).

The normative practice of Communion under the form of bread alone, which was enshrined in the traditional rite (often called

"Tridentine") was founded on doctrinal reasons so central to the Faith that they needed to be compulsorily brought to the mind of those who communicate in both kinds. Thus this custom was called on to play the part of a theological and pastoral guarantee. In practical terms, the conditions laid down for lawful communion under both kinds prove that the Church refuses to allow this practice to wrap itself in the banner of any sort of theological or ecclesiastical campaign.

Since this is the case, communion under both kinds must be practiced precisely as the Holy See has laid down, as the bishops have determined, and this is for "the good of the faithful, and the dignity of the sacrament" in which God gives Himself in the Person of Jesus Christ, who suffered and died *propter nos homines et propter nostram salutem*.

NOTES

1 Constitution *De Sacra Liturgia*, Chap. 2, "Mystery of the Eucharist" art. 55.

2 See also Basil the Great, John Chrysostom, Ambrose, Augustine, Gregory the Great, Isidore of Seville and Bede. cf. J.J. Megivern, Concomitance and Communion, A Study in Eucharistic Doctrine and Practice, Fribourg - New York, 1963, pp 6-12. E.Dublanchy, article "Communion sous les deux espèces" in *Dictionnaire de Théologie Catholique* (henceforth D.T.C.) Paris, vol III, 1923, col. 554-555. N. Iung, article "Communion" in *Dictionnaire du Droit Canonique* (henceforth D.D.C.), Paris, vol. III, 1942, col. 1171-1172. Among many others, Bossuet, *Traité de la Communion sous les deux espèces*, in *OEuvres complètes*, edit. Lachat-Viv÷s, vol 16, 1864, p 225 sq.

3 P.G. 100, 337 sq.

4 Pseudo-Chrysostom, *In Sanctum Pascha*, P.G. 59, 726.

5 Sermon 15 on the Psalms, 118:28, P.L. 15, 1197, 1526.

6 Advers. Haeres. V, 1,2.

7 P. Lebeau, "La Signification de la coupe eucharistique d'après les Pères" in *Studia Patristica. Texte und Untersıchengen*, 107, Berlin, 1970, p 367.

8 Philadelph. 4, 1.

9 Quoted in P.M. Gy, "Les Rites de la Communion eucharistique" in *La Maison Dieu*, 24, 1950, p. 150.

10 cf. G. Daneels, "La Communion sous les deux espèces", in *Concilium* 1965, 2, p. 134. J. Jungmann, *Missarum Solemnia*, Paris, 1954, vol III, p. 315. For respect shown to the Sacred Species in the early centuries, see especially Cyril of Jerusalem, *Mystical Cat.* V, 27; Tertullian, *De Corona Militare* 3; Hippolytus of Rome, Tradit. Apostol. in *Sources Chrétiennes*, XI, p. 67.

11   P.Battifol, *Leçons sur la Messe*, edn. of 1920, Paris, p. 290.

12   F. Nau, "Le texte grec des récits utiles à l'âme d'Anastase" in *Oriens Christianus*, III, 1903, p. 62.

13   J.B. Pitra, *Juris Graecorum Hist. et Mon.* II, p. 136.

14   Mansi, *Collectio*, XI, col. 155. J.J. Megivern, op. cit., p. 27. N. Iung, op. cit., col 1175.

15   M. Jugie, quoted in A Michel, "Communion sous les deux espèces" in *l'Ami du Clergé*, 72, 1962, p. 702.

16   I.H. Dalmais, *Liturgies d'Orient*, Paris 1980, p. 106. E. Herman, article "Eucharistie en Droit Oriental" in D.D.C., Paris, vol V, 1953, col. 542.

17   J.Jungmann, op.cit., p. 317, n. 77.

18   Tertullian, *Ad uxorem*, P.L. 1, 1296; St Cyprian, *De lapsis*, P.L. 4, 486. The historians also cite Dionysius of Alexandria (d. 265), Eusebius of Caesarea (Hist. Eccl. I, vi, 44. P.G. 20, 629), Paulinus of Milan and others.

19   cf J. Duhr, article "Communion frequente" in *Dictionnaire de Spiritualité*, Paris, vol II, 1953, col. 1240.

20   J.J. Megivern, op. cit., p. 20.   cf L. Bouyer, "La Spiritualité du Nouveau Testament et des Pères" in *Hist. de la Spiritualité Chrétienne*, I, Paris, 1960, p. 254, 622.

21   P.M. Gy, "La Relation au Christ dans l'Eucharistie selon S. Bonaventure et S. Thomas d'A." in J. Dore and others, *Sacrements de Jésus-Christ*, Paris, 1983, 82. (article reprinted in *La Liturgie dans l'Histoire*, Paris, 1990.)

22   Sozomon, *Hist. Eccl.* P.G. 117, 1528 sq. Nicephorus Callistus, *Hist. Eccl.* P.G. 146, 953 sq.

23   Humbert, *Adv. Graec. calumnias*, 23, P.L. 143, 951 sq.

24   Leo the Great, *Sermons* 42, 5. P.L. 54, 279 sq.

25   Gregory of Tours, *Hist. Francor.* 10,8; P.L. 71, 535 sq; Mabillon, *Annales Ord. S. Ben.* IX, c. 43, Lucques, 1739, I, p. 239. See also in A. Michel, "Les Décrets du C. de Trente" in Hefele-Leclercq, *Histoire des Conciles*, Paris, vol 10/1, 1938, p. 401, for other arguments used by the Council Fathers.

26   Some liturgical historians today dispute the evidential value of these texts.

27   A. Dublanchy, op. cit., col. 565.

28 Bossuet, op. cit., p. 330-331. Cf J.J. Megivern, "Communion under both species" in *Worship* 37, 1962-3, p. 52.

29 J.J. Megivern, "Communion under both species" ibid., p. 50.

30 cf J.J. Megivern, *Concomitance and Communion* op. cit., p. 241.

31 cf for example M. Auge in *La Liturgia, Eucaristia* vol 3/2 in the series *Anamnesis* by S. Marsili and others, Marieti, edn. of 1994, p. 279. J.J. Megivern, *Concomitance and Communion* op. cit., p. 242.

32 P.M. Gy in *Sacrements de Jésus-Christ,* op. cit., p. 71. (In *La Liturgie...* op. cit., p. 249).

33 P. Browe, *Die eucharistichen Wünder des Mittelalters*, Breslau, 1938, 139-146.

34 J.A. Jungmann, op. cit., p. 125. cf also Megivern, op. cit., p. 242.

35 G. Daneels, op. cit., p. 134.

36 P.M. Gy, in *Sacrements de Jésus-Christ*, op. cit., p. 83, 101.

37 J.J. Megivern, op. cit., pp. 214-36.

38 A.M. Roguet, *L'Eucharistie*, vol II, Commentary on the *Summa Theologica* Desclée, 1967, p. 358.

39 ibid., p. 362. Roguet, like many modern authors, makes a clear distinction between the "sacramental plane", i.e. the symbolism, from the question of the Real Presence.

40 L. Bouyer, *Dictionnaire Théologique*, Paris, 1990, p. 83.

41 A.M. Roguet, op. cit., vol I, 1960, p. 312-3.

42 This perfection is called "primary", cf. IV Sent. d. X, a. 2, q. 3. The process of eating leads to this perfection, cf. IIIa q. 73, a. 2.

43 P. de Vooght, *Jacobellus de Stribro : premier Théologien du Hussitisme*, Louvain, 1972, p. 123.

44 D.R. Holeton, *La Communion des tout-petits enfants. Etude du mouvement eucharistique en Bohème vers la fin du Moyen-Age*, Rome, 1989, pp 86-89.

45 G. Bareille, article "Calixtines" in D.T.C., col. 1364.

46 i.e. the dogmatic legitimacy of communion under one kind only, the presence of the *Totus Christus* under each species.

47   J. Dhur, article "Communion fréquente" in *Dictionnaire de Spiritualité*, Paris, vol. II, col. 1268-1270.   D.R. Holeton, op. cit., pp. 43-58.

48   J.J. Megivern, *Concomitance and communion*, op. cit., p. 248.   cf Y. Congar, *Vraie et fausse réforme dans l'Eglise*, Paris, 1950, p. 548.

49   E. Dublanchy, op. cit. col. 554.   Some modern exegetes and liturgists declare themselves unconvinced by this argument.   Their interpretation is based on quite different premises, we can be sure.   On one side, on Luke 22:17, they emphasise that this cup is not necessarily the eucharistic cup of the institution (see for example X. Leon-Dufour, *Le partage du pain eucharistique selon le Nouveau Testament*, Paris, p. 269; TOB translation, full edition of the New Testament, Paris, 1972, p. 269, notes d and f).   On John 6, the symbolic interpretation claims the adherence of many, such as L.M. Chauvet, who writes that this "is not a discourse on the eucharist as such, but a catechesis on faith in Jesus as Word of God, passed through death for the life of the world, a catechesis expressed throughout in eucharistic language." (*Symbole et sacrement*, Paris, 1990, p. 230. cf also X. Leon-Dufour, ibid., 306-7).   We admit that the pairing of bread and wine, body and blood, or these same elements taken separately can symbolise a complete repast or a twofold repast. (cf. *Vocabulaire de Théologie biblique*, Paris, 1962, pp 165-166 and 991).   Also A.M. Roguet, "As a result, when the Gospel speaks of eating alone, or of eating and drinking, whether it speaks of bread alone, or of bread and of wine, we cannot take any of these texts for or against Communion under both kinds." (op. cit. vol II, p. 361)

50   The Calixtines recognised this authority, even though they claimed that in this matter the Church had been wrong (cf D.R. Holeton, op. cit., pp 237-242).   The reformers on the contrary denied the authority.

51   cf A. Michel, in Hefele-Leclercq, *Histoire des Conciles*, op. cit., vol 10/1, pp 250, 400-401; A.M. Roguet, *L'Eucharistie*, Vol II, op. cit., pp. 351-353; and St Thomas, *Summa*, IIIa q. 64 art 2 ad 1.

52   cf A.Michel, in Hefele-Leclercq, *Histoire des Conciles*, op. cit., vol 10/1, pp 403, 408, 418.   N.B. the Council for various reasons avoided the term "causality", using instead the terms *continuere* and *conferre* (cf. D.-S. 1606).

53   E. Dublanchy, op. cit., col. 572.   We must note that since St Thomas and after Trent the first opinion is the most common, despite e.g. the opinion of the Salmenticenses (*Cursus theol.* vol 18, *De Eucharistia*, disp. XI, d. 6, 2.)   Witness the discussion by the Fathers at Trent (cf A. Michel in Hefele-Leclercq, *Histoire des Conciles*, op. cit., vol 10/1, pp 402-403, 409, 418) and A.M. Roguet, *L'Eucharistie*, op. cit., p. 359.   Among many others, Bossuet held the first opinion, op. cit., p. 331.

54   A. Michel, op. cit., pp. 416-417.

55   S. Pallavicini, *Histoire du Concile de Trente*, Paris, 1863, vol 2, pp 1254-8.

56 Bossuet, *Lettre à Mabillon*, of 12 August 1685.

57 S. Pallavicini, op. cit., p. 1260; A. Michel, op. cit., p. 401.

58 cf. G. Daneeels, op. cit., p. 135.

59 The *Catechism* certainly seems to confirm the most common theological opinion; it goes even further than the position of Trent.

60 On the Canon Law of the Eastern Churches, the *Instruction on the application of the Liturgical Provisions of the Code of Canon Law of the Western Churches*, of 6 January 1996, requires that Communion be distributed *sub utraque*, and that the custom of communicating under the form of bread alone should be abandoned if it derives from a "latinization" of the rites.

61 cf *Eucharisticum Mysterium*, Instruction of the Sacred Congregation of Rites and of the Council (S.C.R.), of 25 March 1967, §32; G.I.R.M. (1969) §241; *Liturgicae Instaurationes*, S.C.R., §6; *Inaestimabile Donum* S.C.R. 17 April 1980, §12, and others, e.g. *Enchiridion Liturgico*, Rome, 2nd edn., 1994, §§459, 517, 658, 977. etc.

62 cited as *La Foi de l'Eglise*, Paris, 1987, p. 347.

63 *Le Nouveau Livre de la Foi - la foi commun des Chrétiens*, Paris 1976, pp 552.

64 In contrast, no one can fail to notice that this does not apply to theologians, many of whom have dealt with this subject. We must observe that their researches and publications do not always or directly constitute an authority which the faithful can or should trust in the way they can rely on their pastors. We can refer to certain popular works where the personal opinion of the author takes it for granted that the rite of Communion under both kinds is superior without any reference to traditional teaching. Such as P. de Cabellec, *Pour mieux vivre l'Eucharistie*, in the series "Actualités de notre Temps", Coutance, 1980, who speaks of it as the "normal" manner and rebukes an "abstract theology which denies an authentic action", p. 44.

65 "The point of view which has governed the choice of articles is that which in France has been called 'liturgical-pastoral' for the past half century" (H. Delhougne, Brepols, vol. I, 1992, introduction, p. v). We shall see what happens in Vol II, which has not yet appeared, though the relevant letters "C" and E" have already appeared in Vol I.

66 Italian encyclopaedias seem to be more ready to discuss the value of this eucharistic rite. e.g. *Enciclopedia di pastorale*, Vol 3, Liturgia, ed. E. Costa, Casale Monferrat, 1988, 229-230; M. Auge, in La *Liturgia, Eucaristia*, vol 3 pt 2 of the series *Anamnesis*, op. cit., p. 279-80.

67 This is virtually a quotation from the Decree re-establishing communion under both kinds in the so-called "Tridentine" rite in 1965. Our reference is to the G.I.R.M.

68 Even though passing the chalice from hand to hand among the communicants is strictly prohibited; see *Liturgicae Instaurationes*, no. 6.

69 A.M. Roguet, "La communion au calice" in *La Vie Spirituelle*, 517, 1965, p. 732. The same author suggests using "tubes of low cost so that they can be burnt after use" (ibid).

70 Nor does it add to the spiritual benefit of the symbolism, for the individual or the congregation. Cf G. Daneels, op. cit., p. 136, putting forward the consideration that "the administration of a sacrament ... must in itself create an athmosphere of faith." The Roman document *Liturgicae Instaurationes* emphasises this in paragraph 6.

71 We can point out that in other areas certain practices which were once condemned for circumstantial reasons were later on recommended, but this was precisely because the circumstances which made them dangerous had totally changed. Is this the case today with regard to the worship of the Blessed Sacrament?

72 Mansi, vol. IX, col. 155.

73 Chapter XIX, P.L. 151, 989 sq.

74 The Council of Clermont says :"*Ne quis communicat ... nisi corpus separatim et sanguinem similiter sumat.*" The Council specified however that intinction could be used in case of necessity, but not without some *cautela* (preparation and precaution). This "necessity" reappears later in the teaching of Pope Paschal II: "*Praeter in parvulis ac omnino infirmis qui panem absorbere non possunt*" (Letter to Pontius, Abbot of Cluny, *Epistolae DXXV*, P.L. 163, 442). Clermont also mentions that intinction can itself constitute a precaution - *cautela* - against the danger of spillage in the case of a whole congregation communicating in the Precious Blood. This precision on the part of the Council did not prevent it from condemning the practice, despite the precautions it mentions. Paschal II also, in his letter to Pontius, rebukes this Abbot for preserving the custom at Cluny. It is worth noting that William of Champeaux (d. 1121), who maintained the practice, still said that it was a "heresy" to affirm the necessity of communion under both kinds (*De Sacramento altaris*, P.L. 163, 1039).

75 Canon 16; cf Hefere-Leclercq, *Histoire des Conciles*, op. cit., vol 7, p. 480.

76 *De sacro altaris mysterio*, I, VI, c. 13; P.L. 217, 866. Innocent III on an earlier occasion took up the argument about the communion of Judas, and wrote: "*Unde constitutum est ab Ecclesia ut eucharistia non detur intincta*". But later on, the Pope produced a much stronger argument: "*constitutum est nihiliminus et pro haeresi extirpanda quae dogmatizavit Christum sub neutra specie totum existere sed sub utraque simul existere totum.*" cf. J.J. Megivern, *Concomitance and Communion*, op. cit., p. 242.

77 E. Dublanchy, op. cit., col 562.

78 cf I Cor. 10:16-22 and 11:20; Psalms 23:5, 105:15; Prov. 9:2; Matth. 26:27-29; Luke 22:17-18. See also especially M. Auge, La *Liturgia, Eucaristia* op. cit., p. 280; Joseph de Sainte-Marie. *L'Eucharistie, Salut du Monde*, Paris, 1981, pp. 301, 303; J. Dupont, "Ceci est mon Corps, Ceci est mon Sang", in *Nouvelle Révue Théolog.* 80, 1958, pp. 1040-41; P Benoit, "Les récits de l'institution et leur portée", in *Lumière et Vie*, 31, 1957, p. 62.

79 Action in the manner of sign does not exclude sacramental action, and if the sacrament actually is the sign (*Summa Theologica*, IIIa, q. 62, art. 1), the sacrament adds a properly efficacious aspect, as a sign transfigured by divine power. (*Vis spiritalis est in sacramentis, inquantum ordinantur a Deo ad effectum spiritalem* art. 4 ad 1). Certainly this presupposes a sacramental theology which depends on a metaphysic of being. "Outmoded system!" say some, and Fr Gy indicated "The largely indispensible character of ontology (cf Ricoeur) and more especially of causality in our present philosophical context." (P.M. Gy, in *Problèmes de théologie sacramentaire*, series *Recherches Actuelles*, II, Paris, 1972, p. 179). Thus a certain line of research, rooted (for example in L.M. Chauvet) in a Hegelian "transcendence", rejects a theology of being, or even "the transcendent", and can assert "in effect, communication of [sacramental] grace should be understood not in a metaphysical format of cause and effect, but in that of symbolism, the communication of the word." (L.M. Chauvet, *Symbol et Sacrement*, op. cit., p. 147). Or again, "This supposes that we leave provisionally on one side any category of causality, preferring those of suymbolism" (X. Leon-Dufour, op. cit., p. 330).

80 A. Ganoczy, *La doctrine catholique des Sacrements*, Paris, 1988, p. 97.

81 This is why St Thomas' discussion in IIIa q. 80, art. 12, on the role of the priest celebrant, in as much as he operates *in persona Christi* and *in persona omnium* remains valid. The alternative, an opposition between these two functions, is considered invalid by modern theologians. Cf. X. Leon-Dufour, op. cit., p. 333, note 9, and the authors quoted there.

82 *Sofres* poll for France-Inter: already in 1986 "less than half of practising Catholics believe in the Real Presence".

83 "The presence [of Christ] in the bread and wine is ... to be understood as the crystallization of his presence in the assembly.... The eucharistic presence can be perceived as the crystallization of the presence of Christ through the Spirit, in the Spirit, in humanity and the universe." L.M. Chauvet, *Thèmes de réflexion sur l'Eucharistie*, (preparatory document for the International Eucharistic Congress, 16-23 July 1981) Paris, 1980, p. 20.

84 *Enciclopedia di pastorale*, Vol 3, *Liturgia*, ed. E.Costa, op. cit., pp. 229-230.

85 cf J.J. Megivern, *Concomitance and communion*, op. cit., p. 242

Homo Adorans
Some concluding remarks at the
end of the Second Colloquium of CIEL

Mgr. Rüdolf Michaël Schmitz (Germany)

Born in March 1957 in the Rhénanie, Mgr. Schmitz was ordained priest in 1982 by His Eminence Cardinal Ratzinger after studying at the German College and the Pontifical Gregorian University. A priest in the Archdiocese of Cologne, he is today a member of the Priestly Institute of Christ the King Sovereign Priest. After a doctorate in dogmatic theology in 1988, he was named curate at Reimscheid, master chaplain of the Order of Malta (1990) and member of the Pontifical Academy of Theology (1991). He obtained a degree in canon law at Munich (1993) and became assistant at the Institute of Canon Law in Munich (1993-1995). Attached to the papal nuncio in Kirghizistan (Central Asia), he has published four books and more than 80 articles in different languages on philosophical, theological and religious themes. He is also academic advisor to the Centre International d'Etudes Liturgiques.

The conclusion of any intellectual endeavour should always at the same time be a beginning. Whether we are dealing with a better understanding of old truths or new insights into familiar practices, the teacher or student of spirituality is permitted to better appreciate both the levels which the human intellect can reach and also the gifts of God's revelation.

And that in fact has been the objective of our colloquium. The sublime gift of the Holy Eucharist and the different ways in which it is venerated ought not simply to be the object of a purely theoretical and dispassionate interest; rather we ought to study them as a vital source of renewal for the Church. Without doubt the organisers and participants at this year's colloquium have from the start shared a common aim, that of saving from neglect the liturgical treasures which the Church has produced down the ages, under the guidance of the Holy Spirit, and of studying them scientifically, a study moreover based on the Faith. It is only in the measure that the liturgical and theological riches connected to the Eucharistic cult remain known in their fullness that they can prevent the impoverishment of those forms of worship which the Church now uses in the service of Almighty God.

I do not think that it would be an exaggeration to say that, this year once again, this aim has been achieved. The broad spectrum of the subjects treated, the in-depth study of specific questions, the participation from the floor as well as from the speakers, the numerous conversations which have taken place outside the conference hall; all this bears witness to the fact that it would be vain to claim, as some do, that the traditional liturgy is sterile. Rather it must be affirmed that our spiritual and intellectual lives will not fail to be enhanced and enriched in the measure that we take on board what has been presented to us: the different theological, liturgical, historical and musicological elements which go, precisely, to make up the worship of the Eucharist. Despite their great and remarkable diversity, the broad spectrum of the subjects treated does not prevent us from recognising a common thread. We have had doctrinal exposés such as that of Bishop Lagrange, the local bishop, on the veneration of the Blessed Eucharist in the teaching of Pope John Paul II, or that of Father Clément on the Church's response to the various Eucharistic heresies, or that again of Herr Graf on the doctrine of *Mediator Dei*. We have had papers about the history of the liturgy, those of Fathers Quoëx and Chanut, Folsom and Lugmayr. Father de Margerie and Father Wladimir have spoken about pastoral theology; Mr Davies and Mr Boogaarts about historical and musicological subjects. All these talks, so rich and impressive, despite their widely different subject matter serve to underline one fundamental truth, a truth which the Church has held dear down the centuries, and which should not be lost sight of now.

All that the Church has done to establish adoration of the Eucharist is inspired by the fact that the human person is by nature destined to worship and adore the presence of the One True God. When this God is present, the Church must, in all the forms of worship which she uses, lead men to that reverence which alone guarantees the adoration rightly due to God. That is the aim of all rites, all theology, all worship. And when the object of our adoration - the necessity of which the Church has come to recognise more clearly down the centuries - when the object of our adoration is no longer the Eucharist, then man loses his very being. The Church has only one objective: to lead all men to the ultimate form of worship, which is that of the world to come, where it is promised that we will "see God as He is" (1 Jn. iii 2).

The mystic glory of this eternal existence for which God has created us we find undiminished in Eucharistic Adoration, in the Sacrifice of the Mass, in Holy Communion, in Exposition of the Blessed Sacrament. All these things lead us towards the worship of eternal homage. That is why I would like to conclude this colloquium with some brief remarks about this fundamental aspect of all Eucharistic worship.

I Adoration is the highest fundamental human attitude

Adoration is the highest form of veneration man can attain. Of the whole visible creation, man alone has the ability to contemplate and worship a superior being. Just as when it comes to philosophy he alone wonders where knowledge comes from, so also when it comes to spirituality he alone is, by definition, *adorationis capax*. But, as so often, to this most noble of abilities corresponds the basest of man's failings. Man, having been brutally torn away in the Fall from the one object of true adoration has, from the contemplation of the Infinite, sunk down into the lowest form of self-obsession. And that is why, although he possesses the ability to worship his Creator without limit, even to go so far as to forget himself, he is at the same time subject to countless temptations which seek to make him take a creature as the object of his greatest veneration.

The model on which these temptations are based is that of the temptation of Our Lord in the wilderness, when our ancient adversary sought, for his ruin, to make Him worship a creature. "He showed to Him all the kingdoms of the world and their glory, and said to Him 'All this I will give Thee, if Thou wilt but bow down and worship me'" (Mt. iv 10; v 9; vi 13). Whenever man ignores this commandment - which corresponds to the most profound part of his very being - then, to borrow the words of Chesterton, "He worships not nothing but everything". Either he enthrones himself as the object of his unlimited adoration, or else in a parody of adoration he worships someone or something which is nothing other than the reflection of his own disordered lusts. Once a man turns away from the proper object of his ability to worship, a vacuum is created which must needs be filled. When God is no longer the object of his adoration, His place is taken by an idol. This idol, which to the sinner in his blindness seems worthy of worship, may have many guises. But whatever the appearance, behind the mask is hidden Satan's smiling face, rejoicing in the fact that once again a creature is taking up his age-old cry of rebellion, *Non serviam* - I will not serve.

Idolatry enslaves. The pitiless tyranny which it wields over a man's spiritual forces can bring him down to the very level of the beasts. Whoever makes himself or another creature the object of his worship brings himself down to the level of that creature. The ability to worship God gives the soul an immense force to reach higher natural and supernatural levels: *anima est quodammodo omnia*.

But when the ability to worship God is turned aside towards created things, man's whole being is perverted. He measures everything by the deceitful yardstick of the thing adored, and, in doing this, he loses sight of the All, the Beautiful, the True, the Good. His world shrinks; he is blinded.

But when a man cultivates true adoration, when that is he makes God the object of this ability which his soul has, then the soul grows and expands. Even a simple person, limited perhaps culturally or intellectually, can have a great soul when it comes to true adoration. Such is the mystery of the Catholic truth which raises up man, in his whole being. This Truth raises his eyes up towards the

235

True, the Beautiful, the Good, and his vision expands because he sees the God Who is present, because he adores Him.   And thus not only his faith and the supernatural force of his soul will grow, but also his understanding of the true value of things.

Whoever submits to the Most High and thus finds his place in the divine order, will have less difficulty in situating other things in their right place according to the hierarchy of values established by God, and will more easily escape from the disorder born of pride which refuses to owe anything to anyone.   He who has, so to speak, found the "middle C" to which all the other notes should correspond, will find himself in harmony with the melody of life which God has noted down for him.   And this "middle C" is, precisely, adoration.

II   The Criteria of True Adoration

This colloquium has very clearly demonstrated that there are several criteria which enable us to make the distinction between true adoration - one which accords with the dignity of human nature and by which God sets us free and exalts us - and false adoration, idolatry.   These criteria are found thoughout the liturgy but they appear especially in the adoration of the Blessed Sacrament.

a) Spirit and Truth

The Lord Himself says, "God is spirit and those who worship Him must worship Him in spirit and in truth" (Jn. iv 24). Some of the papers on dogma presented in this colloquium have had as their aim to underline this truth as a criterion for the correct worship of the Eucharist.   The more the object of worship is illuminated by Revelation, the more the worshipper will be struck by the force of Truth which emanates from that object of his worship, or at least whoever understands it in the measure that the limits of his intellect allow.   Without a doubt this is one of the fundamental differences between human and angelic worship, and also between worship here on earth *in umbris et imaginibus* and worship in our heavenly homeland.   Yet it nonetheless remains true, that without this illumination of truth an intuitive perception of adoration remains flawed. Indeed, if the error is total, it becomes impossible.

b) Spirit and Rite

Worship "in spirit and in truth" cannot dispense with a correct exterior rite. Thus we see that the Church has taken a long time, not without problems, to establish this rite.   For if one wants to produce a ceremonial worthy of the Sublime, then everything is important: each gesture, each vestment, each step.   And this is why respect for the rubrics is important.   It has nothing to do, as is so often supposed, with formalism or a cold legalism.   The spirit created the rite so as to become communicable through the rite.   The worship of God in spirit but without any exterior rite is thus a self-contradiction. Where there is no rite there is no adoration, only chaos.   And thus to claim that a form or rite can become rigid and outmoded and so lose its spirit is mere prejudice.   Those who are outmoded and lose the spirit are those who use the rite but do not understand the spirit which animates it, and believe that in destroying the rite they will free the spirit.   In reality when they destroy the rite they destroy the spirit too, and having lost the spirit they are unable to recreate either rite or spirit.   There is nothing left but chaos.

By contrast those who try to understand the spirit in the rite are borne by the rite to the spirit.   Once one has studied the rites of Eucharistic adoration - as has been done so well here - one reaches the spirit which emanates from them.   Holding the thumb and forefinger joined together after the Consecration, using a Communion plate, carefully preparing the Communion of the sick - what are all these things but the outward and visible sign of interior adoration?   The genuflections, of course, but also every action of Eucharistic adoration cries out with the Apostle Thomas "My Lord and My God".   The spirit of the liturgical rite is adoration.

c) Reverence

The spirit in truth and in rite is the object of a respectful fear or reverence.   The philosopher Dietrich von Hildebrand has well understood that reverence is the virtue of religion *par excellence* and also that it is inseparable from a worship which is based on the knowledge of revealed truth: "Yet the fundamental basis . . . of just behaviour . . . towards Him Who is above us, Him Who from above speaks to us of the absolute, of the Kingdom, of the Supernatural, of God, is reverence.   It is the mother of all the virtues, of all religion.   It is the basis and the beginning first of all because it makes our minds able to receive true knowledge . . . He alone who venerates is capable of true exaltation . . . of true love, of true obedience".[1]   Nonetheless, for man, reverence cannot develop except by respect   for external rites.   We are so much the slaves of our senses that we cannot live out a purely intellectual and spiritual reverence, as do, for instance, the angels.   Only someone who is attached to an external rite can practise reverence, reverence which leads him on to a still deeper knowledge.   We should not therefore be surprised that the suppression of rites has been accompanied by a lack of reverence towards the Blessed Eucharist, to such an extent that now we are threatened by the definitive decomposition of the Eucharistic truths.

237

Reverence, understood as a respectful fear, is not the same thing as servile fear. One can rightly say that the whole liturgy is a holy representation in which earth and heaven meet. There each one has his own place, which he ought to keep and in which he ought humbly to respect the rites willed by God and protected by the spirit.

Inasmuch as a man acts in this way with a desire to penetrate ever more deeply the mysteries presented to him, reverence, perfected in its rites and expressed in liturgical actions, will open up to him such a profound knowledge that he will have to fall to his knees in wonder and praise. But at the same time he will also see how all things form part of an order, an order which demands reverence towards its Creator, an order which signifies that God Himself is present in the world. Thus, the spirit of true adoration in the liturgy allows the adorer to discover "the mystery of the infinite depths which are to be found in each being as something which comes from the hand of God".[2] Whoever preserves with reverence the liturgical rite comes not only to adore but also to understand. As in the life of the Church, liturgy and wisdom, music and art, spirit and rite flow together in his life in a harmony which gives us already a foretaste of what will be given to us in the world to come.

III Our Goal

In order to reach this end and so lead all men to the eternal worship of heaven, the Church has always sought to orient the human gift of adoration in this world towards the one object on earth which is worthy of it: Almighty God, made flesh in Jesus Christ, present in the Most Holy Sacrament of the Eucharist. The battles which she has had to wage to affirm and deepen faith in the Real Presence, have served to show forth the reverence which is God's due, but also to show clearly to the Christian people that not only is the Lord present, but also that even in the way we move, we owe him some form of concrete display of adoration. As Mary Magdalene annointed the Lord with a precious ointment and wiped His feet with her hair, so also the sin-soiled man, be he priest or layman, who enters into contact with the Eucharist, is bound by *tractatio Sanctissimi* in accordance with his state, one which corresponds to the greatest reverence.

To better recall this objective of the Church's liturgy is the aim of this year's colloquiium. It is not polemics or a policy of splendid isolation which will revive the spirit of reverence and adoration but rather a deepening and broad diffusion of our knowledge. The great achievement of the organisers has been to go along this road and to have assembled, once more this year, speakers capable of presenting and explaining the relationship between truth, rite and reverence, thus promoting even more the idea of adoration as a fundamental attitude of Eucharistic worship. We thank them all. But, above all, we ought to give thanks to Him who has looked down on our wretchedness and has not willed to hide His face from our worship, the Almighty God made present amongst us in Jesus Christ His Only Son. Those who, thanks to the lectures we have heard in this colloquium, now understand better the depths of the adoration which comes from the eternal heights into this world, and which takes form under liturgical rites, will understand that I would like to conclude with these words:

Misericordias Domini in aeternum cantabo.

---

(1) Dietrich von Hildebrand: *Liturgie und Personnlichkeit*, St Ottilien 1989, p. 43

(2) ibid. p.50

A Report of the second Colloquium of CIEL

Notre-Dame-du-Laus
9th to 11th October 1996

The Centre International d'Etudes Liturgiques (C.I.E.L.), founded in 1994 by a group of Catholic lay people, held its second study conference on the *traditional* Roman Liturgy, from the 9th to the 11th October 1996, in the sanctuary of Notre-Dame-du-Laus, in the diocese of Gap (France), on the theme *Veneration and Administration of the Eucharist.*

The participants

Almost a hundred participants, lay and ecclesiastical, were present, and came from France, Italy, Austria, Germany, Switzerland, Great Britain and Gabon, all anxious to study liturgical questions thoroughly, and to form themselves better in the spirit of the Church.

For three days, simple members of the faithful, those responsible for associations, parish priests, religious, and ecclesiastical superiors, were able to follow scientific lectures, participate in liturgical ceremonies celebrated according to the traditional rite, and exchange points of view and pastoral experiences in an atmosphere of study and fidelity to the Magisterium of the Church.

Amongst those present were: Bishop Lagrange, Bishop of Gap, Bishop Jacqueline, former Nuncio in Morocco, Dom Courau, Abbot of Triors, Father Bisig, Superior of the Fraternity of Saint Peter, Monsignor Wach, Prior of the Institute of Christ the King, the Reverend Father Wladimir, Superior of the Opus Mariae, Mr Michael Davies, President of the International Association of *Una Voce*, Mr Mario Seno, President of *Una Voce* Italy, Mrs Monica Reinschmitt, President of the Association *Pro Missa Tridentina*, Mr Christophe Geffroy, Director of *La Nef*, and Miss Béatrice Toulza, President of the movement *Jeune Chrétienté.*

The lectures

After the singing of the *Veni Creator*, Loïc Mérian, President of CIEL, outlined what had been achieved since the first colloquium, underlining especially the publication of the Proceedings, which had been very widely circulated - in particular to the French bishops and French-speaking communities - as well as the foundation of branches in other countries, giving CIEL an increasingly international character, and allowing the publication of the Proceedings in several languages.

It then fell to Bishop Lagrange to initiate the work of the colloquium with a lecture on the veneration of the Eucharist in the teachings of His Holiness John Paul II, stating from the outset the object to which all the contributions were to tend: the real and substantial Presence of Christ in the Eucharist, source of all spiritual life and the object of adoration.

The ten lectures which followed explored three principal aspects of the subject :

1) It was appropriate in the first place to demonstrate the historical evolution of Eucharistic veneration, and to explain how, in the face of errors, the Church had been able to establish its doctrine more precisely. This was carried out by Father Clément, professor of liturgy, who gave the general principles of this deepening of the doctrine in the face of error. Father Chanut, a historian, took the matter further in the particular case of the rite of Exposition, showing the very close bond which the liturgy helped develop between the teaching of the faith and the living faith of the people. Michael Davies, president of *Una Voce*, painted a detailed picture of the Anglican reform of Eucharistic rites, and of the radical theological differences which this demonstrated in relation to the Catholic faith. Professor Graf, through the encyclical *Mediator Dei*, brought the proceedings to the contemporary era.

2) It is through the liturgical rites that the Church has, through the centuries, most directly set out the faith to the faithful. For this reason the Reverend Father Folsom, professor at the Pontifical Institute of Saint Anselm, and then Father Quoëx, professor of liturgy, demonstrated the evolution of these rites of the veneration of the Eucharist, and showed the profound origin and theological and spiritual importance of each gesture, expressed more or less solemnly in the different liturgical books. Father Lugmayr, speaking on the subject of the Communion rite, and the Reverend Father Wladimir, Superior of Opus Mariae, discussing Communion under both kinds, showed that the practice of the Church had always moved towards a veneration, ever more profoundly marked, of the Eucharistic species.

3) Finally, Bishop Lagrange, the bishop of Gap, speaking on the teachings of the Holy Father on the subject, and the well-known theologian Reverend Father de Margerie,

examining the question of frequent Communion; Professor Boogaarts of the University of Utrecht, on the question of Eucharistic hymns, and then Monsignor Schmitz, member of the Pontifical Academy of Theology in his concluding remarks, all returned to the essential point: the adoration which is due to the Saviour really and substantially present under the Eucharistic species.

The liturgical ceremonies

This reality, present at the heart of the Church's life and liturgy, was truly at the heart of the debates and lectures, which were not restricted to intellectual reflection, but led also to contemplation. So the liturgical ceremonies celebrated according to the liturgical books of 1962 (pontifical Masses celebrated by Bishop Lagrange, Dom Courau and Bishop Jacqueline, and the singing together of the Office of Compline each evening), made possible a better penetration of these rites, with which the Church surrounds the Eucharistic treasure.

A time for exchange of views

The conference was also an ideal opportunity for the exchange of views between lay people and priests present from many countries, those responsible for various associations, and members of the ecclesiastical hierarchy. The debates occasioned by the lectures, and the leisure time set aside for meetings allowed everyone, in a spirit of fraternity and friendship, the better to experience the universality of the Church spread throughout the world.

The Proceedings

The Proceedings of the colloquium will be published in French, then in English, German and Italian, from January 1997. The French edition can be ordered at a price of 140 FF (post free).

The Proceedings of the first colloquium held in October 1995 are available in French, under the title « La Liturgie trésor de l'Eglise », at a price of 180 FF, post free.

242

Dom Hervé Courau OSB, Abbot of Triors, with Fr. Emmanuel OSB of Le Barroux, Pontifical High Mass at the Colloquium.

Right: Bishop Georges Lagrange in the dining hall.

Below: Delegates in the conference hall.

Fr. Bisig, Superior General of the Fraternity of St. Peter, with CIEL's Ulrich Bork and Monika Rheinschmitt of *Pro Missa Tridentina*.

Left: Fr. Gy OP (right) and Fr. Lugmayr FSSP.

Below: A clerical chat. Facing the camera, from left to right are Fr. Wladimir OM, Fr. Chanut and Mgr. Wach

L. to R.: Fr. Clément, Mgr. Schmitz and Fr. Wladimir

Bishop Lagrange, *centre*, with Bishop Jacqueline and Fr. de Margerie SJ

CIEL Gen. Sec., Cathérine Chamaillet, *left*, with another delegate.

Above: Cardinal Stickler celebrates Low Mass at the 1995 Colloquium.
Below: Cardinal Stickler with Mgr. Wach and other clergy.

Acknowledgements

Those in charge of the Centre International d'Etudes Liturgiques wish to thank all those who contributed to the success of this second colloquium, in particular His Lordship Bishop Lagrange who welcomed the activities of the colloquium in his diocese and celebrated the opening Mass, Father Cler, Rector of the sanctuary of Notre-Dame-du-Laus, Father Marie-Olivier, Vice Rector, and the welcoming team of the sanctuary.

They thank also Bishop Jacqueline and Dom Courau who celebrated the High Masses of the colloquium, Father Bosi, the Institute of Christ the King Sovereign Priest, the Canonical Institute of Opus Mariae, the Priestly Fraternity of Saint Peter, as well as the abbey of Sainte Madeleine du Barroux whose presence allowed for the solemnity of the liturgical ceremonies.

CIEL also thanks the numerous priests and laypeople who helped in the publication of the Proceedings:

Mr Ulrich Bork, Miss Christine de Cacqueray, Miss Catherine Dilée, Mrs Marjorie Diot, Miss Armelle Doutrebente, Mr Joachim Ferrera, Mr Christophe Geoffroy, Mr Henri Ha Duy, Mrs Nicole Hall, Mr Hourst, Miss Anne de La Goutte, Mr Jacques Lapluye, Miss Marie-France Maisonneuve, Mrs Claude Mallié, Mrs Sylvie Marquant, Mr Christophe Mourra, Miss de Rengervé, Mrs Monika Reinschmitt, Mr David Smith, Mrs Ségolène Smith, Mr Vincent Thomas, Miss Alex Tollet, Miss Béatrice Toulza, Miss Simone Wallon.

The following associations: JEUNE CHRETIENTE, NOTRE-DAME de CHRETIENTE, UNA VOCE, PRO MISSA TRIDENTINA and the journal LA NEF.

For the English Edition:

We should like like to thank all those many people who have helped towards the launch of CIEL UK and the publication of this book, amongst whom are:

Monsignor Canon Frederick Miles
Father Andrew Wadsworth
The Priestly Association of St. John Fisher
Priests of the Brompton and Oxford Oratories

Mr Gordon Dimon
Miss Merryn Howell
Mr David Joyce
Mr Anthony de Mello
Mrs Eleanor Murphy
Mr Michael Price
Mr Tony Scotland
Mr William Tomlinson

Principal Benefactors:

Prince Rupert Loewenstein
Mr Christopher Newton
Mr Denis Whitehouse
Miss Elisabeth Hare

Translators:

Father Jerome Bertram Cong. Orat., MA, FSA
Father Martin Edwards MA, STL
Father Nicholas Kearney MA, M Theol, MPhil
Father Andrew Wadsworth GTCL, LTCL, LRAM
Father David McCready MTheol, Lic. Theol. Cath.
Prince Konrad Loewenstein BA, MA
Mrs Carol Byrne MA, PhD(Dunhelm)
Mr G. Ken Connelly MA(Cantab)
Mr Peter Crozier MA, MIL
Mr Ferdi D. McDermott MA
Mr Peter Spurgeon MIL, MITI
Mrs Ruth Real BA
Miss Penelope Renold MA(London)
Mrs Henrietta Tyler

Second Translators:

Father Aidan Nichols OP, MA(Oxon), STL, PhD Ed, Dip. Theol (Oxon)
Father Ignatius Harrison Cong. Orat., MA, BD
Father B Davenport
Dr John M. Tennant MA(Cantab)
Mr David Smith BSc
Mr James Murphy BA(Dunhelm)

248

Background to the
International Centre of Liturgical Studies

Loïc MERIAN, president of C.I.E.L.,
explains the *raisons d'être* of this association of lay Catholics.

What is the C.I.E.L.?

Loic MERIAN: C.I.E.L. (*Centre International d'Etudes Liturgiques* in French) was founded in 1994, by a group of French lay Catholics. Its aim is to make known and to increase the understanding of the traditional liturgy of the Latin Church (that is to say the liturgical forms used in the Latin Church up until 1969) in total fidelity to the Holy See.

Why this objective?

Since the last liturgical reforms, a number of liturgical experts have drawn frequent attention to major theological and pastoral deviations to be seen today. In this context, the traditional Latin liturgy is a very important point of reference, too often today considered the concern of merely a few nostalgics. This is illustrated by the fact that for the last twenty years the traditional Latin liturgy has not been considered an interesting and living subject for researchers and university students. Since the 70s, it has been, as it were, "marginalised" from Church life and from the fields of interest of theological experts.

Consequently, the aim of those in charge of CIEL has been to put the traditional liturgy back in the place it deserves, in particular by re-introducing it into the intellectual world in order to "demarginalise" it and to point out its unique riches and dynamism.

How do you hope to achieve this aim?

By organising an academic colloquium each year, bringing together international specialists from various ecclesiastical discplines. Through the quality of their work, they provide a demonstration of the spiritual and doctrinal riches of the traditional Roman rite and thus supply the basis for future work to be undertaken in the years to come.

The aims of these colloquia are thus threefold:

*   to bring together experts who rarely have the occasion to meet one another due to their geographic separation, allowing them to exchange their opinions;
*   to allow clergy and laity interested in these subjects to benefit from these activities;
*   finally, to ensure publication of these studies in French, English, Italian and German, and widespread distribution of the Proceedings of these colloquia to the faithful and to universities and seminaries.

Thus the liturgy will be shown to have a living character and the promotion of the traditional liturgy can therefore be assured by a truly intellectual and academic work.

Are these colloquia reserved for experts?

Not at all! Our colloquia are open to all. Is the liturgy not public worship? It is therefore the concern of both clergy and laity alike. There are, of course, eminent personalities amongst our participants, prelates (cardinals, bishops, abbots), superiors of religious communities, university professors, and leaders of lay associations and movements. But many of the participants, from more than ten countries of the world, are also parish priests, religious and a large number of simple laymen wanting to learn more about the traditional liturgy.

Are there not already a number of church institutions officially in charge of liturgical questions?

Of course. But there are also, as in all spheres, a number of local initiatives fostering a deeper understanding of the meaning of the Catholic liturgy, for priests and faithful. The particularity of our enterprise is to propose a place to meet and to reflect on liturgical questions relatively openly and in a way that shows that the traditional Roman liturgy is not an archaism.
Furthermore, we do not wish this colloquium to be confined to studies distant from reality and open only to experts. We would like the pastoral dimension to remain important, so as to produce tangible fruits from these works.

What are your links with ecclesiastical authorities?

Although run by laymen who look after the organisation of the colloquia and the publication of the Proceedings, our Centre wishes to maintain a close link with Church authorities, both through our invited speakers and through contacts at Rome as well as in the dioceses. Our activities are carried out in the service of the Church, and we undertake our work, respectful of the Church authorities.

Are lectures the only activity during the colloquia?

Of course the colloquium is not only made up of lectures. A point must also be made of the magnificent ceremonies celebrated according to the liturgical texts of 1962 which allow each and all to unite at the foot of the altar or to join in chant at evening Compline. There again it is not simply an exercise in intellectual speculation. Furthermore, the allotted free time - meals, aperitifs, meetings - provides occasion for contact and exchange of views.

Does your activity have an international character?

It is certain that the universality of the Church encourages us to make our colloquia international meeting-places. Our guest speakers and our participants come from the five continents, and year after year, new local correspondents relay the work of CIEL in their countries. We would indeed like the colloquia Proceedings to be available throughout the world. The publication of the Proceedings in French, German, English and Italian allows them to be sent free of charge to all the bishops, seminaries, ecclesiastical libraries, and Roman congregations that use these languages. It is a great task, but which, alone, can help to advance thought on these liturgical questions.

What are the fruits of the first colloquia?

The first two colloquia have shown that the faithful attached to the traditional liturgy represent a dynamic movement in the Church. The youthfulness of a number of the participants and even of some of the speakers was particularly remarked. Here is a dynamism which must be reckoned with. Many contacts have been made, and the Proceedings have been sent to a number of bishops, seminaries and religious superiors. It is an encouraging enterprise as a number of meetings have stemmed from it.

What future for the traditional Roman liturgy?

As our disoriented contemporaries turn finally to sects or seek certainties in other religions, is it not time to show them the inestimable benefits of the Catholic liturgy?

It is the casket of divine omnipotence, which is offered to us in a redeeming sacrifice. God is there, truly present amongst us, at the heart of our Masses. Each gesture, each symbol of the liturgy is an affirmation of faith. The traditional liturgy, by its sacred character, its theological solidity, carries with it certainties, hope and joy. The proof is in the multiplication of parish communities or religious communities which use it.

Pontifical High Mass celebrated by Bishop Georges Lagrange
in the presence of HE Cardinal Stickler, at CIEL's first colloquium

Proceedings of the first colloquium of the International Centre of Liturgical Studies

"La Liturgie, trésor de l'Eglise"

Notre-Dame-du-Laus (Diocese of Gap, France)
9th to 11th October 1995

Proceedings available in French from CIEL, France
One volume of 266 pages with photographs - 160 FF post free

Contents:

The third colloquium of
the International Centre of Liturgical Studies (CIEL)

25-27 September 1997

"Introibo ad altare Dei"
Sacrifice, Altar and Eucharistic Action

CIEL will be holding its third international colloquium of historical, theological and canonical studies on the Roman rite, from 24th to 26th September 1997, in the Paris area. Contributors will be drawn from various nationalities and these liturgists, historians, theologians and canonists will tackle different themes, to enable a better understanding of the liturgy of the Roman Church. These studies will concentrate particularly on the strong link which unites the Eucharistic Sacrifice and the sacred altar.

Lectures will deal with the following subjects:

* Sacrifice and sacred meal in the history of religions
* Meal and Eucharistic Sacrifice in the teaching of the Magisterium
* The liturgical rites of the meal and Sacrifice
* St. Thomas Aquinas' teaching on the Sacrifice of the Mass
* The notion of sacrifice in the Protestant churches
* The altar, place of sacrifice and sacred space in the religious building
* From table to stone altar: a historical analysis
* The rites of the consecration of the altar
* The place of the altar in the Eucharistic rites

The lectures will be delivered in the language of each individual speaker. Translations in several languages will be distributed to participants.

To register, please contact the Secretariat of CIEL.
Full details are available on request (see page 255 for addresses).

The International Structure of CIEL

For more information about CIEL, the organisation of its colloquia, or the publication of the Proceedings in different languages, contact our national secretariats:

CIEL: France

Loic Mérian (Président)
Antoine Villepelet (Vice-président)
Catherine Chamaillet (Déléguée Générale)

BP 34, Paris Convention, 75518 Paris cedex 15, France
Tel.: +33 (0) 1 40 43 17 50
Fax: +33 (0) 1 40 43 05 50
Email: merian@club-internet.fr

CIEL: U.K.

Mrs. Nicole Hall
CIEL U.K., P.O. Box 180, Hemel Hempstead, HP3 0UJ
Tel.: +44 (0) 1442 833642
Fax: +44 (0) 1442 834142
Email: prmhall@aol.com

CIEL: Deutschland

Ulrich Bork
Luise-Zeize-Str. 44D, 12683 Berlin, Deutschland
Tel.: +49 (0) 30 543076 040
Fax: +49 (0) 30 543 76 041
Email: PMT.Stuttgart@t-online.de

CIEL: Italia

Alberto Rosada
Via Giulia 187, 00186 Roma, Italia
Tel./Fax: +39 (0) 6 6868 353